D0248868

_VIRTUALLY YOU

ALSO BY ELIAS ABOUJAOUDE, MD

Compulsive Acts: A Psychiatrist's Tales of Ritual and Obsession

_VIRTUALLY YOU

The Dangerous Powers of the E-Personality

_Elias Aboujaoude, MD

W. W. Norton & Company
New York • London

Names and identifying details have been changed to protect the privacy
of all individuals whose stories appear in this book.

For information about permission to reproduce
selections from this book, write to Permissions,
W. W. Norton & Company, Inc.,
500 Fifth Avenue, New York, NY 10110

For information about special discounts for bulk purchases,
please contact W. W. Norton Special Sales at
specialsales@wwnorton.com or 800-233-4830

Manufacturing by RR Donnelley, Harrisonburg
Book design by Marysarah Quinn
Production manager: Devon Zahn

Library of Congress Cataloging-in-Publication Data

Aboujaoude, Elias, 1971–
Virtually you : the dangerous powers of the
e-personality / Elias Aboujaoude.
     p. cm.
Includes bibliographical references and index.
ISBN 978-0-393-07064-4 (hardcover)
1. Internet addiction. 2. Internet—Psychological aspects.
3. Internet—Social aspects. 4. Personality disorders. I. Title.
RC569.5.I54A26 2011
616.85'84—dc22

                                   2010043483

W. W. Norton & Company, Inc.
500 Fifth Avenue, New York, N.Y. 10110
www.wwnorton.com

W. W. Norton & Company Ltd.
Castle House, 75/76 Wells Street, London W1T 3QT

1 2 3 4 5 6 7 8 9 0

TO MY MOTHER

_CONTENTS

_PREFACE

MY PATIENTS, many of whom have obsessive compulsive disorder and as a result are highly superstitious, would probably caution me against starting a book on the Internet with a reference to online death and virtual estate planning. But as I was pondering how to introduce a book on this Internet life, an article that suggested I start preparing for my online afterlife arrived in my in-box. The news story introduced me to two Web sites that apparently any responsible netizen should bookmark: MyLasteMail.com, where I can leave special messages for loved ones to receive after I die—an online legacy "they can treasure forever," according to the site; and MyWebWill.com, which offers to carry out my last digital wishes, such as forwarding my passwords to designated relatives, deactivating my accounts, making one final Facebook status update and sending one last tweet on my behalf, and even ensuring that my World of Warcraft character finds a new stable home. Metaphysics, rest assured, is for the most part beyond the scope of this book, especially to the extent that the afterlife the article was concerned about is that of our avatar—an entity that, as we will see, differs in important ways from who the dying person really is. Still, it may be appropriate to bring up MyLasteMail and MyWebWill before Amazon or YouTube, because they suggest how highly evolved and "complete" our Web experience has become. This evolution, to the point where we are now born online as someone rather different, live abundantly there, then die and have a legacy to worry about, is, I will argue, sometimes happening at the expense of our offline life and evolution, and our overall psychological equilibrium. And this is very much the subject of the book.

Although I had never contemplated the digital hereafter, I have, for a long time, wondered about what it means to go online. As a Stanford medical student during the dot-com years, I was keenly aware of our campus's role as technology incubator for nearby Silicon Valley, and often marveled at the Internet's power to attract fellow classmates away from the "certainty" of medicine and into a career in an unknown new world.

A few years later, as a psychiatrist at the Stanford University School of Medicine, where I am director of the OCD Clinic and the Impulse Control Disorders Clinic, I started seeing the ways in which the Internet facilitates dramatic shifts in identity and behavior. The compulsive nature of some people's Internet use can be compared to OCD, and the euphoric "high" some experience is similar to what we see in impulse control disorders such as pathological gambling. For those reasons, it made sense that individuals with Internet-related psychological disturbances would be referred to my practice. My approach to diagnosing and treating them was also informed by research: I helped lead the largest U.S. study on problematic Internet use published to date. The study, which looked at the Internet habits of over 2,500 U.S. adults, revealed alarming rates of online pathological behavior that cut across geographic, socioeconomic, age, and gender differences. The data we collected confirmed what my years of experience as a Silicon Valley resident, student, observer, and psychiatrist have taught me: that while the Internet is a force for good in many arenas, it also has the power to interfere with our home lives, our romantic relationships, our careers, our parenting abilities—and our very concept of who we are.

The way we see and evaluate ourselves is changing as a function of new personality traits born and nurtured in the virtual world. These include an exaggerated sense of our abilities, a superior attitude toward others, a new moral code that we adopt online, a proneness to impulsive behavior, and a tendency to regress to childlike states when faced with an open browser. Together, these traits combine into a "whole new you." However, unlike other experiences that pretend to deliver this transformation but are hardly transformative, the Internet is, indeed, fundamentally changing us. The ways in which we act, interact, speak, read, think, and negotiate urges and goals online are remarkably different from the ways in which we handled these activities offline. What may be more remarkable, however, is that our online traits are unconsciously being imported into our offline life, so that our idea of what a real-life community should be, for example, is being reconfigured in the image of a chat room, and our offline persona increasingly resembles that of our avatar. Even with no browser window in sight, on an island that DSL somehow forgot—our age's equivalent of the proverbial "deserted island"—the ways in which we would act, interact, speak, read, think, and negotiate urges and goals would all be very different from the ways in which these occurred Before Google.

Because of its ubiquity and deep penetration, the Internet is the main vehicle for this transformation and the main focus here, but other mediums can also transport us into a virtual experience. Video games, "smart" phones, and iPads all share important features with the Internet, and all illustrate to varying degrees the psychological processes and real-life consequences that are the subject of this book. As such, I will refer to research and anecdotes pertaining to those other digital pastimes in order to make my argument more relevant and, I would hope, more comprehensive. (It has also become impossible to define the boundaries between various information-age appendages, as our iPhone becomes our personal daily planner, our gaming console, and our Internet browser.) It is all one big digital life, or afterlife; the Internet just happens to have been our introduction, a "gateway drug," of sorts, that has opened the door wide to other "addictions."

There is no doubt that the Internet (and our other digital crutches) has radically and irreversibly changed the way we work, play, see the world, and relate to one another. Yet the very significant and often negative psychological transformations that have ensued have gone largely unexplored. I try, in *Virtually You*, to look past gross domestic product gains and other uncontroversial, largely positive, things the Internet has brought about to focus, instead, on those. I recognize the good in cyberspace but strive for an assessment of the Internet that is more mindful of our psyche, and try to give the reader the tools and questions necessary to reach such an assessment. I will have succeeded if the reader starts approaching virtual life a little bit more self-consciously, if not necessarily less frequently. I harbor no illusions about the latter.

_VIRTUALLY YOU

_CHAPTER 1
E-PERSONALITY

THERE IS A GOOD chance you bought this book online. You may have even researched it and placed the order at work. You knew that, technically, you're not supposed to prowl Amazon on company time, but you have become so good at using the Internet to multitask that you also know that a half hour of title browsing in the office will ultimately have little effect on your day's productivity. When the book arrives, and you sit down to start reading it, it is possible that a browser window that you can still see through the corner of your eye will begin flashing, indicating a new e-mail in your in-box, or that your iPhone will start beeping, announcing a new text message. The book, I hope, will hold your interest long enough so that you are able to shield yourself from the distractions and finish reading it in a few days, at which point you may decide to tweet your praise or criticism to your followers, or post your thoughts on Facebook for your friends to see. Ultimately, you may choose to sell it on eBay or donate it at booksforsoldiers.com. And that's if you bought the paper version.

Few would contest the fact that the communication, information, economic, and social landscapes have been completely redrawn by the virtual revolution. We simply do *everything* online today and do it so seamlessly that it is easy to forget how relatively young the medium still is. Even when we do not need to be online, as when we are trying to focus on a book, the new norm dictates that a browser remain open on a nearby laptop or smart phone. The Internet and all it brings have become so ingrained in our experiences that the state of being totally logged off and out of reach now strikes us as a bit unusual, perhaps even unnatural.

Yet for all of the change wrought by the virtual world and thoroughly incorporated into our lives at this point, the more subtle reconfiguring of our *psychological* landscape that has taken place along the way is often lost on us. To the extent that most of us discuss the Internet's effects on our psychology at all, we tend to gravitate toward the romantic, the social, and the clinical. We swap stories about online love and heartbreak and laud the mutual support we find in virtual communities of kindred souls. We marvel at how the Internet can connect us with so many individuals who share an esoteric interest we thought nobody else could have. We talk excitedly of reconnecting with an old acquaintance with whom we had fallen out of touch and feel a hint of self-importance as we watch our circle of online "friends" grow into the hundreds or even thousands. We research psychological ailments such as ADHD, depression, and anorexia, self-diagnose or diagnose each other, then look up treatment options. And as we watch each other liberally share credit card information with Web sites familiar and unfamiliar, some of us, without a hint of irony, even offer tips on how to prevent Internet-mediated identity theft. But what, *really*, of that "identity" in the virtual age? Is theft—at least that kind of theft—the only threat it faces? Is our bank account number or the three-digit security code on the back of our credit card the only identifying detail we stand to lose? Are the unfortunate ten million Americans whose information is stolen annually the only victims of identity theft? The answer, most definitely, is no. From a psychological perspective, something is happening to our identity—something seems to be hijacking it—each and every time we log on, and all one billion or so netizens have something deeply personal to be concerned about and protective of.

I really like my college friend Laurie,* but it takes work. The challenge is to constantly separate the flesh-and-blood human being—with all the real memories attached to her real person—from the carefree spirit, blithely roaming through cyberspace, spreading unnecessary confusion and pain in concentric ripples that seem to originate somewhere near her laptop. I do mostly well with my challenge, phoning her, when possible, instead of e-mailing, never, ever cc'ing her on a message, and constantly reminding myself that there's Laurie and there's *virtual* Laurie, and that the person coming to my college reunion party, or inviting me to join her book club, or babysitting for her neighbors, is the real one, not her virtual cousin. But when an outsider unfamiliar with her dual personality falls in the gap between the two Lauries, and I see the repercussions in her life and in the lives of people around her, Laurie's predicament comes alive for me again.

Laurie was thirty-five and working as an executive recruiter in San Francisco when she started seeing Dennis. The two met only six weeks before she had to leave on an extended job assignment in Japan. Perhaps because they knew they would have to separate temporarily in a short period of time, Laurie and Dennis found themselves compressing the usual stages of courtship, and by the time he dropped her off at the airport for her early flight to Tokyo, the couple had decided to put on hold their independent searches for a home because, "you never know, we might be living together a year from now."

During their forced separation, e-mail quickly became the most convenient communication method for the new couple. But as the weeks went by and as they exchanged missives through the ether, Dennis began to feel alienated from Laurie; and, she could tell that his ardor was starting to fade. Fearing for the future of the relationship—and despite the reservations I expressed to her—Laurie began to share with me, her

---

* Names and identifying details have been changed to protect the privacy of all individuals whose stories appear in this book.

"psychiatrist friend," their e-mail exchanges, looking for some insight into what was going on.

As I read through Laurie's messages, I could quickly see a problem: Her lengthy e-mails struck me—and most probably Dennis—as highly unrepresentative of the woman I had come to know and like as a friend. Dennis's e-mails gushed with the emotion and longing appropriate to the early stages of courtship, but they were still tempered by logic—one "got" them. Laurie's line of thinking, on the other hand, was difficult to follow. In a typical flight of ideas from one of her e-mails, I (and Dennis) found her bouncing around from the cherry blossom festivals in Japan, to the real estate market in San Francisco, to the cost of sushi in Japan, to how she missed nibbling on her boyfriend's ear, and, finally, to complaints about her boss's terse e-mails! In e-mail exchange after e-mail exchange, Laurie came across as disorganized, unfocused, and utterly incapable of linear thinking—traits that are distinctly unattractive and that in no way reflected the successful, college-educated young professional that Dennis and I both knew.

Inevitably, Dennis's feelings continued to cool as he grew more confused by Laurie's messages, something that caused Laurie's despair to mount, which then manifested itself in the form of further disorganization in her e-mails. Increasingly, her e-mails resembled a hyperactive Internet browser with no pop-up blocker: multiple unrelated windows competing for attention, flashing graphics in all corners, and banner ads running up and down the screen at all times. When I tried to explain to my mystified friend that her lack of any sense of order and prioritizing in her e-mails might be to blame—how, for instance, she seemed to give equal weight to missing her boyfriend and the alarming level of mercury in Japanese maguro—Laurie could not understand. "But it's only e-mail!" she complained. "I thought one could free-associate online." Of course, one can free-associate online, but Laurie's dramatically different online personality proved devastating to the relationship: A very disoriented Dennis broke it off a few months later.

Laurie is hardly alone in having two "operation manuals"—one for online interacting, one for offline interacting. Her own boss seemed to show a similar dichotomy. It is ironic that one of the things Laurie complained about in her messages was his e-mail style. She was disturbed by what she perceived as his overly aggressive, impatient tone. Without necessarily intending it, his terse e-mails, with their brusque salutation ("Laurie-"), curt signature ("-Jim"), and total disregard for grammatical rules in between ("need tokyo report by end of biz pacific time 2day") made him seem disrespectful and critical, even as he was entrusting her with the company's first overseas branch, and even as he was authorizing her raise. Because she no longer had his warm, real-life presence two offices down the hall to soften the rough edges of his online style, Laurie began to read the worst into his words and assume the worst about his intentions. So, just as Laurie's online personality was wreaking havoc with her romantic relationship, her boss's online personality was causing her significant professional stress.

According to the Digital Future Project, an annual examination of the social impact of online technology conducted at the University of Southern California Annenberg School for Communication, the number of hours Americans spend online has risen in the past few years to an average of 15.3 hours per week in 2008. Internet users reported being involved in the following activities at least weekly: e-mail (96 percent go into it), Internet surfing without a specific destination (71 percent), looking for news online (60 percent), finding product information (43 percent), conducting online banking or other financial services (38 percent), instant messaging (37 percent), playing online games (35 percent), and searching for humorous content (25 percent). Then, too, membership in online communities has more than doubled in the last three years, with more than half of online community members (54 percent) logging into their community at least once a day. A full 71 percent of members said that their community is very important or extremely important to them, and 55 percent said they feel as strongly about their online communities as they do about their offline ones. All of these online transactions afford unparalleled opportunity—to reach out to friends and family, to purchase goods without having to enter a brick-and-mortar store, to stay informed about the world around us, and so on. What goes unrecognized, however, is the new personality that all these activities define, and which now exists, increasingly uncomfortably, alongside what we have always thought of as our only personality.

The result of all these online interactions is the unwitting creation of an e-identity, a virtual whole that is greater than its parts and that, despite not being real, is full of life and vitality. Unfettered by old rules of behaving, social exchange, etiquette, or even netiquette, this virtual personality is more assertive, less restrained, a little bit on the dark side, and decidedly sexier. Its advantages cannot be underestimated: This "e-personality" can act as a liberating force for the real-life individual, allowing the person to transcend debilitating shyness, let go of stultifying inhibitions, and forge connections and friendships that would be impossible otherwise. In many cases, the virtual version nicely complements the actual person and acts as an extension of his real-life persona. Seen under the best possible light, it is bolder, stronger, and more efficient than the real-life original. It is what makes voicing an unpopular point of view and organizing against an injustice easier to do over instant messaging and on social networking sites. It spurs action and confers bravery and takes cyber-disobedience from Facebook to Freedom Square in Tehran, in the form of hundreds of thousands of wired and suddenly emboldened freedom lovers, carrying out what was dubbed Iran's "Twitter Revolution" in the summer of 2009. (On the eve of renewed student protests later in the year, one of the first measures taken by the Iranian government was to choke off Internet access.)

It is also what makes breaking up with a significant other easier over e-mail and allows us to put an end, less messily or so we think, to an unsatisfying relationship that has gone on too long, without the awkwardness of a conversation that we know we should have but which we keep delaying. Seen from this perspective, this is our action-oriented side at its most efficient best, moving past mountains of inertia, cutting through layers of real life red tape, social etiquette, and business protocol, to expeditiously and relatively painlessly consummate all manner of transactions in cyberspace. Given these advantages, having a virtual persona can be like acquiring the proverbial third hand: It empowers the person sitting at the computer desk and can even serve as an incentive to become more assertive, effective, and efficient offline as well.

For my friend Laurie and many others, however, the flip side of enhanced productivity, expediency, and courage can be confusion, pain, and disorientation in the real world. That is so because the online self is also dangerous and irresponsible, running roughshod over our caution and self-control. It can encourage us to pursue unrealistic or unhealthy goals; it can make us feel smarter and more knowledgeable than is warranted; and it can encourage us to behave more selfishly and reck lessly. By promising both immediate fantasy fulfillment and anonymity, the Internet makes it difficult to resist going to eBay and buying that unneeded leather jacket or waltzing into a "social network" and pretending to be thinner, more popular, and more successful than we really are. It allows us to reinvent the portions of ourselves we are unhappy with, and it offers the freedom to engage in behaviors that our more responsible selves might put a stop to in the harsh light of day. As the Internet presents itself as a godsend and the answer to old yearnings and needs, it is creating unfamiliar and dangerous challenges—ones that strike at the core of who we are or who we want to be. Indeed, if logging on begins as an attempt to fulfill our human need for self-expression and connectedness, it often gives voice to some less mature and antisocial impulses, aspects of ourselves that have historically been kept in check by culture, expectation, religion, and what one might call the social contract. The consequences of allowing these psychological forces to go unchecked can be far-reaching.

One needs to look beyond the unquestionable universe of new

opportunities that the virtual world represents—a revolution equal in scope and potential to the Industrial Revolution—to see the dramatic transformations taking place in the most basic ways we behave, communicate, and identify ourselves in the world. When we log on to the Internet, or lose ourselves in a texting exchange, we become, to varying degrees, different individuals. Unconsciously, we take on a new personality that in some cases bears little resemblance to the one familiar to us from our offline lives. It takes but a moment of self-reflection to realize that our typed words often do not sound like us, our online purchases are less thought out than those at the local mall, our cyberspace hookups are less responsible, and our online personal profiles, well, stretch credulity. It takes but a little self-scrutiny to be hit by the realization that we really should know better than to text and drive. Yet in that "state," we feel free, invincible and immune, like "nothing can touch me now." Why should we want to log off?

The person we become can be a conscious creation of our wild imaginations, as on the Web site Second Life, where over sixteen million virtual "residents"—cyberspace avatars built from scratch—live in a parallel world of work, play, and romance. Or it can be a deliberate repackaging of our most attractive or attention-grabbing traits, as on social networking sites like MySpace, which has over 100 million active accounts, or Facebook, with over 500 million users. Whether on Second Life, MySpace, or Facebook, subscribers consciously and intentionally reinvent their biographies in part or in whole, presenting to the large virtual audience a new version of themselves, one that may in some cases bear little resemblance to the "real me." More often than not, however, this new self emerges unintentionally and unconsciously, through e-mail, blogging, texting, message boards, e-tail, sexual pursuits, and innumerable other interactions in cyberspace. Assessing the breadth and nature of a person's online activities, then holding them up against the real-life person we think we know, we can appreciate how foreign and removed virtual personality can be. Indeed, the totality of my experience as a psychiatrist treating Internet-related disorders and as a researcher has convinced me that fundamental psychological shifts are occurring within us as we spend time online or using related digital media. These shifts unfold spontaneously, almost naturally—nobody "teaches" us to become more daring or less diplomatic over e-mail; it just happens. On the surface, these newly acquired characteristics serve to make us feel more potent and happier: Having an e-personality that seems freer and more resilient can offer a welcome break from the tensions and inhibitions of our real circumstances. Taking on that personality online, over a couple of hours at night or between stressful meetings during the workday, can be seen as therapeutic. It relaxes and destresses and offers us an opportunity to transcend or temporarily forget the conditions around us.

But these shifts, empowering and fun as they may be in cyberspace, exact a heavy price in the real world, where their effects are experienced in two ways. First, the traits we take on online can become incorporated into our *offline* personality, so that we may, for example, become excessively daring or less diplomatic in our day-to-day interactions and relationships, even when there is no open browser or iPhone in sight. The second way is through the direct toll our online adventures take: The cost of feeling too powerful or having too much fun online is typically felt away from the screen, in the form of tension at home, as when new Facebook friends start taking too much time away from family; conflict in the workplace, as when the boss reprimands us for tactless e-mails when we are otherwise rather tactful; or distraction in the classroom, because the pace of our online activities has compromised our attention span.

Consider Liz and Richard, two patients I treated for compulsive shopping and pathological gambling, respectively, in my Impulse Control Disorders Clinic. Impulse control disorders fall within the obsessive-compulsive spectrum of psychological conditions. They share with OCD repetitive, anxious thoughts that intrude on the person's mind (the obsession equivalent) and ritualized behaviors that calm the anxiety down (the compulsion equivalent). Unlike OCD, which is never pleasurable, impulse control disorders are often thrilling, even euphoria-inducing in the moment, but lead to much distress and remorse in the long run. While I had some experience diagnosing and treating real-life impulse control disorders, Liz's and Richard's cases came with a new twist to their age-old problems: Their impulsivity seemed exclusively virtual.

Liz, a forty-four-year-old homemaker with no previous psychiatric problems, came to me for help with out-of-control e-tail expenditures. She had heard a radio ad for a clinical trial we were doing at Stanford University to test Celexa, a serotonin-based antidepressant, in the treatment of compulsive shoppers. She hoped she would qualify to be in the study. "For every dress I like, I have to buy three, each in a different color," she told me at our initial meeting, sounding puzzled at her own behavior. "Then, for each color I get, I have to buy two additional sizes—what if I gain weight, what if I lose weight?" Meanwhile, Liz's brick-and-mortar shopping habits remained relatively reasonable. She made it a point to tell me how she had just missed the annual Labor Day weekend sale at the big furniture outlet near where she lives—an event she looked forward to year after year. "I didn't think I could afford it. Not this year. Not with my online spending," she explained. Then, sounding almost nostalgic for her days of responsible shopping, she added, "I never lost control at a real store the way I lose control online. Until I discovered Buy.com, I was actually putting money aside for retirement. What is it about me?"

Or what is it about the Internet? I encouraged Liz to ask herself this question and to explore how the medium itself might be contributing to her behavior. The idea seemed to resonate. "I guess if it's online, somehow it doesn't feel real," she said. "Or not *as* real. It's innocent and fun. Almost guilt-free—just like a computer game. And how bad can a computer game be?"

Quite bad, unfortunately, as Liz discovered. Her online shopping sprees had already caused her to file for bankruptcy, which is what finally prompted her to seek help in my clinic. Although her problem was clearly shopping-based, it wasn't the traditional "compulsive buying disorder" our study was recruiting for. Instead of those crowded modern-day cathedrals we call malls, Liz's problem manifested itself solely in virtual joints that are always open and where parking is never a problem. Most of our experience with compulsive shopping, and most of what had been described in the psychiatric literature, involved real acquisitions from real stores. Our screening questionnaire for the study, which included questions about the role of in-store advertising, the effect of product display, whether she shopped alone or with friends, and how much effort was involved in getting to her favorite stores—all seemed irrelevant and fell woefully short of "capturing" her problem. Yet Liz was undoubtedly a compulsive shopper, only on to something new, when our research premise was stuck in a twentieth-century understanding of her condition. Even though I couldn't take her into the study, I continued to see Liz in my clinic.

For Richard, a thirty-six-year-old married Human Resources specialist and father of two, it was the threat of divorce that made him make his first appointment. For years, his gambling habits were what one might call "social," not remarkably different from what his coworkers would describe in conversations around the water cooler on Monday mornings. Like them, Richard enjoyed the occasional weekend skiing trip to Reno, a three-hour drive from home, where he and his wife would sometimes play the slot machines in their hotel lobby well into the night. Beyond that, however, he never sought it out and never stopped to try his luck at the local Indian casino, despite a couple of memorable wins in Reno that might have served to draw him back to a gaming institution. Simply put, when it came to gambling, Richard could take it or leave it.

A single spam e-mail in his in-box, however, led Richard to a virtual casino that became his undoing. It started with an offer for a free trial of an online Texas Hold 'em game that Richard took advantage of one night when he was having trouble falling asleep. Before long, he was waiting for his wife to go to bed in order to log on, eventually using her credit card to do so after exhausting his promotional account and maxing out his personal credit cards. Intriguingly, on his morning drive to work, Richard would speed past the Indian casino, counting the minutes till he could get to his desk and log on to his favorite gambling Web site. "It's a very different experience than being in a real casino," he explained to me, opening his wallet to show unused coupons he had received from the Reno resort where he had won big. "See, they're always mailing me offers for a free stay, free meals, free shows," he said. "None of it seems to move me. Somehow it feels better online. You're free of inhibitions, whether they're your own or imposed on you by other people. It's just you and your computer screen, with no one to disapprove of you or give you dirty looks, and no one to remind you of your responsibilities and your credit card debt." But Richard could not avoid disapproval indefinitely. It caught up with him when reality, in the form of his wife leaving him with their two kids, encroached on his virtual life.

How might one treat Liz and Richard? Selective serotonin reuptake inhibitors, or SSRIs, are a family of drugs that are thought to work by increasing levels of serotonin in the brain. Prozac and Celexa are two examples. They are well established as generally safe and effective antidepressants, and, in addition, they have been shown in double-blind, placebo-controlled studies to be effective in people with OCD. (Double-blind, placebo-controlled studies are those in which neither investigator nor subject knows who is taking active drug and who is taking placebo; they are considered the gold-standard in testing the efficacy of a medication.) Because of their proven usefulness in OCD, some SSRIs have been studied in impulse control disorders as well, including compulsive shopping and pathological gambling. While the overall results are mixed, two SSRIs have shown some promise: Celexa in compulsive shopping and Paxil in pathological gambling.

A form of psychotherapy known as cognitive-behavioral therapy, or

CBT, is also effective and is often recommended as first-line treatment. Cognitive-behavioral therapy aims to correct faulty assumptions people make about situations, such as a compulsive shopper's belief that buying more things somehow leads to improved self-esteem, or a gambler's belief in special talents that make him or her more likely to win a game of pure chance. As their thoughts are confronted, patients are gradually weaned off problematic behaviors such as mall or casino visits, often with the help of relaxation tools that can bring down the accompanying anxiety.

Cognitive-behavioral therapy and SSRIs, however, have been shown to work on real-life compulsions, such as the compulsion to shop and gamble the old-fashioned way. For Liz and Richard, it felt like the real-life person who would be taking my Celexa or Paxil prescription, or who would be working with me in a CBT mode, was somehow not the one getting in trouble or in need of acute treatment; it was some virtual extension thereof—a foreign entity, one much more difficult to reach than the person sitting in my office. That is why it seemed like the first step in treatment should consist of something that was much more obvious and that did not require an MD or a licensed therapist to administer—namely, suspending their Internet subscription. In asking them to log off, I felt that I was bolstering their real personality, which now seemed under serious assault by a virtual version of it, with terrible consequences. Increased awareness, through therapy, of how virtual and real life interact and sometimes clash, as well as relaxation tools and possible SSRIs, were all reasonable options to explore—afterward.

Unlike Laurie, whose e-personality was less obvious to her and slowly did its damage as she watched in shock and disbelief, both Liz and Richard realized that they were essentially different people online. They saw the other personality take over, even as they did not understand the cause or who to blame. They identified a difficult-to-resist force that was making them engage in problematic behaviors in cyberspace and recognized that those behaviors stood in stark contrast to their normal offline actions. They were helpless but aware, their transformation too dramatic and costly to go unnoticed.

Many more people are like Laurie than Richard or Liz in their online lives. They give in to the virtual self more subtly, even unconsciously, and are almost unaware of the significant changes taking place. Without fully realizing it, they fire off e-mails that offend colleagues; they click the "buy" button to purchase an unnecessary item when they already feel anxious about the next mortgage payment; they post pictures and identifying details about themselves as they complain about Web security; and they make blog entries that brim with exaggerated self-confidence and other qualities that are not normal to them. And when something goes wrong, when they get in trouble, they are caught off guard. Their reaction falls in the narrow range between "I thought I was behaving the way I always do!" and "I thought I was just being myself!" In reality, they were behaving quite differently even if they didn't really know it.

The overwhelming majority of these individuals don't max out their credit cards or declare bankruptcy, although they probably do spend more than they can afford. Their colleagues don't corner them in the hallway with questions about the "out-of-character" e-mail they sent, although they might start thinking differently of them. Their spouses may well be annoyed and confused but don't necessarily leave them. Because their symptoms are subtle, they never make it to a psychiatrist's office, and neither should they—they are not psychiatrically ill in any accepted definition of "ill," and they do not require SSRIs or CBT. But they are transformed, too—their personality a bit hijacked. And to the degree that this transformation is changing their lives and redesigning our culture, to the degree that the effects of their e-personality do not go away when they hit the "hibernate" key on their computers or log off at the end of a long day, that transformation and those effects deserve to be understood, studied, and discussed.

While Laurie, Liz, and Richard had different levels of awareness of how they changed online, they were all "honest" in their cyberspace interactions. They did not set out to give themselves a personality transplant—it just happened. Many of us, however, use the Internet to *actively* reconfigure aspects of who we are, often with the hope that somehow this will make our real-life selves better, more popular, or more attractive. Not that we are necessarily wanting to defraud other people and lie to them. Rather, it is often a well-meaning dishonesty, a white lie, more fantasy than malicious misrepresentation, and with the goal of breaking free of the confines that help make us who we are.

Fraud should be the last thing that comes to my mind when thinking of my patient Jill, but there is no way around the deceitfulness that marked her foray into online dating. A highly intelligent, always conservatively dressed English teacher, Jill suffered from a severe social anxiety problem that had crippled her romantic life and survived many attempts at medication treatment and psychotherapy. With Jill still celibate at twenty-nine, her previous psychiatrist wisely recommended online dating as a good way to confront the problem. His idea was for her to "break the ice" through a gradual, nonthreatening e-mail and picture exchange, which would ensure that a basic attraction was present and fundamental compatibilities were met. Such an approach would minimize the possibility of rejection or a significant personality clash at the first meeting, along with the overwhelming anxiety this would generate for someone with social phobia. That is how, armed with an online dating service subscription and almost-thirty desperation, Jill finally met Tom.

Actually, Jill sort of met Tom. Her online persona, the one that Tom started courting, was an exalted version of the shy, inhibited woman sitting in my office. For starters, she called herself Tess, changing her name in part to protect confidentiality. However, well beyond the name change, Jill felt a strange pull to embellish, or rather reinvent, other aspects of who she was. Instead of an English teacher—too boring and drab, she thought—Jill became a sales rep who used a combination of natural gregariousness, which she did not possess, and borderline-provocative dress, which I could not imagine her wearing, to convince architects to try the new line of high-end Italian furniture she was pro-moting. She even intentionally dumbed down her syntax—a sacred cow for her in the classroom—and opted instead to communicate with Tom in simple, declarative sentences and plenty of emoticons. ("They make emotions much easier," she explained.) Gone from her e-mails, then, was the SAT-style vocabulary she modeled for her students, and in came playful monosyllabic words and truncated forms (cuz for because, pic for picture, u for you, hugz for hugs). Coming across as too brainy was the kiss of death, Jill thought, even if she was communicating with a doctor-in-training like Tom.

This online version of Jill appealed to Tom, and over a six-month e-mail courtship, something that can only be called love (or maybe "luv") developed between the two: an irrational need to check in with the other on an exhaustingly frequent basis, for no other reason than to make sure the person is still desired with the same intensity expressed in the last e-mail, sent only ten minutes before. Along with this need, of course, came internal restlessness and agitation if the e-mail, text, or instant messaging ping did not arrive when expected. All in all, how-ever, this was thrilling restlessness and agitation, and a completely novel experience that Jill would cherish in her mind as a much delayed first romance, finally.

But then Jill turned thirty, and online love suddenly took on a juve-nile air she could no longer tolerate. The cuzes in her e-mails became embarrassments for the schoolteacher, and the lols (for laughing out loud) stopped being funny. Utilizing big, difficult-to-truncate descrip-tors like "inane" and "asinine," Jill described to me the discomfort, even shame, that she started feeling with her online love story. She stopped seeing her psychiatrist, saying she was turning into somebody she didn't recognize under his care, and wanted to start seeing me instead. She still loved Tom, however, and my role was to help her transpose her online relationship into the real world, "because I don't want to give up who I am." I tried to explain to her how this was not an easy task, how I had no special psychotherapeutic skills to help her carry it out safely and successfully, and how she should consider going back to her former psychiatrist, who knew her better and who had the right instinct when he recommended online dating, even if she ended up taking it too far—but Jill would not listen or reason. She was a woman in virtual love.

As I quickly found out, what stoked Jill's anxiety even more than entering the fourth decade of life was that, several months into their courtship, Tom was not insisting on meeting in person. Jill had enough insight into her psychology to realize how, in many ways, this had been the perfect relationship for her, providing an outlet for libidinal energy without the unbearable stress of social performance and interpersonal contact. But why wasn't Tom more persistent? What was *his* problem? This question plagued Jill and, more than any other consideration, made her insist on the fateful meeting. Despite his cold feet and her untruths, she was still intent on trying to bring her virtual romance to a smooth landing in the real world, and I was to help her navigate this emotional minefield.

Where to meet, what to wear, and in what order to begin correcting the many fallacies that separated Jill from Tess? My patient struggled mightily with these questions as she prepared to meet her online love. As it turned out, however, she needn't have worried at all. Or, perhaps more accurately, she should have been doubly worried, for Tom had a few secrets of his own to confess. For starters, he was really Ted, and the doctor Jill thought she had landed was a pharmacist who had always wanted to go to medical school. The two were playing the same game: Jill was increasing her appeal by pretending to be less socially inhibited, and Tom was increasing his by elevating himself on the socioeconomic and alpha male ladder. Somewhere in cyberspace their trajectories collided, with much potential and heartache resulting.

Yet, far from con artists, Tom and Jill were using the virtual world to overcome limitations that they felt were unjust, and both were helpless in front of a game that had self-perpetuating, snowballing tendencies built into it—and real rewards associated with it, too. For, regardless of how we might judge it and regardless of the outcome, it would be impossible to deny the intensity, even the genuineness, of the pleasurable, ego-boosting emotions/emoticons that the Internet helped generate between "Tess" and "Tom," whoever they really were.

For them, the face-to-face meeting must have been a terrifying reminder of all the old anxieties, inhibitions, and "baggage" that they were able to ignore for a long while online—a reminder of what mere mortals they still were. In its ultimate philosophical interpretation, this confrontation with reality was a brutal reminder of death itself, the devastating death of an ideal personality that they wished they had— freer, sexier and, in their eyes, more worthy of being loved than the one they were stuck with in real life. And neither he nor she could tolerate it. According to Jill, the meeting ended with the couple, having shared a string of disappointing revelations, separately leaving the café where they had met, having decided not to pursue a relationship that was too burdened by lies to have a true chance at success. That evening, they logged on from their home computers, found each other online, chatted briefly, then found a reason to log off. From what I could glean, it was a perfectly pleasant but superficial IM exchange, devoid of "blame game"–type accusations, but also of any big love pronouncements. They would not, the following day, obsessively check e-mail to see if the other person had sent a sweet note.

As this story might suggest, our e-personality can be in competition with the real-life one, constantly reminding us of our shortcomings and of the rosier trajectories our lives could have taken. That is so because of how quickly we manufacture, and buy into, fantasies online. Unconsciously, we give free rein to our imagination, allowing it to imbue our ambassador in cyberspace with special attributes of intelligence, status, and charisma that we do not normally possess, or at least do not possess nearly to the same degree. This, alas, does not always result in the real person sitting behind the computer screen feeling smarter, more successful, or more charismatic. To the contrary, we often begin to prefer the online version of who we are. Our lives as we have known them, with our in-between IQs, so-so jobs, and bodies that leave something to be desired, now become boring in comparison with the online lives we have built or Photoshopped for ourselves, where the various details that make up our virtual identity (and seemingly everybody else's) are all above average. In the worst cases, one of two outcomes follows: self-hatred, i.e., something that resembles depression, or a total immersion in virtual life, i.e., something that resembles psychosis. While I certainly do not mean to suggest that the roughly 160 million regular Internet users in the United States are suffering from depression or psychosis, an argument can be made about how the Internet can produce depression-*like* and psychotic-*like* states in many of us. The Internet responds to our need for escapism by helping us generate phantasms and illusions, but that online phantasmagoria can in some cases lead to low self-esteem and/or a divorce from reality.

What can one make, psychologically speaking, of the online/offline schism shared to varying degrees by Jill, Tom, Liz, Richard, Laurie, and perhaps even her boss? What templates from the history of psychiatry might help us understand the fracturing of identity that seems to be taking place, albeit to different levels, among them? Might "dissociation," a well-known clinical phenomenon wherein thoughts and behaviors are not adequately integrated into consciousness and memory, be relevant to their experiences? For people who transform into something very different online, and for the many among us who transform to lesser degrees in front of our browsers, might e-personality represent a twenty-first-century "alter" of sorts?

Before the current fad of overdiagnosing bipolar illness, before the attention deficit disorder fad that preceded it, the psychiatric diagnosis en vogue was multiple personality disorder, or MPD. Briefly visiting the history of that disorder, and examining some research studies into it, might shed some light on the concept of parallel personalities today, including the idea of a parallel e-personality.

The "patient zero" in the MPD epidemic was Shirley Ardell Mason, known to the world as Sybil Dorsett. Dr. Cornelia Wilbur, the psychiatrist who treated Sybil in New York, is said to have used hypnosis to identify sixteen separate personalities in her patient. She blamed Sybil's disintegration on unspeakable childhood abuse at the hands of a disturbed mother. Before Sybil, fewer than a hundred cases of MPD had been reported in the scientific literature worldwide, the most famous being that of Chris Costner Sizemore, whose story was dramatized in the 1957 movie *The Three Faces of Eve*. However, a veritable avalanche of MPD case reports was unleashed in the late seventies, along with journal articles, medical texts, and specialized conferences, when Ardell Mason was fictionalized as Sybil in a best-selling book and a 1976 made-for-TV movie.

As MPD became a household ailment, overeager clinicians, determined to find it, started diagnosing it in normal people who just "didn't feel like themselves." Or when depression, say, was the more appropriate diagnosis, some clinicians might diagnose MPD instead, using the faulty logic that the patient was not depressed but, rather, that one of her depressive "multiples" had taken hold. As a result of the frenzy, rates of MPD climbed feverishly and suspiciously, reaching, at the height of interest in the condition, 1 to 2 percent of the U.S. population (that is, several million, but probably still a fraction of the number who subscribe to Second Life and such sites today!).

Another suspicious observation was the growth in the number of personalities *within* each case. The classic literature had mostly described dual personality, but a certain one-upmanship set in among therapists and patients alike in the aftermath of Sybil, with each competing to diagnose, or be diagnosed with, more personalities than the last one. (Even Eve, not to be outdone by Sybil's sixteen personalities, revisited her story, amending it to claim twenty-two, up from three in her original account.) The expanded repertoire of personalities did not, however, include a digital personality—the MPD epidemic was spreading from the mid-1970s to the late 1980s, Internet light-years before Second Life.

Serious questions have been raised over the years about Sybil's story and about her doctor, severely undermining confidence in the MPD diagnosis. Dr. Herbert Spiegel, a prominent New York psychiatrist and hypnotist who knew Sybil and Dr. Wilbur, sowed doubts about the latter, describing her as "profoundly ignorant of the whole hypnosis phenomenon," and suggesting she may have caused the emergence of alter personalities in her patient through amateurish experimentation with hypnosis. As for psychiatry's early embrace of the MPD phenomenon, he described it as "a hysterical response to hysteria."

All this continues to fuel skepticism about the disorder—a skepticism that one has to contend with when introducing the idea of an online personality that may differ in significant respects from the familiar offline one. Yet Sybil and the idea of a parallel identity live on, not just in the movies and in our cultural consciousness but in science as well. And for good reason: Despite the controversies, evidence of brain pathology in patients with MPD has emerged from some well-designed scientific studies. One such study, published in 2006, used magnetic resonance imaging (MRI) to compare the size of the hippocampus and amygdala, two brain regions crucial in memory functions and emotional regulation, respectively, in fifteen female subjects with MPD and twenty-three healthy controls. The researchers found significantly smaller volumes (20 to 30 percent smaller) among patients with MPD, compared to healthy controls.

Another study, conducted at Harvard and published in 1999, reported measurable biological changes taking place in the brain of one patient as she switched between personalities. Using functional MRI, an imaging technique that measures brain activity as opposed to only size or anatomic structure, researchers imaged the brain of a forty-seven-year-old woman with long-standing MPD. When the adult waking self was instructed to switch to her eight-year-old child alter, activity in the hippocampus was seen to decrease. "Now we can watch multiple personalities emerge in the brain," the *New Scientist* announced on its cover, rather hyperbolically.

Despite their limitations, such studies lend some legitimacy to MPD as a real disease and support including it in the *Diagnostic and Statistical Manual of Mental Disorders*, or *DSM*. The *DSM*, published by the American Psychiatric Association, is the worldwide Bible of psychiatric diagnosticating. In its most recent edition, revised in 2000, MPD is given the new name of "dissociative identity disorder" (perhaps to "dissociate" it from the heavy historical baggage attached to MPD). It is included within the larger category of "dissociative disorders," a group of conditions that share the important symptom of "dissociation."

We are all capable of some degree of dissociation, defined as a disruption of the normal integration of thoughts and behaviors into consciousness and memory, so that for a period of time certain information is not integrated, or "associated," with other information as it normally and logically would be. Everyday examples include daydreaming and performing certain familiar tasks automatically and almost without an awareness that one is doing so. Patients with full-blown dissociative disorders, however, are more severely and more pervasively disconnected and, as a result, are much more impaired.

I would argue that mindless Web surfing, without forethought or plan, and without awareness of the passage of time or any real-life anchoring, is our era's very common version of the symptom of dissociation. It is probably where the Sybil discussion should be today. While I have yet to encounter a true case of MPD the way the *DSM* defines it—as "two or more distinct identities or personality states, each with its own . . . pattern of perceiving, relating to, and thinking about the environment and self" and which "recurrently take control of the person's behavior"—I believe my dearth of experience treating this condition is the result of its extreme rarity, not its nonexistence. (When patients have been referred to me with the MPD label, my own evaluation invariably led me to believe either that the diagnosis was the result of the patient's vivid imagination, usually combined with a fascination with Sybil or another hero/heroine of the MPD movement, or that the condition was iatrogenic—from the Greek root for "brought forth by a healer." The latter refers to illnesses caused by medical intervention, whether the

leukemia that follows cancer chemotherapy or the splitting of personalities in response to ideas suggested by an overzealous hypnotist.) So,
while I wait to meet a patient with true MPD as defined in the *DSM*, I
wonder whether, for people like Laurie, Liz, Richard, Jill, and Tom, who
clearly dissociate into something quite foreign online, and for the many
among us who dissociate to lesser extremes whenever we type Google
.com, e-personality can be seen as a kind of latter-day alter, too.

How else can one understand this slipping in and out of
impulsiveness—helpless online, relatively in control off—that characterized Richard and Liz, for example, and that seemed to correlate
directly with whether they were in front of an Internet browser? As an
uncontrolled experiment, I asked Richard to complete the Dissociative
Experiences Scale, a twenty-eight-item questionnaire that assesses an
individual's proneness to dissociate, and that is used to help diagnose
MPD, among other accepted dissociative disorders. On question after
question, I might as well have been Dr. Cornelia Wilbur administer-
ing the questionnaire to Sybil Dorsett! Richard's proneness to dissociate
was impressive, with the Internet being the almost exclusive vehicle for
that dissociation. Statements from the questionnaire that he identified
strongly with included: "Some people sometimes have the experience
of feeling that their body does not seem to belong to them"; "Some
people find that in one situation they may act so differently compared
with another situation that they feel almost as if they were two different
people"; "Some people sometimes find that in certain situations they are
able to do things with amazing . . . spontaneity that would usually be difficult for them"; and, "Some people find that they sometimes . . . are not
aware of the passage of time." Examples abound for other individuals
who, like Richard, saw their lives drastically changed as a consequence
of gambles, purchases, and other decisions made during an Internet-
powered "switch." While not bona fide multiples, their online trance-
like states nevertheless point to prominent and frequent dissociation-like
episodes, with much accompanying damage to the waking self.

My clinical experience with heavy video and Internet game users suggests that they, too, experience dissociation phenomena and score high on dissociation questionnaires, and research studies are beginning to point to biological changes in their brains that might help explain the process. Good studies of the changes occurring in the brain of someone who is going on an Amazon shopping spree, skipping school to linger on Facebook, or undergoing metamorphosis on a Match.com profile have yet to be conducted, but the effects of video games on our brains have already received some amount of research attention. Because the two experiences are similar, data from video game studies are relevant and can help us make some basic inferences about the Internet experience— whether it is World of Warcraft or Second Life, both games involve an interactive, immersive medium and a good dose of reality simulation (or, perhaps more appropriately, reality evasion).

In a 1998 study published in the journal *Nature*, positron emission tomography, or PET, scans were used to measure the levels of the neuro-transmitter dopamine in the brain during a video game. Dopamine is a major player in the "pleasure system" of the brain and is released during rewarding experiences such as sex, eating, and gambling, and after using addictive substances like alcohol and drugs. (It is also implicated in cognitive functions like attention and memory, among other vital processes.) The euphoria that is sometimes induced by cocaine use, for example, has been shown to correlate with dopamine release in several "reward centers" in the brain. The video game that researchers studied involved using a mouse to navigate a tank through a battlefield while destroying enemy tanks for a monetary reward. Eight male participants, aged thirty-six to forty-six, were recruited to have their brains imaged during a fifty-minute video game session. Analysis of the scans revealed a significant rise in dopamine release during the game in a part of the brain called the striatum. Moreover, the degree of dopamine release seemed to correlate with performance level. For the first time, a technology-enabled *behavior*, in this case playing a video game, was shown to have a similar effect on the brain as an abusable substance.

DNA studies seem to be substantiating the dopamine-virtual games link and the comparison to substance use. In a 2007 study led by Harvard psychiatrist Perry Renshaw, seventy nine teenage boys who engaged in excessive online video game play (an average of 2.3 hours per day) were compared to a control group of seventy-five teenage boys whose participation in online play was more reasonable (an average of 0.8 hours per day). The researchers analyzed DNA samples from both groups, focusing on two genes known to be involved in dopamine transmission (a gene for a dopamine receptor and a gene for an enzyme that breaks down dopamine). The results showed that the group who engaged in excessive Internet video game play had versions of the two genes that are known to be present in individuals with alcohol and nicotine dependence. Like the previous study, this one seems to suggest that because of how our brains are wired, and because of what gets some of our brain neurotransmitters, including dopamine, flowing, some of us might be easy victims to the screen pyrotechnics of computer games and, possibly, some Web sites and other related platforms.

Crucial as it likely is, dopamine is hardly all that is involved in transfixing us to a virtual interface. Another study, published in 1992 in the journal *Brain Research*, used PET scans to track the metabolism of glucose in the brains of eight young men before and after they spent several weeks practicing Tetris. Tetris is a game of dropping blocks; points are scored for each block that comes to rest on the gradually rising pile, with the goal of preventing the pile from reaching the top. The players' PET scans showed that with increased practice, brain glucose metabolism decreased, suggesting that subjects were using fewer brain circuits and/or fewer neurons per circuit after practicing the task. One has to wonder what happens to those underutilized neurons as we spend an increasing number of hours repetitively playing a computer game we have perfected or, by extension, obliviously clicking through familiar Web sites. Might one "lose it" if one does not use it? The effects of idling in cyberspace on our IQ, attention span, and retention capability will be discussed later. For now, suffice it to say that preliminary scientific evidence is pointing to real, measurable changes that occur in our brain chemistry as we interact with the virtual world. These changes might explain how our consciousness and overall "association" with the world around us are affected when we sit for too long at the game console or spend another afternoon aimlessly browsing. Once elucidated, they could help explain the biological underpinnings for what we are calling online dissociation or e-personality.

Regardless of the neurotransmitter cocktail at work, one downstream effect is certain and seems to characterize every e-personality: We all have less inhibitions online and act out more frequently and more intensely than we would "in person." The normal brake system, which under usual circumstances helps keep thoughts and behaviors in check, constantly malfunctions on the information superhighway. This chronic malfunction has been called the "online disinhibition effect." It is the stably unstable foundation upon which we will stack the building blocks of e-personality.

Several features unique to the Internet medium help promote online disinhibition, writes Rider University psychologist Dr. John Suler. Those include *anonymity, invisibility*, the *loss of boundaries* between individuals, and the *lack of any real hierarchy* in cyberspace. According to a *New Yorker* cartoon, "On the Internet, nobody knows you're a dog." When, by remaining anonymous, "people have the opportunity to separate their actions online from their in-person lifestyle and identity, they feel less vulnerable about self-disclosing and acting out." The first step in Jill and Ted's radical makeover was a new name they gave themselves. Once they "became" Tess and Tom, other details of the embellishment process followed easily. If we can change or hide our name, our most personal and most identifying marker, other components of our ID become natural fodder for Photoshop. Anonymity can make it possible for people to "convince themselves that those online behaviors 'aren't me at all,'" writes Suler. If they "aren't me," it follows that they don't reflect on me and that I'm not responsible for their consequences. This gives us carte blanche to engage in them with more abandon. As we will see, however, and as anyone who has ever sent an impulsive e-mail or text to a boss, colleague, or friend will agree, lack of anonymity hardly protects us from disinhibited actions. Some of our most regrettable online gaffes carry our proud signatures at the bottom of the message.

Like anonymity, being invisible also encourages online disinhibition. Richard talked about how being able to avoid the disapproving gaze of people helped him maintain his gambling. Being out of sight facilitates problematic actions, not to mention all sorts of outpourings over e-mail, on blogs, in text messages, and in chat rooms. Along with anonymity, invisibility is what makes possible a popular blog with the revolting title: "A Man and His Rant: Online Verbal Diarrhea, Delivered Fresh." As Suler reminds us, people in real life will avert their eyes and look away when discussing something personal or embarrassing. Traditional psychoanalysts sat behind their patients—that is, outside their field of vision—to encourage them to open up about their most heavily guarded secrets and traumas. Similarly, the person we are e-mailing or texting is invisible to us. (People we wrote letters to were also invisible, but that experience was more solitary than interactive in that a response could not be expected in real time or near–real time.) Not seeing who we are interacting with increases the chance of a heart-to-heart and of unrestrained effusions of the very personal kind. Depending on what it is that gets shared and whom we are sharing it with, that is not necessarily a good thing.

The absence of the face-to-face cues that normally guide our offline interactions can erase boundaries among people in cyberspace, also contributing to disinhibition in the virtual world. An e-mail from somebody might be experienced as an internal voice in our head. "When reading another's message, one might also 'hear' the online companion's voice using one's own voice," Suler writes. People often move their lips or make speech sounds as they read, which can make them project their own voice into the other person's text. The result can be that the conversation is experienced as taking place in one's own head, much more a soliloquy than the dialog that it really is between two separate entities. Since talking to oneself is generally considered safer than talking to someone else, the result is more indiscriminate openness and less responsible disclosures, not to mention a dissolution of boundaries between "self" and the "other." This dissolution, we will see, does not help our universal goal of psychological independence and healthy autonomy.

Finally, the lack of true status differential in cyberspace also encourages disinhibition. Typically, authority figures, such as parents, teachers, and police officers, announce and assert themselves through various visible trappings of strength and influence that arrive with them. Those include age stigmata, costume, body build, body language, and the many details that define one's environment and create a "halo" of power. Online, however, people are separated from the real-life markers of their authority. On the Internet's level playing field, everyone is equal and equal to the megabyte-per-second speed of his connection. We are all peers in cyberspace, and what's a little disinhibition among friends? (One could even argue that traditional authority figures are at a disadvantage in that online status differential, to the extent that it can exist, might correlate with a Web site's "bells and whistles" and its ability to engage us and make us want to come back. Most teachers, parents, and government agencies, however, lack the know-how or originality to produce a catchy site one would want to bookmark. In the parent-child context, this in some cases is giving rise to parents being digitally beholden to their children, and a sort of reversal of normal parenting, as we will see.)

All individuals in this chapter's vignettes dissociated into less inhibited versions of their real selves, which led them to behave and express themselves differently than they normally would. That split between the virtual and offline self, not just in extreme cases but in our mundane existences, can be potentially destructive in many spheres of life. Whether one is psychologically devastated by it or merely confused and brokenhearted, we all have a relatively disinhibited e-personality that belongs somewhere on a spectrum that, toward its more extreme end, also traverses those of Laurie, Liz, Richard, Jill, and Tom.

But besides overarching, always-present disinhibition, e-personality, like any personality, has other defining features—those stubborn traits that characterize it and that tend to remain constant over time. Having laid here the groundwork for our multiplicity, or at least duplicity, in the Internet age, I will focus, in the next chapters, on the predominant undercurrents that are unleashed in the virtual world and that tend to mark e-personality. More specifically, against this background of dis-inhibited, dissociated personhood, five psychological forces will vie to assert themselves: grandiosity, or the feeling that the sky is the limit when it comes to what we can accomplish online; narcissism, or how we tend to think of ourselves as the center of gravity of the World Wide Web; darkness, or how the Internet nurtures our morbid side; regression, or the remarkable immaturity we seem capable of once we log on; and impulsivity, or the urge-driven lifestyle many fall into online. Those are the transformations (and fractures) that occur in our identity as we sit in front of our browsers, and that is the "Net effect."

Liz, the homemaker with no absolute need for the Internet, and who could no longer afford her Internet subscription anyway, still could not act on my recommendation that she cut off her Internet service. She simply could not envision herself without an online outlet. All she would agree to was a temporary downgrading of her connection from high-speed DSL to dial-up. That helped, but only to a point. Starting Celexa did not, unfortunately, result in added benefit. She continues to suffer through the consequences of bankruptcy and ruined credit.

Richard went cold turkey, both at home and at work, after success-fully petitioning his boss for a demotion to a position that did not require computer access. (He left the Human Resources office and became the company's night-shift security guard.) I worried, at first, that he might start frequenting real gaming institutions to compensate, that he was at risk for substituting one problem for another. That, fortunately, did not happen. Using therapy-acquired relaxation tools, he gradually found it easier to ride the anxiety wave that accompanied the unfulfilled urge. Eventually, better alternatives replaced the problematic behavior: Richard started running again and took up an extreme sport that probably comes with its own dopamine rush—rock climbing. With time, he was also able to reintroduce the browser into his life in a more responsible way, with the added security of a sophisticated software program that blocked most gambling Web sites, and with the help of new legislation that made it more difficult for Americans to access online casinos. A year after I met him, his wife and kids had moved back in.

My friend Laurie remains single in San Francisco but has a very active presence on eHarmony, Chemistry, and JDate (an online service aimed at Jewish singles; Laurie is not Jewish). I continue to prefer face-to-face or phone exchanges over online communication with her, and she can now appreciate why. Although she no longer sees them as an indictment of her performance, she still complains about her boss's digital missives, and says that they have only gotten more annoying: His economy of words has become even stricter since he started sending text messages from his smart phone, instead of using his laptop to e-mail her. Because he now had the 140-character limit to contend with, and because of the inconvenience of typing on a cell phone keypad, he has dropped salutations and signatures altogether. So, instead of the "Laurie-" greeting and "-Jim" signature that used to drive her mad, all my friend gets now is a one-liner communicating, seemingly still in English, the order of business for the day.

Jill's appointments with me gradually petered out until she disappeared from my practice altogether. She was missing more and more the liberated person she was in cyberspace, and was feeling increasingly hopeless about ever achieving that same lightness of being offline. I tried to convey to her that reproducing that level of freedom in real life was not feasible or even advisable, but I was ultimately unsuccessful. Still, although Jill terminated her care with me and returned to her former psychiatrist, I cannot say that I completely failed her: Toward the end of our work together, her Match profile claimed qualities that lay halfway between those of Jill and Tess—a sign of progress, I suppose.

To the extent that the "thief" is not a fourteen-year-old hacker in a faraway land or the geek next door (forgive the stereotypes) but rather our own virtual alter, something more insidious than traditional identity theft is happening in the fifty-six innocent seconds that we spend, on average, on every Web page we visit; something that goes to the core of who we are and who we want to be. These fifty-six-second breathers add up to nothing short of a parallel identity we construct for ourselves, so that for every real being with an Internet hookup, there exists now a virtual version living side by side. The term "digital divide," which has typically been used to denote the gap between those who have access to information technology and those who do not, would perfectly describe the fracture emerging within our own psyches as we conduct more and more of life in virtual terms. To varying degrees, every time we type in a password and hit "enter," we cross from one side of the schism to another. Doing so smoothly and in a psychologically healthy way is becoming an increasingly difficult challenge, but one that we have to manage if we want to preserve those things about us that we hold dear. As part of earthquake country, Silicon Valley, the birthplace of the Internet, has learned to live with its fault lines. How are we negotiating ours? And will we prove as resilient and agile?

_CHAPTER 2

DELUSIONS OF GRANDEUR

It was the midnineties. I was a medical student at Stanford University, still becoming comfortable with using e-mail, when a Silicon Valley Internet startup began flirting with me. I could not ignore their overtures: Chris, a former classmate who hated the human anatomy course and dropped out to pursue Internet gold instead, worked there and was now trying to recruit me. I could command the compensation I wanted, he said, as long as it was in shares, not real dollars. If it had been actual money, I might have more seriously considered the offer: Even though I had done well in my human anatomy class, I can't say I enjoyed it, and I hated embryology and statistics, even calling the latter "sadistics." But I wasn't comfortable with the concept of shares, even one hundred thousand of them, or 10 percent of the value of the company, which was equal to Chris's piece.

As I halfheartedly negotiated with them, it was hard to find much in common with the man I had known in medical school. I could barely see past the 639 skeletal muscles in the human body, while Chris thought in gold rush equations and boundless rates of return. I was still memorizing, sometimes in Latin, medical terms coined by the Roman anatomist Galen, while Chris spoke the strange vernacular of a new era, throwing around phrases like "angel investors," "dot-com incubator," "stock options," and the one that to this day will cause any heart in Silicon Valley to flutter—"going public." "Here's finally something that will really 'end business as usual,'" he joked between pie charts and Excel spreadsheets.

The possibilities of this new world launched Chris outside the certainties of Newtonian physics—it did seem like his apple would not fall—whereas "Boring Me" still craved old-fashioned security and the grounding experience of laying my hands on a patient during examination and listening to his or her heartbeat through a stethoscope. I couldn't quite convince myself to take the leap and join a start-up that was going "where no one had gone before." The risk of a job that could go terribly poorly or terribly well—a risk that is thrilling to many twentysomethings—was too great for me to bear. So in the end, my cautious nature prevailed and I declined the offer.

But I did follow news of his start-up, from a distance that was geographically short (Stanford University is in the heart of Silicon Valley) but light-years away in terms of "feel." Ensconced within the rigid structure of ossified medical education—a position of relative safety that, barring any disasters, would result in an MD degree and a job—I watched Chris's dot-com company closely. How could I not? How could I disappoint the voyeur in me when the magnetism of the new medium was drawing me, and countless others in the area, so forcefully? The unsolicited e-mails his company spammed me with, probably along with a million other recipients, were in a sense very wanted: I craved information on how their fund-raising was going, how their business model was evolving, and how much money Chris was going to make—and I was *not* going to make—once the company went public. And with every piece of good news carried in every e-mail, with every positive newspaper article on his company's prospects, I felt someone take a bite out of my apple, until it completely vanished on the day of the initial public offering (IPO). Chris's company was valued at several hundred million dollars, transforming him, in an instant, into a very rich man.

Since its early days, the Internet has nurtured lofty ambitions—entrepreneurial and otherwise—and a certain rush to participate in a mass experiment with nearly limitless potential. It has encouraged big dreams and bold behavior, and fostered risk taking that we might not be comfortable with in the real world. Consider, for example, how many times you've sent an e-mail to a colleague or superior that is more strongly worded than your typical face-to-face communications. Protected by the space between our message and the recipient's reaction, we feel emboldened to express ourselves more freely and more aggressively; the Internet imbues us with a newfound sense of daring, even though our actual circumstances—in this case, office politics and our need to maintain good relations with our superior—haven't changed at all. My classmate Chris was similarly emboldened, though for different reasons: The Internet lured him with the possibility of untold riches, just as it lures many people in with the promise of easy wealth, health, and happiness. Grandiosity, defined as an exaggerated belief in one's importance and one's abilities, seems to be in the Internet's DNA. In someone who has manic depressive illness (also known as bipolar disorder), grandiosity can reach delusional proportions, as the person starts believing he is a movie star or has three PhDs when this is not the case. But we hardly have to be literally delusional or in the throes of clinical mania to think too highly of ourselves and of our chances of success online.

Why not dream "big" in cyberspace in an age that has produced startling Web success stories, like those of Larry Page and Sergey Brin, the thirty-seven-year-old cofounders of Google whose combined net worth, according to *Forbes*, is more than $30 billion; Pierre Omidyar, the forty-three-year-old founder of eBay, whose net worth is almost $9 billion; and Mark Zuckerberg, the twenty-six-year-old founder of Facebook, who transformed himself into the youngest ever self-made billionaire? The possibility of such success, so early in life, still feeds the grandiose notions of many starry-eyed Internet entrepreneurs, although, as we will see, online grandiosity is hardly limited to excessive confidence in one's business idea or chances for financial reward. Rather, it is at play each time we act as though we are invincible and each time we blind ourselves to the unfavorable odds of making it online, whatever it is that we are attempting.

According to official Google history, Larry Page and Sergey Brin met at Stanford in 1995, when Larry, 22, a University of Michigan student considering the university, was assigned Sergey, 21, to show him around campus. A year later, by then Stanford computer science graduate students, the two collaborated on a search engine they called BackRub. BackRub operated on Stanford's servers for over a year, until it started taking too much bandwidth, as far as the university was concerned. The two then took their search engine off campus and renamed it Google, a play on the mathematical term "googol." "BackRub" might have given the wrong impression, like "don't bother us, we're too tranquil post-massage," when the restless pair were intent on shaking things up and going places. A more ambitious name was clearly in order.

Finding inspiration in the "googol" conveys the reach of Brin and Page's early aspirations. The googol represents the numeral one, followed by one hundred zeros, or 10^{100}. As an indication of a googol's vastness, it is estimated that the number of atoms in the known universe is 10^{79}, or less than a googol. The term was coined in 1938 by the mathematician Edward Kasner to illustrate the concept of infinity by comparing it to an unimaginably large number. According to the story, Kasner asked his nine-year-old nephew what name he would give to a really large number, and "googol" was the boy's response. In choosing a derivative of this mathematical term, Google's founders let us in, very early, on their immodest goal—organizing an amount of information that approaches infinity on the World Wide Web.

Through initiatives like Google Books, which aims to create a universal library by digitizing every book in the public domain, and Google Earth, which photographically maps our planet's topography up to a six-inch resolution in some areas, one can say that the founders' dream has become reality. With the degree of Google's penetration into our lives and our times (to the tune of over five billion hits a month) and its accomplishments so far, two old company jokes in the Silicon Valley April Fool's Day tradition now strike us as disturbingly prescient, as though they, too, are ambitious company goals that time and technology will sooner or later make happen: On April 1, 2000, Google unveiled the MentalPlex, a tool by which it claimed to read users' minds as they stared—hat and glasses removed, as per the instructions—at a circle that looks like a spinning beach ball; and, in 2004, it announced plans to open the Googlunaplex, a research facility on the moon. That should not be confused with the "Googleplex"—the company's headquarters in Mountain View, California, Planet Earth—which itself is a play on "*googol*plex," a number even larger than the googol and represented by one followed by a googol of zeros, or 10 duotrigintillion in the American system for naming very large numbers . . .

Sixty billion is grandiose enough, thank you, and represents the dollar value of items sold on eBay in 2008 by its 80 million or so users. The figure grew from $14.83, the price fetched by the very first item transacted on the Web site—a broken laser pointer sold by Pierre Omidyar. According to company lore, Omidyar contacted the winning bidder personally to make sure he knew that the laser pointer he just bought was broken. "I'm a collector of broken laser pointers," the man told him, a response that must have made Omidyar realize that his idea to take the personal garage sale online would succeed even beyond his expectations. Indeed, regardless of what your collecting proclivities may be, you are guaranteed to be able to expand or shed your collection on eBay. However, as the following chapters will show, it is sometimes the one-of-a-kind items that occasionally go on sale, and the interventions that the company is forced to make into the marketplace as a result, that may say more about us, both as eBayers and as virtual beings in a more general sense. In 1999, for instance, a human kidney was auctioned off, and bids surpassed $5 million before the listing was pulled. In 2001, eBay had to ban the sale of seats to view executions. Even more desperately, in 2001, Adam Burtle, a twenty-year-old University of Washington student and part-time car mechanic, put his soul up for auction. It went for $400 to a buyer identified only as a Des Moines, Iowa, woman. She seemed unbothered by Burtle's product disclaimer: "I make no warranties as to the condition of the soul." The woman had an eBay feedback rating of zero—meaning she had no record of any previous transactions on the site before bidding on the man's soul. Maybe she had everything else.

Mark Zuckerberg is not in the business of selling souls. Rather, he makes his money helping souls connect and reconnect through the popular interface he created. "Hacker. Dropout. CEO" is how *Fast Company*, a high-tech magazine, titled its 2007 feature on him. According to the article, when Zuckerberg found out that Harvard did not offer a student directory with photos and basic information—that is, a face book—the then barely sophomoric student hacked into Harvard's student records to produce Facemash, a Web site that randomly paired pictures of undergraduates with invited visitors to determine which one was "hotter." Four hours and 22,000 photo views later, Harvard suspended Zuckerberg's Internet connection. An uproar and an apology ensued, and a decision by Zuckerberg to pursue his project in a more roundabout way: He set up the Facebook template and let students fill in their own information. Within two weeks of its launch in early 2004, half the Harvard student body had signed up. That summer, Zuckerberg dropped out to head West, relocating to Silicon Valley. By 2007, he was fielding one-billion-dollar offers to buy his baby and lecturing the World Economic Forum at Davos—"It was great. I wore shoes."

Zuckerberg's story shows us that the promise of unprecedented success coming to hardworking entrepreneurs or lucky visionaries by way of the Internet is very alive today in the Web 2.0 movement. The term refers to companies that thrived after the late 1990s crash and that tend to exploit the social networking potential of the Internet. That is the same promise that fueled early Internet enthusiasts like Omidyar,

Page and Brin, and my classmate Chris. For them, there was nothing but positive potential in cyberspace. They dreamed big, on the googol scale, and felt as though they were on the verge of colonizing a new world. Their dreams seemed justified because the virtual world brought back the promise of great adventure and major discovery. From a business standpoint, it was different from any other money-generating medium ever tested before, and so, the story went, old-school financial and other rules no longer applied. With the support of venture capitalists eager for a piece of the dot-com pie, they half-hatched ideas and built them into companies, often lavishly spending on infrastructure in a way that far exceeded revenue. "Get big fast" was their motto, and it seemed perfectly feasible and realistic. (It is also the title of a book that chronicles the rise of Amazon and the tactics of its founder, Jeff Bezos.) Once big enough, they pursued one of two lucrative exit strategies: They sold out to a bigger company or filed an IPO. Their success stories are fondly remembered in Silicon Valley and frequently retold, like the foundational myths of a revered civilization.

When historians write the definitive story of the dot-com boom, they will probably say it began on August 9, 1995, the day of the Netscape IPO. According to MarketWatch's John Shinal, "The stock offering's success showed that huge fortunes could be made by selling shares in a Web start-up, even though the company itself had yet to make a dollar of profit. . . . The IPO's success—which made millions for early Netscape investors, including not a few 20-somethings—was like a gunshot whose echoes reverberated from Silicon Valley to Wall Street." The notion, revolutionary at the time, that investors were willing to buy stock in a still unprofitable company based on wild projections of immense future returns was beginning to take hold, encouraging Internet start-ups with shaky foundations and questionable business models to proliferate. "Before Netscape there were no little old ladies from Pasadena or Peoria pestering their brokers about how to get in on hot dot com IPOs." After Netscape, millions of mom-and-pop investors bought into the idea that investing in the Internet was the sure path to the good life, and exercised their viral power to jack up values of start-up company shares. The Internet had made tech investing accessible and sexy to the non-wired masses, and made money virtual—an even less tangible and further removed concept than the plastic of credit cards often cited as an example of our reckless out-of-touchness with finances. "People thought it was limitless, that things could only go up," a San Francisco investment banker told Shinal. One no longer needed any finance or technology background to see tremendous, unrealistic potential in the Internet. It was going to make us all rich. Welcome, irrational exuberance.

" . . . Clearly, sustained low inflation implies less uncertainty about the future, and lower risk premiums imply higher prices of stocks and other earning assets. We can see that in the inverse relationship exhibited by price/earnings ratios and the rate of inflation in the past. But how do we know when irrational exuberance has unduly escalated asset values, which then become subject to unexpected and prolonged contractions . . . ?" "Irrational exuberance," the phrase that so perfectly captured the dot-com euphoria, almost got lost in the midst of a typically dehydrated speech delivered on December 5, 1996, by Alan Greenspan, then chairman of the Federal Reserve. If it was meant as a cautionary message, it was heeded for about a nanosecond. The dot-com cauldron bubbled on, just as irrationally and exuberantly, for four more years, culminating on March 10, 2000, when the tech-heavy NASDAQ stock exchange index hit a record high of 5132.52. (As a comparison, the NASDAQ ended 2009 at 2269.15.) A few days later, a loud pop was heard in Silicon Valley. The Internet bubble had burst, and dot-com stocks began a devastating slide, leading the way to a staggering seven-trillion-dollar drop in the total market value of U.S.-listed stocks. Two hundred thousand people in "Sili Valley" were newly unemployed, including Chris, whose company's stock value evaporated overnight. Dot-com was now synonymous with "dot gone." Just as the Internet had promised and delivered unprecedented success, it was also producing some spectacular falls. Just as it had helped people defy gravity during the ascent, it also rejected moderation when it came time to land. We were awakened from a collective dream, our grandiosity seriously—but, as we will see, not fatally—wounded.

The roughest of all the dot-com landings was probably that of the online grocer Webvan. A darling of investors big (Jim Barksdale, former Netscape CEO, and Louis Borders, cofounder of Borders Bookstores) and small (our clinic clerk), Webvan attracted more funding than any other e-tailer except Amazon, with its ambitious plan to deliver groceries to consumers in a thirty-minute window out of huge automated distribution centers, each the size of eighteen supermarkets. Serving seven U.S. markets, with plans to expand to twenty-six, Webvan had just inked a one-billion-dollar deal with Bechtel to build a string of warehouses worth $30 million each, and had just acquired HomeGrocer, one of its leading rivals, for $1.2 billion. But its lavish spending on infrastructure without the customer base to match it, its disastrous tendency to overlook short-term operating costs, and its unsustainable cash burn-through rate proved too strong a current even for this fearless Internet fish to swim against, ultimately leading to its dramatic demise. When Webvan filed for Chapter 11 bankruptcy protection in July 2001, its stock had plummeted to $.06 from a high of over $30 during its November 1999 IPO.

Webvan's legacy today survives in the form of thousands of sturdy, bright plastic shopping bins that make excellent storage containers—I should know; I bought two on eBay—and as a business school case study in how a start-up cannot operate with total disregard for the constraints imposed on it by offline business reality. In a 2001 article titled "Sweeping Webvan into the Dustbin of History," Nicholas Hodson and Tim Laseter accuse Webvan of "historical innocence," an assessment that reflects the naivete of this Internet enterprise. They argue that any casual student of retail history would know that radically new business models win only by using significantly lower prices to attract price-sensitive customers—those most likely to switch retail allegiances. Webvan, along with many other now-defunct e-tailers, ignored this lesson from history, employing, instead, plenty of flash to accomplish the rather preposterous goal of making brick-and-mortar stores obsolete.

Grandiosity, in the manic and bipolar sense, is as applicable as "historical innocence" here. For somebody suffering from bipolar mania, it might mean thinking he can excel at a number of unfamiliar endeavors for which he is unqualified, or that he can drive against traffic because he is too talented and above the usual rules. For Webvan's "grocers," but also for countless Internet wealth, thrill, and fame seekers, it means operating outside the realm of history, economy, rationality, and, in some cases, the law. Such "innocence," and on all these fronts, recalls other moments of discovery in our history that also brought out the grandiose trait in people's personalities, most recently the Wild West.

Part of the Internet's ongoing allure lies in its ability to rekindle a strong instinct that had not dared express itself since the frontier days of the Wild West—an adventurous streak that has been long dormant, and which has found its outlet online. It turns us into Internet Explorers®, on the verge of finding gold in the Sierras, or, to go further back in history, it gives us the illusion of being part of something like the Northwest Passage expedition. In fact, it is hard to think about the early days of Internet expansion without conjuring up the image of California frontiersmen or drawing a parallel between Brin & Page and Lewis & Clark. The comparison is hardly new, but just as apt today as it was in 1998, when Andrew Morriss, professor of law and business at the University of Illinois, was among the first to make it. He described how Americans in 1848 received news that the vast, sleepy province they had just acquired from Mexico was brimming with riches, prompting many a young man to go West, and beginning an almost fifty-year rush on western minerals. "The California gold rush alone offered tens of thousands of people, drawn from every corner of the globe, the chance to pick gold up off the ground," writes Morriss. "Not surprisingly, they flocked to California and spread out across the West in search of more gold. In the process, they turned what had been a quiet provincial back-water into a fast-growing, diversified economy." Cyberspace, Morriss argues, is the analogous virgin territory of our time and exerts the same pull. (Was it a coincidence that at their company's weekly movie night, my classmate Chris and his start-up buddies seemed to only show bad spaghetti Westerns?)

Morriss disagrees, however, with Hollywood's depiction of the Wild West, where "no epic was complete without the villain with the pencil-thin mustache preying on the innocent widow and her helpless children." Beyond the common notion of infinite bounty, his comparison with the Wild West stresses a more controversial quality that he believes the two epochs also share. In his view, there is a similarity in the essential *goodness* of both historical periods and in their ability to self-police (similar, I sup-pose, to the now-defunct "self-policing" system adopted in the early days of eBay, wherein buyers and sellers were trusted to rate one another). Morriss summarizes, and largely dismisses, warnings, already loud in 1998, that the Internet is full of all manner of predators. Such concerns, in his view, serve as pretexts for government interventionists and central planning enthusiasts when what the Internet requires to flourish is what worked well for the Wild West: free rein and a laissez-faire disposition. He accepts that the original infrastructure of the Internet was funded by the government, but describes that version of cyberspace as a boring place populated almost entirely by academics, "much like pre-gold rush California"; and who would want to be surrounded almost entirely by academics? "The nineteenth century west was a place of almost limit-less opportunity," he writes, "where, through market transactions and voluntary action, tens of thousands of strangers developed institutions that allowed them to take advantage of that opportunity in communities of peace and good order. . . . If we are lucky, the Internet will turn out to be just like the American Wild West."

A year earlier, John Ashcroft, then a U.S. senator, opined—in response to a Clinton administration request to give the government the capability to read computer communications—that the limitless potential of the new medium would be seriously challenged by such hindrances as Internet monitoring and taxation. "We should not harness the Internet with a confusing array of intrusive regulations and controls," he said. The best way to support the new medium was to try something that worked in the past: "Online communication is akin to the Wild West of the 19th century. To best settle this new frontier, we should unleash American know-how and ingenuity." In other words, allow the Internet to grow organically, in the heads and on the shoulders of grandiose, manic-y dreamers. Old rules and common fears do not belong in cyberspace and could only impede the dynamic and beautiful process that was naturally unfolding. (Although it was not the point Ashcroft was trying to make, he was probably right to stress *American* know-how and ingenuity: An innovation that is so radical and that makes such tabula rasa with history could have only been made in America, maybe even California.)

The opportunity-creating, frontier-busting parallels with the Wild West that Morriss and Ashcroft were among the first to point out have only become more apparent with time. The sense of being outside of normal rules, and of operating in an economic, legal, and ethical vacuum, and the gold mine of opportunity this creates in people's minds, encourage the large-scale dreaming that defines many online lives. It helps explain why it is difficult *not* to be irrational or exuberant when it comes to our online activities, from investing in start-up stocks, to seeking fame at all costs, to reckless sexual pairings, to impossible-to-fund shopping sprees.

It is harder, however, to agree with these people's early faith in the Internet's essential peace and goodness. (Or, for that matter, the Wild West's.) As the White House's 2009 decision to appoint a "cybersecurity czar" indicates, we know too much now about online financial scams, child pornography rings, cyberstalking, malware, spyware, phishing, "sniffing," and "squatting" not to think that this new Wild West is, indeed, in need of a sheriff. Yet the notion, still alive, that mostly good things happen online, and that little serious or irreversible damage can result from our dealings in the virtual world, remains behind some of our exaggerated initiatives in cyberspace. It is as though a bad outcome, should it happen in the virtual world, will only lead to *virtual* pain—our real lives will proceed blithely.

Consider bankruptcy, for example. Once money goes virtual, debt stops scaring us. Studies like the 2003 UCLA Internet Report suggest that over 20 percent of American Internet users spend more money online than they intend to, and research by Baylor University business professor James Roberts confirms that younger adults—the very demographic most likely to shop online—are most prone to compulsive shopping. According to his research, 10 percent of the so-called millennial generation (defined as those born between 1982 and 1990) can be classified as compulsive buyers, compared to the 1 to 3 percent of baby boomers and 5 percent of Gen Xers. The rates are even higher for younger shoppers born in the nineties: Researchers at the University of Sussex, England, found that 44 percent of adolescents aged sixteen to eighteen are compulsive online shoppers. Is it any wonder that in 2008 total U.S. consumer debt reached $2.52 trillion; that the average American with a credit file is responsible for $16,635 in debt, excluding mortgages; and that the personal savings rate has hovered close to 0 percent for the past several years? When money goes virtual, numbers like these become possible because they don't mean anything anymore. One could argue that our relationship with the dollar increasingly resembles a Second Life resident's relationship with the Linden (L$), the site's official currency. In some ways, it feels just as ungrounded and just as dissociated from its real-life implications.

Along these lines, one has to wonder what role the Internet may have played in the devastating housing bubble and credit meltdown of 2008 and 2009, both of which followed relatively quickly after the dot-com bubble and bust. It is worth noting that four of the top-ten online advertisers in 2007 sold mortgage services, with Low Rate Source ranking number one, and that countless Web sites were in the business of encouraging consumers, including those with marginal credit histories, to bid on properties they could not afford. All of a sudden, too many of us with no real-estate background or relevant qualifications were looking for second homes to "flip," almost as a side hobby. This, too, can be seen as a bout of grandiose thinking, one that online life, by making us allergic to gravity and anything that holds us back, may have helped facilitate. After all, owning a virtual home is relatively painless: All you have to do to build your Second Life McMansion is borrow a few Lindens. Should you default on your loan, the most painful outcome possible is that your Second Life subscription might get suspended or canceled. They call it "real" estate for a reason, yet many of us approached first, second, and vacation homes as though they were virtual property, castles we built in the sky. The awakening, or "correction," that followed was/is surely very painful, but only as painful as the buying binge that preceded it was dissociated.

Dreaming big often translates into a Webvan-style bankruptcy, not to mention the nonfinancial bankruptcies. As a culture with a foot firmly in cyberspace, we seem to be in more danger than before of swinging between bubble and burst, between feast and famine, because of an e-personality that dreams unrealistically big and, because of it, risks bigger disappointments and more dramatic falls.

Even for those insightful or experienced enough to recognize a bubble when they see one, it is still difficult not to get swept up in it. The Internet can make us feel singularly left out if we choose to resist. When we see our friends and colleagues land a "zip zero zilch nada no down payment required" mortgage on zerodownloan.com, or take their business or dating life online, or find a great deal on smartbargains.com, we can start to feel like we are missing out on the windfall/mate/deal of a lifetime if we fail to do the same. To not participate is to miss the boat. How many hours are spent researching books on Amazon, recipes on Epicurious, shoes on Zappos, hotels on TripAdvisor, investment yields on BankRate, and men and women on Match? The Internet offers an exponential increase in the rate of success for our grand quest, whether it is a missing knob for a vintage oven or a date that we are after, because of the exponential increase in exposure and access it affords us. This echoes the stratospheric IPO valuations of the early dot-com days and is today's diluted and much more personal manifestation of the start-up frenzy that created the bubble. Both are the outcomes of the same conquistador mentality. Online, we are all still prospectors at heart, looking for a bonanza like everybody else. And so, many among us believe that if we join enough chat rooms, consult enough blogs, listen to enough podcasts, and look at enough three-dimensional pictures, we can finally discover the unique, perfect, most exquisite . . . can opener!

While the Internet offered, and continues to offer, the thrill of major discovery and the potential for entrepreneurial success, today's version of the froth of the late nineties is more subtle. Online grandiose thinking is no longer reflected in the NASDAQ, or followed live on MSNBC, and our e-personality's outsized dreams are no longer limited to unspeakable wealth. Rather, the online quest has become more personal, and often involves a search for the best possible version of something or someone—and an unshakeable conviction that that version simply *must* exist somewhere in cyberspace, and that with the right search engine and the right search terms we will undoubtedly hunt it down. A subscriber to Match.com, for example, has access to fifteen million potential matches. For a man looking to meet a woman, the site allows him to specify her geographic location, ethnicity, height range, body type (many gradations from "slender" to "big and beautiful"), eye color, hair color, religion, educational level, languages spoken, job, salary range, marital status, whether she smokes or drinks, whether she has or wants kids, and whether any kids live with her. With such a large pool of candidates to choose from, and such sophisticated tools to help him narrow down his search and zero in on the perfect match, a man is justified in feeling that he can find *exactly* what he is looking for. His dream of finding that perfect someone—or that perfect anything—is now within reach, or so it seems.

The Internet has become the sure means to almost every brilliant goal, the one common road to myriad things we fantasize about and want to see realized. The conviction that the virtual world will help us "get there" justifies our lack of moderation: If our online expedition is expensive, time-consuming, or even of questionable morality or legality, at least it can be rationalized as a quest for a state of perfection that we now know exists and can be found; at least it can be done in the name of discovery and dream fulfillment. Our e-personality is happier, almost by definition, because it can set for itself unrealistic goals considered elusive in normal life, and then amuse itself confidently trying to achieve them.

Although the Internet has been with us, more or less in its current form, for nearly fifteen years, the conquistador mentality remains at the heart of our quixotic approach to the virtual world, as I have argued. And conquistadors were not in it for the anonymity. They marked the terrain with monuments, headstones, blood, and babies. They nurtured their legend and celebrated their conquests. In a similar way, but lacking much of the pathos, a cult of fame often marks people's approach to the Internet, only in cyberspace it is typically short-term, disposable fame that one is after—more grandiose than grand. Most of us, of course, will never achieve any significant degree of recognition from our blog, Facebook page, Match profile, or other virtual endeavors. Still, overnight celebrity stories can stoke our own dreams of the proverbial fifteen minutes of fame. But even if we do not become a breakout Internet celebrity, chances are we are participating in the creation of one. For instance, who among us has not watched, or marveled at, the fame and reach of such online celebrities as gossip blogger Perez Hilton, YouTube superstars Obama Girl and lonelygirl15, and Christian Lander of the wildly successful satirical blog Stuff White People Like? Who has not been forwarded a link to their videos, or has not cc'd one around? The fact that in March 2009 there were over six billion videos posted on YouTube is a testament to our online ambitions: While not everybody is looking for fame, many amateurs are competing to be the next Tila Tequila, the MySpace celebrity who was given her own MTV reality show, or, especially, the next Justin Bieber, the sixteen-year-old whose homemade videos, posted on YouTube when he was twelve, launched him into superstardom, eventually sweeping up the world with a highly infectious case of "Bieber fever." Not to mention the thousands of "citizen journalists" posting their work on CNN's iReport.com—where the banner reads: "Your stories. No boundaries. You won't believe what people are uploading"—and hoping to make the jump from the Web site to the cable news channel.

"Broadcast Yourself" is what YouTube's banner implores its users to do. Matt Harding is one of the millions of people who have taken this message to heart, broadcasting "Dancing," a four-and-a-half-minute video of himself dancing in sixty-nine different locations worldwide, to over ten million viewers. Here is how the *New York Times* described his dance in a 2008 article:

> . . . a big, doughy-looking fellow in shorts and hiking boots performing an arm-swinging, knee-pumping step that could charitably be called goofy. It's the kind of semi-ironic dance that boys do by themselves at junior high mixers when they're too embarrassed to partner with actual girls.

According to the *Times*, Harding had skipped college at the recommendation of his father, who found it pointless to pay tuition for someone he felt was so unmotivated, and worked at a video game store before embarking on the travels that led to "Dancing." On the video, he is often seen dancing in the company of others—New Guinea bushmen, Bollywood dancers, Tokyo waitresses, South African street children—all imitating his "flailing chicken step." The contagiousness of the dance, as seen in the international cast of dance partners on the video, was also reflected in the response by online viewers who wasted no time in trying to outdo it, and to blog and vlog—for video blogging—all over it. The end result for Harding was a publicity contract with a chewing gum company, an appearance on *Good Morning America*, and, of course, the *New York Times* article. His father must have been proud. Never in real life did he expect his son to succeed.

A Google search of Matt Harding today yields 541,000 results. Rudolf Nureyev, considered by some the best ballet dancer the world has known? A mere 300,000. As Harding's story indicates, online fame is easier to attain and is uniquely democratic; everyone is entitled to grandiose dreams, and everyone's grandiosity stands a reasonable chance of being "rewarded." No birthright privileges or special qualifications, like talent or looks, are required. One need not speak English to succeed wildly in English-speaking countries. Consider the example of Mahir Cagri, a man from Izmir, Turkey, whose Internet celebrity peaked in 1999, when his picture-laden personal homepage, which related in effusive, broken English his hospitality and some of his favorite things, became a hit among millions of Web users: "I like music, I have many many music enstrumans my home I can play"; "Who is want to come TURKEY I can invitate. . . . She can stay my home. . . . ."; and "I kiss you!!!!!" Countless fans, especially women, from around the world kissed Cagri back, posting pictures of their puckered lips on their own Web sites, along with a personal dedication to the gushy Turk. *Madtv* and *Late Show with David Letterman* appearances followed, and another star was born.

If the planets of cyberspace line up, nonhuman "celebrities" can happen, too. Any especially supplicating e-mail from a banking institution in Nigeria, any urban legend, any animation short can aspire to be the next "Dancing Baby." The 3-D digital rendition of a lifeless baby dancing for several seconds circulated among millions of Internet users in the late nineties, and was eventually featured in a Blockbuster commercial and on the popular TV series *Ally McBeal.* As proof that the baby "made it," many parodies competed to snatch fame away from him, including "Drunken Baby," "Samurai Baby," and "Rasta Baby."

The animation file, much like the I Kiss You Web site and Harding's videos, is an example of an Internet meme, an online phenomenon that spreads virally across the ether, temporarily forcing a place for him/her/it in our zeitgeist, thereby satisfying someone's grandiose yearnings (his narcissistic yearnings, too, no doubt, but more on those later), and encouraging them in countless others. Memes are behind the celebrity manufacturing behemoth that is the Internet, and most of us partake in spreading them around, sometimes hoping that our own profile, video, Web site, or blog will also catch on, bringing Web traffic in our direction.

In his 1976 book *The Selfish Gene,* British author Richard Dawkins defined the meme as a unit of cultural information, like a belief or practice, that is transmitted from one person to another by repetition, in a manner similar to the biological transmission of genes. The word is derived from the Greek *mimos,* the root for "mimic," and points to the power of imitation in propagating culture. Applied to the Internet, memes offer a framework for understanding how quickly a phenomenon can metastasize online, efficiently spreading to "all four corners" of the wired globe until the whole World Wide Web is audience to the sensation du jour. Internet memes spread from in-box to in-box, very much like a computer virus although they are not called that, transferring the genetic material of one day in the life of cyberspace. However, unlike real DNA, which is passed vertically from one generation to another, memes, including Internet memes, travel horizontally, compressing the requisite twenty-five-year generation length to disseminate, instantly, the hot issues, and "hotties," of the moment.

Web sites like somethingawful.com, bored.com, snopes.com, and dipity.com chronicle and timeline the lives of Internet memes. To reacquaint oneself with memes of days past is to realize how evanescent

Internet fame is and how suspect the online grandiosity that fed it. It is a lesson in how Warhol's fifteen minutes, fleeting enough in pre-virtual readymade culture, have been further condensed by the Internet, metaphorically reduced to a "flicker" of relevance on flickr.com, the popular picture-sharing Web site. Because it is easier to copy and reproduce big dreams online than in real life, everything from celebrity status to discovery to second homes to "going public" seems that much closer and that much easier to close in on. The price we pay for online mimetic propagation, however, is twofold: the usually ephemeral nature of whatever it is we are propagating, and its typically inferior quality.

According to Gary Marshall, of London's Middlesex University, there is, in cyberspace, "a premium on short, catchy memes as opposed to more complex [ones]. Infectiousness assumes an importance far greater than that of attributes that may well have greater long-term value such as utility and authority." The grandiose objectives that mark many people's online lives tend to lie on the superficial side and are more preoccupied with reproducing short-lived attention than something substantive or lasting—a "flailing chicken step" will always generate more hits, which is the goal, than any intelligent contribution in an online forum of ideas. A Web site's utmost goal may be for users to bookmark it and add it to their list of "favorites." It will do anything in its means to catch our attention and earn that distinction. Many of us take the same approach, and do not mind if our contributions are not meaningful enough to last beyond those fifteen minutes. Everything online is transient anyway. No teenager in my extended family would be caught dead on MySpace today. They have all migrated to Facebook, whose administrators, in turn, live in fear that users will abandon them en masse in favor of Twitter or the next trendy network. It's only a matter of time. If our love affair with e-mail has given way to a love of texting, anything can happen. Transience is the new norm, and that does not seem to bother us.

"There is nothing, or next to nothing, in human behavior that is not learned, and all learning is based on imitation," writes French philosopher René Girard. "If human beings suddenly ceased imitating, all forms of culture would vanish." Much of what we do is to imitate others. That includes imitating them in what or whom they desire, in hopes of achieving the same enhanced level of being we think they possess. "If the model, who is apparently already endowed with superior being, desires some object, that object must surely be capable of conferring an even greater plenitude of being." As Girard sees it, it is not so much fame or a second home or a sexual partner that provokes us, but another person's desire for them. Rather than a binary relationship between a wanted object and the person wanting it, then, desire is *triangular*. It involves the desired object, the person (me) seeking it, and another person who is after the same thing I want and on whom I model my own desire. Given that the Internet is the domain, par excellence, of unregulated desire— a subject I will explore more fully later—as well as of imitation and reproduction, as "Rasta," "Samurai," and the other dancing babies from this chapter suggest, we can appreciate the bloody competition that is likely to follow ("bloody" because two or more people are now after the same thing and because our model is also our rival). The conflict that results provides one mechanism for understanding how the Internet, a medium of memes and mimetic desiring, is awash in so much violence and hostility.

Whether it is little old ladies stampeding to jack up the stock of a questionable dot-com start-up, wide-eyed young entrepreneurs convinced they will take the next Facebook public, a working-class couple applying for a second home mortgage at zerodownloans.com because their neighbors did so, or fame seekers who would love nothing better than to become virtual memes, people online often seem to be elbowing one another in a grandiose race, blinding themselves in the process to some eternal truths and past lessons, and to the inevitability of the bankruptcies and busts to come. Sadder yet is that we do not always learn from the bankruptcy or bust when it does happen. The hold that grandiosity has over our online psyche is such that it seems to require only a short period of time before it recovers and comes roaring back again. How else, after the "dot gone" bloodbath, can one explain the popularity in Silicon Valley of t-shirts and bumper stickers that read "I want to be irrationally exuberant again"?

But must one rain on people's dreams? Would we have visionaries, idealists, and artists if dreamers ceased dreaming? Why call what they engage in "grandiosity" and give it a clinical tinge? To the extent that the virtual world enriches our dream life, it can enrich our real life, too. It can help us open new windows and think up new possibilities, and what is the human condition if not a sense of restlessness with the moment and a constant striving for a better tomorrow? This restlessness, this striving, have found in the virtual world a formidably powerful but tricky means to some age-old goals. Yes, there is a way to use the Internet to imagine better days and then help make them happen. In reality, however, many of the scenarios we dream up in cyberspace are either not worth the REM sleep that produced them or are so engrossing that we refuse to wake up when waking up should, eventually, be the objective; the way we translate beautiful visions into an improved reality.

Like Webvan and the groceries it tried to deliver, online grandiosity tends to have a limited shelf life. Nearly fifteen years into the Internet revolution, this should be rather obvious, yet we still approach virtual life with supersized notions and the Napoleonic conviction that, while glory is fleeting, obscurity is forever. Never mind that so many of our online pursuits are hardly imperial—in our new value system, it is better to be a passing meme than an unknown soldier.

CHAPTER 3

NARCISSISM

CLOSELY LINKED TO grandiose thinking is *narcissism*, another character trait that is nurtured by the Web and that marks many people's e-personalities. According to the *DSM*, people with narcissistic personality disorder not only are grandiose but have a "need for admiration" and a "lack of empathy." *DSM*-certified narcissists usually believe they are "'special' and unique and can only be understood by, or should associate with, other special or high-status people." Their attitudes tend toward the "arrogant" and "haughty," and they have an exaggerated sense of entitlement, with "unreasonable expectations of especially favorable treatment or automatic compliance with [their] expectations." They are often "interpersonally exploitative," which means they will ignore the needs of others and even manipulate them in order to achieve their own goals.

Narcissists are self-worshippers who want you to worship them, too. They can only conceive of themselves on a pedestal, and can only conceive of you in the audience, preferably in the backseats. They are "full of themselves," like some grandiose individuals can be. In addition, they are often full of low regard for the other, because of the other's inferiority and inability to measure up. While grandiose people can fly so high and be so removed from reality that they make the observer feel unanchored himself, a narcissist will make you feel exploited and taken for a ride. One gives you vertigo; the other, a bad taste in your mouth.

According to epidemiological studies, less than 1 percent of the population meet criteria for pathological narcissism as defined in the *DSM*. (Studies also suggest that men are more likely to be afflicted than women.) However, with the Internet encouraging and sustaining some of the features that make up narcissistic personality disorder, it is quite possible that this figure has now become an underestimate.

A tour of the online evidence for narcissism takes the person from the ridiculous to the sublime. The popularity of "narcissurfing," a new word that made many 2007 "word of the year" lists, points to many people's obsession with the online footprint they are leaving (hint: bigger is better). This does not refer to the healthy concern about what is being written about someone online, and how, for example, it might affect that person's chances of getting a job. Rather, it is a celebration of the number of results a person's self-search yields. Here is how UrbanDictionary.com, a slang dictionary compiled by online users, defines it, along with the example it supplies of its usage in daily speak:

> **Narcissurfing**: Googling yourself to see where, when, and how often you show up on the Internet.
> JOE: I wonder why Tom was so late to work this morning?
> TIM: I guess he stayed up all night narcissurfing.
> JOE: The guy is such a narcissist.

The shift from e- to i- in prefixing Internet URLs and naming electronic "apps" parallels the rise of the self-absorbed online Narcissus. Like the Judeo-Christian God, the "I" is omnipresent in cyberspace and in what is now being appropriately called "personal media." From "i"Tunes to "i"Pod to "i"Phone, the entire digital world, and not just Apple, is at the disposal of the first-person singular pronoun. (Not to mention the iPad, whose name brought up hyperpersonal hygiene issues for some women, and caused tweets like: "Heavy flow? There's an app for that!")

The Internet is more I-centric than ever and all about you. Yahoo!, for example, seeking to make a comeback and regain territory from Google, launched a global branding campaign in late 2009 that played up this very characteristic. It was titled "It's Y!ou" and included ads such as: "Now the Internet Has a Personality. Yours."; "There's a New Master of the Digital Universe. It's Y!ou"; and "The Internet Is under New Management. Yours." By 2010, the campaign had turned even more personal, with slogans such as: "Your Own Personal Everything." and "The Web, Myself and I."

EarthLink's ubiquitous tagline, "EarthLink revolves around you," makes the same point below the signature at the bottom of e-mails that its users send. So does the "Mi-Fi," a new gadget that brings you your own portable Wi-Fi bubble, a private hot spot that follows you wherever you go, like a cloud constantly over your head. As for the iPhone, downloading iBubbleWrap from your online Apple store can calm your nerves by giving you virtual bubble wrap to pop: "Unlike real bubble wrap, iBubbleWrap never runs out of bubbles to pop and you always have it with you." If you get that satisfaction from popping whiteheads, instead, Zit Picker lets you pinch and pop Veronica's incoming pimples, or those of any friend whose picture you direct the program to pull from your album. Even less useful, iCycle keeps a guy alert to the hormonal shifts of the woman in his life: "Enjoy peace and quiet in your relationships. Prevent arguments and unnecessary misunderstandings, save money, plan your dates, vacations, weekend trips and major discussions within her 'best time period' of the month." Someone needs to get an iLife!

More than ever, virtual and digital technology aims to satisfy our every last need and to put us in the driver's seat. Not only can we choose our online news source to read, we can modify it in dramatic ways. We can specify, for instance, which news topics we want on the "front page" and which ones we'd like moved to the end or filtered out completely. As one writer remarked before, instead of CNN, the *Washington Post*, or the *Daily Oklahoman*, we can sip our morning coffee reading "The Daily Me." Similarly, in the age of podcasting, live feeds, virtual music libraries, and iPods, it is now possible to listen only to songs that we know we like. Also, with Web sites such as Hulu and digital video recorders such as TiVo, we have more power than at any other time to watch only the shows we want, when we want to, even speeding through the commercials. Complaining about this culture of customization is slightly disingenuous—we all crave tools that save us time and that reflect our individuality and unique tastes. But two unintended consequences cannot be ignored. First, as we increasingly choose to expose ourselves only to the ideas, entertainment, and even people that appeal to us, we are undermining the common experiences essential to a sense of community and fragmenting ourselves along narrow lines of interest. This state has been called iSolation, when the Internet was supposed to broaden our horizons, diversify our interests, and help us commune with the world. The second consequence might be more relevant to a discussion of narcissism: As we get accustomed to having even our most minor needs, such as the need to pop bubble wrap, accommodated to this degree, we may be growing more entitled.

Very Short List is a good online resource that succinctly reviews, in regular e-mails sent to subscribers, interesting highlights from the world of science and pop culture, including cyberculture. Being chosen to receive those feeds—that is, being "Very Short Listed"—may have unconsciously tickled my own narcissistic fantasies, but, in reality, anyone with an e-mail address can instantly join and claim that privilege. One VSL feed that landed in my in-box brought me news of a 2008 study on Facebook narcissism conducted by Laura Buffardi and Keith Campbell, of the Department of Psychology at the University of Georgia, in Athens. Very Short List accurately and succinctly summarized the take-home findings from the well-designed study.

According to VSL, Facebook provides "the perfect forum for . . . narcissistic tendencies: Instead of looking in the mirror too long, [narcissists] can spend all day online, updating their profiles and basking in their own bright light." To illustrate their point, VSL refers readers to the Facebook profile of Ashley Alexandra Dupré, the high-priced call girl whose services cost Eliot Spitzer, the governor of New York—and, some might say, a raging narcissist himself, but that's a different story— his job in 2008. I suppose VSL surmised that a non-narcissist would have had enough with "networking" after the scandal and would have chosen out of shame if nothing else to disappear from the public eye for a little while and temporarily suspend her membership with the site.

In their own minds, narcissists have always felt perfect, but the Internet may be giving them the opportunity to show off even more and to fall in love with themselves all over again. Venues such as Facebook and MySpace are very effective outlets of self-promotion through heavily edited biographical information, flattering pictures, and the large numbers of shallow Web-based relationships advertised on people's profiles, and meant to imply popularity ("I'm so cool I have three hundred friends on Facebook"). Dupré's MySpace page—she has one there, too—counts over 14,000, and Facebook found it necessary to lift its 5,000-friend limit to embrace the increasingly promotional role it plays in people's lives. People can now use the site to broaden their audience base even further and quickly communicate with their legions of fans. Twitter, to be discussed in more detail later, more straightforwardly calls those "followers."

In Buffardi and Campbell's study, which was published in the journal *Personality and Social Psychology Bulletin,* 129 undergraduate Facebook page owners were recruited to be interviewed and have their Facebook pages analyzed. Researchers administered the Narcissistic Personality Inventory, or NPI, a forty-item personality test designed to detect narcissistic traits by asking test takers to choose between statements such as "My body is nothing special" versus "I like to look at my body," and "There is a lot I can learn from other people" versus "I am more capable than other people." (In the foregoing sample pairs, the second statement is awarded one point, whereas the first statement is awarded no points. Higher total scores on the NPI correlate with higher degrees of narcissism.)

In addition, independent raters who did not meet the study participants analyzed their Facebook pages using a number of objective and subjective criteria. The objective criteria were based on Facebook-specific features such as the number of friends listed, the number of virtual groups the page owner belonged to, the number of lines of text in the "About Me" section, and the number of Wall posts—messages posted on the owner's bulletin board. The hypothesis was that Facebook users with the greatest number of friends, virtual group affiliations, Wall posts, and lines of self-description were more likely to be narcissistic in real life, as judged by their NPI scores.

The subjective criteria analyzed included the contents of the "About Me" section (rated as self-absorbed, self-important, self-promoting, or self-conscious) and the amount of clothing worn in the main photo (rated as attractive, self-promoting, sexy, vain, or modest). The scores on the objective and subjective measures of narcissism as seen on the Facebook page were then tallied and compared to the participants' NPI scores.

The results showed that users with higher NPI scores—that is, more narcissism in real life—were seen as sexier and more self-promoting in their photograph. The independent raters were able to accurately detect the owner's level of narcissism based solely on the profile's content. (I guess there is something to the old designation of personal Web pages as "vanity sites.") Perhaps more telling, however, is that higher scores on the NPI were linked to higher numbers of Facebook interactions with other users. The more narcissistic, the more interactive. Buffardi and Campbell conclude that "because narcissists have more social contacts on Facebook than the non-narcissists, the average user will experience a social network that over-represents narcissists. . . . [This] raises the possibility that—because of elevated exposure to narcissistic individuals and self-promotion—norms of expression on social networking sites will be pulled in the direction of greater self-promotion."

Mark Leary, a Duke University psychologist, raised similar concerns about the implications of the study. He describes Facebook as essentially a "self-presentational vehicle" that is "a little bit like advertising." Since we expect ads to be self-promoting, we are now in a situation where "the rules of advertising apply to ordinary human beings." We objectify ourselves, cherry-picking and highlighting our most favorable attributes, then merchandize them in the same way a car or shampoo ad might. Venues like Facebook and MySpace, and the many online dating sites, turn us into virtual billboards, flaunting our sometimes invented attributes. The goal is to stop (Internet) traffic whatever it takes—not an easy feat given all the other virtual billboards one could be looking at. One wonders how, over time, this would not translate into rising levels of narcissism. Indeed, it is hard to feel normal and reasonably sociable having only six Facebook friends when your classmate at school or colleague at work links to over two hundred. How else to prevent a painful inferiority complex, then, than to quickly and drastically reconfigure your online identity in a way that raises your popularity index and self-esteem? This is what I will call entering "God mode," and it might be as narcissistic an act as we are capable of.

We all have in the back of our minds a fitter-for-survival version of ourselves that we wish could be real—one that is free of the inhibitions that hold us back and of various character and physical "deficits," like IQ and sex appeal limitations. This gap between the idealized version and reality often serves to motivate people toward self-betterment through ways that include education, hard work, and even spirituality. It is what encourages people on the bottom end of the office hierarchy to prove themselves and earn a promotion, and what inspires overweight individuals to exercise. It is what prompts an anxious person to work harder to break out of his anxious shell. It is also what gives us a dose of humility. For many people today, however, the Internet promises a shortcut to that difficult-to-attain perfect model—one that goes through Photoshop, Dreamweaver, and other software of dissimulation to painlessly and efficiently turn them into someone else that they perceive as much better than themselves.

The Internet can provide a safe space for self-conscious or otherwise inhibited individuals to connect with one another. I have often "prescribed" online dating to socially anxious patients, as Jill's doctor did before me, and have taken the liberty to suggest it to busy friends as well. What has repeatedly struck me, however, is how difficult it is to resist the opportunity for online reinvention. While all the cultures of the world have felt a seasonal need for disguise—think Halloween, Mardi Gras, Venetian masquerades, and Rio carnivals—reinvention and pretense are now pervasive and constant, thanks to a large degree to the Internet. As a result, it is more difficult than ever to tell when one's mask is on and when it is off. Whether we are pretending to be someone more accomplished in a chat room or embellishing what we have to offer in an online personal ad, we rely upon the distance afforded us by the Internet—the distance between writer and audience—in order to deceive. It is this distance, much greater online than it is offline, that allows some of us to create wildly airbrushed copies of ourselves in cyberspace. And it is this distance that allows the mythical version of who we are to emerge. For if John and Jane Doe represent the nondescript all-too-real everyman and everywoman, e-John and e-Jane are their mythologized, full-of-life online versions. They are today's answer to the age-old lure of the alter ego, Latin for the "other I," and they are on the prowl in cyberspace. All this makes a reality check from Plato timely again.

According to Plato's theory of ideal forms, objects and events are only shadows of their perfect versions. Those versions, which he called "Forms," belong to a different realm altogether, and while we can understand them intellectually, they are frustratingly difficult to attain in the sensible world. The beauty of a flower we pick, for instance, is a decay-prone example of the perfect, eternal, and changeless original. A drafts-man's penciled line, however straight, remains imperceptibly crooked when judged against the standard of absolute straightness. Even justice, as in Plato's recounting of Socrates' trial, is only an imperfect, unfair copy of some elusive, unattainable Justice that exists elsewhere. Beauty, Straightness, and Justice, as well as the highest form of them all—the Form of the Good—are all ideals that the best human life should strive to understand and emulate, accepting all along that it will never completely achieve them. The Christian tradition, in part through the work of theologians Saint Augustine and Saint Thomas Aquinas, fur-ther cemented this notion, fusing the Form of the Good with God (the so-called hellenization of Christianity), and forcing upon humanity an added dose of modesty and realism vis-à-vis a superior realm or being.

For better or worse, we have been liberated from that inferiority com-plex. The Internet has the power to transform us into self-infatuated demigods. According to Richard Dawkins, God-unfriendly author of *The God Delusion*, people on Second Life act in a "God-like way." He is right: A higher game level with additional administrative rights and enhanced access is even referred to as "God mode," and comes with a "God menu" that allows the person greater control over Second Life real estate, avatars, and players. Important questions follow from becoming accustomed to such privileges in cyberspace: Why put up with some character weaknesses when we can pretend to be omnipotent? Why struggle to advance at our job if we can be the reigning boss of our own little corner in the blogosphere? Why work hard to socially integrate if we can count five hundred friends between MySpace and Facebook? With his virtual life as perfect and empowering as he made it, my patient Alex no longer found reason to improve himself offline, eventually los-ing patience with reality altogether.

Alex did not start out a narcissist, but he changed into something that resembles one when the Internet convinced him that his "Form," in all its perfection, was now accessible to him. The result is that he fell in love with his picture and ended up inadvertently exploiting people he cared about. I told his story in my book *Compulsive Acts*, and reprise it in summary form here, with a somewhat different focus.

Alex was an anxious twentysomething who came to see me at the urging of his fiancée, Natalie. He had serendipitously joined an online community that advocated dropping out of normal life and living, virtually, whatever alternate existence one wished to have. There, for the first time, Alex's identity was his to perfect as he saw fit, with no IQ, socio-economic, or psychological barriers. If, as was Alex's case, one is plagued with social anxiety, one can still be the most outgoing, life-of-the-party character there is. Simply put, one can pick and choose the individual genes that make up one's DNA—a fascinating concept that in real life might be called eugenics and might bring up memories of Nazi selective breeding. And it got Alex hooked.

Using the site's sophisticated graphics, Alex invented Sasha, a gregarious former high school jock, now in his midthirties, who is CEO of a high-tech company. "I then meticulously painted in his hair, streak by streak, and picked 'azure blue' for his eye color and 'snow white' for his teeth. I paid for a fully loaded subscription so I could buy real estate right on the edge of Lake Eternity, with great views over downtown."

Unlike Jill, my extremely shy patient who also took extreme liberties redefining herself, Alex did not just pretend to possess qualities he always dreamed of having; he appeared to be "living out" his new life. Just recounting the experience in my office seemed to imbue him with newfound self-confidence: I could hear his voice grow steadier and see his body elongate into a much more comfortable position from the almost fetal curl he was in at the beginning of our first session.

Before long, Alex's obsession with Sasha became an all-consuming, almost philosophical pursuit, and he started doubting the value of real life compared to the "full" one he created for himself in the virtual world. Suddenly, the life he had always known—with its little problems and myriad anxieties—*that* life became the "second" one. He would check, at least once an hour, Sasha's mailbox, but didn't mind letting his mail pile up at home. And, when he had a choice of going to an open house with his fiancée or going online to work some more on Sasha's virtual home, there was no doubting where his priorities lay and where his heart was.

His fiancée was growing increasingly frustrated by a game that had become Alex's main focus. Yet she still thought of it as essentially a juvenile pastime that her twenty-nine-year-old husband-to-be would soon outgrow. She stopped being patient, however, and stopped thinking of it as a game when he introduced her to Nadia.

Nadia was another virtual resident Alex met on the site who then became Sasha's virtual girlfriend. With her permission, Alex reworked her features, from her waist size to the number of freckles on her cheeks. "I might as well have been Michelangelo working on a sculpture—nothing, *nothing*, ever gave me such a high before," he told me. "And, the more time I spent online with Nadia, whether at the movies, cooking dinner in Sasha's kitchen, or even in bed, the more resentful Natalie became."

Alex, in the form of Sasha, had embarked on some form of a romantic relationship with Nadia, an online character he designed. The woman he fell in love with was his own creation, which might imply that he was really in love with himself. Too similar to the story of Narcissus staring at his reflection in the pond—we know to anticipate a bad outcome.

Natalie had many qualities, not the least of which might have been that she was real. Unfortunately, as Alex later told me, real had become overrated. "Who needs Natalie when one can have Nadia?" is the question he seemed to be struggling with. Like most real-life girlfriends and boyfriends, Natalie came with too much baggage. Alex had perfected himself online, or so he thought, and nothing short of a masterpiece girlfriend was worth his time anymore. But Alex was not interested in "processing" any of this. He had come to see me at the insistence of his fiancée, and as soon as he made the final decision to leave her, he canceled his appointments.

Moved by Natalie's predicament, and still intent on trying to help him, I decided to go visit Alex myself. He agreed. I approached the Internet with trepidation as I typed the site's address. Once on the homepage, I chose the name "Doc" for my guest registration and was given the option to either build my own unique body or accept a generic one. I took the latter option and used the mouse to guide myself to where we were supposed to meet.

I recognized Sasha immediately. The good looks Alex had described gave him away.

"Hello, is this Alex?" I typed as a bubble rose over my head carrying my words. Alex prompted me for the password we had agreed on. "Shrink," I typed, then quickly got into the meat of our "session."

I asked Alex whether he felt he had crossed a dangerous line and created a complete rupture between who he is online and who he used to be. Alex agreed that he had, but did not see that as something bad. "I'm trying to understand what reality really is, and I happen to think this is very important work." Over a long exchange, I suggested that he keep a foot in both worlds; that he reflect, if he must, on what reality is, but do it in a way that didn't make him completely withdraw from a life in which his existence, fraught as it was, still had meaning. But I was ultimately unsuccessful.

"I'm sorry. I'm just not invested enough in your reality at this point." At that point Alex logged off, his avatar melting into the chat room's background.

Feeling what I can best describe as bereavement, I lingered alone, hoping that he would come back, maybe with a change of heart or a follow-up question. To kill time, I used the pop-up menu to pick out a face—"sad and forlorn"—for my generic body, and personalized other details of my appearance. But Alex never returned. Another resident of the community, however, did materialize: A balding man with an older face on a younger body, and wearing a white bathrobe with matching slippers.

"You look sad and forlorn," the man said, rather robotically, immediately upon seeing me. "Can I help you?"

I tried to exit, but the man would not let me. "You look sad and forlorn. Can I help you?" he kept repeating.

Despite feeling detained, I was moved by this stranger's insistence on helping another stranger based on nothing but a standard facial expression I had borrowed. Something about his mechanical kindness was both endearing and intriguing. "I'm Doc," I typed, curious to find out more about him. "Who are you?"

"I am God," the man responded. "You look sad and forlorn. Can I help you?"

I had gone online to try to save a patient from a God-like version of himself and his girlfriend, only to find God. Are there any mere mortals around here? Where am I? Mount Olympus?

While the Internet encourages dreams of wealth, health, and happiness—all of which can seem but a mouse click away—it also feeds self-distortion and delusion, by which I mean the ability to enhance or perfect oneself online simply by grossly misrepresenting one's identity, like Alex did, or aspects of that identity, like most of us do, to varying degrees. Given our natural propensity for self-improvement, we spend hours "clicking away," allowing our Internet-empowered imagination to produce new and vastly improved copies of our generic selves—versions that might be more at home in Plato's universe of ideals than in any version of the real world that we have come to know. What is worse is that in some cases we start believing the misrepresentation. We buy into how unique and popular and attractive we are. All of a sudden, our real-life friends, fiancés, partners, and spouses are no longer good enough. We start expecting to be admired and to want to associate only with equally admiration-worthy people. This is one way virtual life can encourage narcissistic tendencies in people.

Some have compared the extreme misrepresentation that takes place online to a parapsychotic state. Defined as a radical break from reality, and found in severe psychiatric illnesses such as schizophrenia, psychosis is one of the most serious symptoms mental health professionals treat. Many virtual reality addicts, like Alex, can be far more functional in society than most schizophrenic patients can, unfortunately, ever hope to be. However, the degree of their retreat into the virtual world has in some cases been likened to what is seen in someone who has withdrawn into a hallucinatory, parallel reality as a result of schizophrenia-like symptoms. Psychoanalyst Patricia L. Gibbs of the Michigan Psychoanalytic Institute goes so far in comparing the two states as to call the denial of reality that the Internet can facilitate "ordinary everyday psychosis."

Gibbs describes how hallucinations in an individual with schizophrenia—typically voices originating inside his head—are interpreted in Freudian psychoanalysis as the concrete form that an unbearable, unconscious conflict in the person's mind takes. Ambivalence about an abusive mother, for example, can, according to psychoanalytic theory, give rise to hallucinations. For Gibbs, immersion in virtual reality serves the same purpose; it takes painful conflicts and turns them into something that she sees as approaching psychosis. "The Internet can also be seen as serving the . . . anxiety-reducing function of transforming the reality of painful unconscious conflicts . . . into a more bearable hallucinatory virtual reality," she says. "Use of the Internet/computer, then, serve[s] the same function as hallucinations, namely to alter a too-painful . . . reality." In other words, the Internet took Alex, a somewhat detached, conflicted young man, and reduced his anxiety by turning him into Sasha, a *totally* detached version of himself—one that is as real as a hallucination.

Still, we hardly need to subscribe to Second Life, or to fall in love with an online picture, as Alex did, to be capable of some degree of online "hallucinating." The Internet, not a therapist's couch or a friend's arms, is where many people go today to sublimate all sorts of conflicts. The elongated padded chaise of the traditional analyst's office has morphed into the iPhone's "touch screen," and people pour their souls out, express their worst fears, hate their mothers, and kiss and make peace—all in blogs, on Facebook, and in texting or e-mail. For "all of us," Gibbs writes, online ordinary everyday psychosis "affords us control over an otherwise too painful reality."

And what I and others are, rather liberally, comparing to psychosis is seen on both ends of the online transaction. It operates in people who, like Alex, deny reality to the point of creating wildly revised online versions of themselves and then buy into them. It also operates in their deluded audiences—people who are clamoring to be listed as their friends, or are praying to get their e-mails to them answered while willfully suspending disbelief about the information these objects of their adoration are feeding them. According to the University of Southern California's 2008 Digital Future Project, as many as half of Internet users find that most or all of the information available online to be generally reliable. While some people may feel too threatened by what they see or read, my professional experience has convinced me that exaggerations like those listed in personal ads and on Match profiles, Facebook, and MySpace are more likely to inspire desire and awe than doubt and avoidance of the Internet. The person behind Nadia, Alex's virtual girlfriend, fell for a supposed jock CEO without pausing to question his real identity. Alex, who *knew* of her fakeness—he perfected her himself with software—felt invested enough in that relationship to justify breaking up with his fiancée. It hardly mattered to him that his perfect Second Life girlfriend might, in real life, be a shriveled old man living in New Zealand.

Like Alex and Nadia, people are inclined to accept online lies about others if the lies give them the illusion of approaching a perfect ideal they want to own or be with. Too quickly, they buy into the product being promoted, few questions asked. And just as online advertising seems to work and is causing traditional newspapers to fold for lack of advertising revenue, online *self*-advertising works, too, and is causing real-life relationships to fold as cyber–alter egos play make-believe then crash and burn on the first contact with reality. I will elaborate on this point more, with research studies and "mainstream" examples, in the love and relationships chapter.

It is paradoxical, no doubt. The desire for "contact with reality" is often greater the more perfect and godlike the online misrepresentation is. I cannot confirm it because he did not continue to work with me, but I imagine Alex and the person behind Nadia eventually talked about meeting in real life, despite the numerous "red flags." Indeed, we dream of taking all that Facebook sexiness offline, and fantasize about occupying the same pedestal in the office or in our marriage that we occupy in the blogosphere. If the person is a true narcissist, he will get an even bigger ego boost from a living, breathing, clapping audience. Even as we chase Plato's ideals in cyberspace, most of us refuse to settle for entirely "platonic" relationships and still want to consummate our virtual bonds in reality. Because of the strong pull to make what works so well in cyberspace also work offline, we start confusing the online narratives we have woven with the real world, which is where the danger begins. A somewhat extreme story from a genuinely psychotic patient helps illustrate the risks of virtual alter egos on the loose offline.

Wendy was a forty-two-year-old landscaper whom I treated for bipolar disorder. She thought she had found love online after meeting Omar, a thirty-three-year-old Jordanian man, on a singles' Web site. Instead of presenting an obstacle to their love, the fact that Omar lived in the Middle East initially fueled Wendy's romanticism with exotic notions imported from *A Thousand and One Nights* and Elizabeth Taylor and Richard Burton's *Cleopatra*. Their love could not subsist on imagination alone, however. Wendy very much wanted to meet Omar in person, but her limited financial resources and his visa problems precluded that. So, in her strong desire to be with Omar, Wendy, now psychotic from bipolar mania, started believing that a neck rash she developed one morning—a known but relatively uncommon side effect of the new mood stabilizer I had just prescribed—was actually a hickey that resulted from their intense session of online making out the night before. Here was tangible proof of perfect love, consummated.

Thankfully, most people do not buy into online representations to the point of developing virtual hickeys. Most of our online "psychosis" is a lot more "ordinary" and "everyday," and our brushes with online perfection tend to be less dramatic and extreme. One hardly needs to be psychotic or take make-believe to Second Life levels to be seriously faking it or to cause real harm. In that sense, my patient's Ron experience with Craigslist misrepresentation may be more relevant.

Ron, a pleasant, unassuming thirty-three-year-old man with a big heart and average looks, came to see me for depression symptoms happening in the context of romantic disappointment and social isolation. Ron, who is gay, had been spending an increasing amount of time looking for love on Craigslist, the hugely popular classifieds Web site serving fifty million users in fifty countries, and receiving twelve billion page views per month. In Craigslist ad after Craigslist ad, however, Ron saw nothing but threatening profiles by guys purporting to have gym-toned physiques and impeccable "stats" (for "statistics," a reference to numerical information people publicize in gay and straight ads, including height, weight, waist, chest and shoulder circumferences, and more private data on other accoutrements of masculinity or femininity). "Where did all the other guy-next-door types go?" he wondered. Because he felt he could in no way match the perfection before his eyes, Ron rarely answered an ad and felt too self-conscious posting a truthful one himself.

Realizing that his chances for meeting a match were slim, and feeling rather inferior about what he had to offer, Ron became increasingly isolated and, as a result, depressed. When I suggested that he should perhaps consider meeting someone the "old-fashioned" way—that is, in a social setting or at a club—he answered that dating in his community of urban gay friends has gone completely virtual, and that he would come across as too behind the times, even "pathetic," going to bars by himself. "Craigslist killed the gay bar," he said. Despite Ron's commitment to getting better and his engagement in psychotherapy, my work with him on how online misrepresentation might be holding him back, and might be creating an inferiority complex in his mind about his looks and his potential, seemed stuck. The stalemate, however, was rather dramatically broken when Ron came across "The Craigslist M4M Dictionary" e-mail, a Rosetta stone of sorts that was circulating among similarly befuddled users of the personals section of the Web site. Reading the "diction-ary" seemed to give Ron a newfound sense of hope, and crystallized in his mind the problem with pretense on Craigslist. I can confidently say that it accomplished what several weeks of psychotherapy had failed to achieve, and Ron was quick to share it with me.

According to the user's guide to Craigslist, "swimmer's build" in a gay personal ad typically describes the physique of "someone who probably never swam a lap in his life"; "jock" is a guy "who tries very hard to be manly but probably is deathly afraid of sports"; "beefy" is code for "fat ass"; and "8X5," when referring to a guy's manhood, most commonly describes a member that is "six inches long and barely four inches in circumference." Even the once-fixed inch is subject to online recalibra-tion! As we all go, to varying degrees, into "God mode," surely nothing is sacred anymore.

Regardless of the extent of the exaggeration, the scenarios people concoct and the overblown attributes they give themselves don't stay "there" (a reference to There.com, a virtual community of avatars à la Second Life). Sooner or later, many will come in contact with reality. While the friction that ensues does not, in the overwhelming majority of cases, involve literal blood, it is still a difficult-to-take, psychologi-cally violent, and very rude awakening. And it still involves death—the metaphorical death of an unattainable, much too perfect, alter ego: one that should have probably stayed an abstract notion in Plato's universe of Forms, rather than something to try to breathe life into.

God may be dead, as Nietzsche famously proclaimed in the nine-teenth century, but the need for some kind of omnipotent, perfect Form obviously persists. People, however, have stopped looking upward or outward for it. The virtual world is helping convince them that the Form is—look no further—within us, not in some distant forbidden realm that requires patience, humility, or spiritual attunement to break into. All we need to release our inner God is a pulpit and an audience, both of which the Internet supplies in great abundance. Too bad that the corollary to being in God mode in cyberspace is an explosion of narcissism and self-centeredness.

I suspect Richard Dawkins, arguably the world's most celebrated atheist, would partially agree. In his view, faith is a pernicious meme, much like the "Dancing Baby" of the previous chapter, only more pervasive and malicious. As he sees it, believers in a supernatural God are victims of indoctrination by organized religion and by exploiters of childhood innocence and impressionability; only atheists can be rational, independent thinkers. In *The God Delusion*, he aims to refute what he calls "the God hypothesis" by proving that God as an all-knowing, all-powerful designer is a figment of humanity's collective imagination. God is more than dead, he seems to be saying; he never existed in the first place and amounts to nothing but bad fiction. "The God of the Old Testament is arguably the most unpleasant character in all fiction," he writes, then recites a long list of less than endearing attributes: "jealous and proud of it; a petty, unjust, unforgiving control-freak; a vindictive, bloodthirsty ethnic cleanser; a misogynistic, homophobic, racist, infanticidal, genocidal, filicidal, pestilential, megalomaniacal, sadomasochistic, capriciously malevolent bully." Sounds like an antisocial narcissist! Why would anyone want to associate with such a character, much less *be* him? Dawkins does not give an entirely convincing answer to this question, or an entirely rational refutation of the God hypothesis—maybe some people have an innate need for faith the way they have a need for bad fiction. Still, he seems to agree that God is to be found online these days. As he said, people act "God-like" on Second Life. And, by the way, "I have been in there myself as an avatar," he tells us, "incognito." And so, in a speech to his fellow Second Lifers, Dawkins was broadcast through a video feed into an auditorium on the mythology-laced Elysian Isle, a Second Life island purchased by the Random House Group, his publishers, to advertise its authors. Two details caught my attention as I watched the speech: The inside of the auditorium looked suspiciously like a church, and Dawkins would not say what his Second Life avatar was . . .

The Second Coming may be here. As virtual technology liberates our alter egos and makes quasi-psychotic denial of reality possible, more of us are playing God, which is the height of narcissism. As we will see, the deity being revealed has some of the unattractive qualities of that unfriendly character from the Old Testament.

CHAPTER 4

ORDINARY EVERYDAY VICIOUSNESS

RAFFI WAS A forty-year-old married man who came to see me for what he described as "self-esteem issues." As the only son of first-generation Italian immigrants, he grew up in a religious household feeling pampered and doted on. The altar boy who did well in school and excelled in sports became a successful civil engineer, marrying his high school sweetheart and forming a family that also included two beautiful teenage daughters. The couple of years before our first appointment, however, had been very trying. Two years ago, at the age of thirteen, one daughter was diagnosed with diabetes. Shortly after that, his beloved mother died unexpectedly of a heart attack. And when the recession hit, Raffi was laid off as part of a restructuring of his company, becoming unemployed for the first time since finishing college. Multiple job interviews had led nowhere.

The string of family and professional losses happening in a relatively short period of time led to clinical depression, which further compounded the situation by taking away Raffi's energy and his motivation to exercise, eat healthily, and take care of his physical appearance. The once vibrant forty-year-old with the boyish looks and charmed life started seeing himself as fat, unemployable, and all-around worthless.

His wife of fifteen years, still working and as striking and active as when they first fell in love during their senior year, tried to be supportive. In his state of extreme vulnerability and low self-esteem, however, all Raffi could focus on was how she *must* be having an affair. Not that he had any reason to suspect infidelity: Any extramarital activities his wife partook in seemed to focus on attending diabetes support groups and investigating insulin pumps for her child. But "she has to be having an affair because I have nothing to offer," went his faulty logic. "Just look at her and look at me."

About ten years before this, in the "old days," Raffi might have worked hard to convince himself she wasn't. He may have sought a "reality check" from a friend or therapist. He may have tried to seek reassurance from his wife that she still loved him and that she would stay by his side until the dark clouds had passed and they were able to go back to their normal lives. If all alternatives failed, he might, out of desperation and as a last resort, decide to hire a private eye. But this was today, a time for shortcuts and immediate results, so Raffi decided to "cut to the chase" and start with the desperate act right away. Only instead of a costly detective, he installed keyloggers on his wife's laptop.

Keyloggers is a family of easily downloadable, relatively inexpensive software programs that track (or log) the keys struck on a computer keyboard without the person using it knowing that his actions are being monitored. They have some defendable applications: They can be used to control kids' Internet surfing habits and can help maintain an automatic backup for one's typed data. Increasingly, however, their main use is as spying tools for people who want to snoop on one another in personal and business affairs—a way to extend one's knowledge of, and potentially control over, the other person into the virtual realm.

It is now generally accepted that if there is "dirt" to be found in someone's life, a good place to start looking for it is in that person's e-mail or text message in-box. Only a clean in-box is proof of a clean record, so Raffi prayed for a chaste log of e-mails that would exonerate his wife. He quickly retrieved her passwords and, for six months, scrutinized her outgoing and incoming messages. He studied her saved contacts and researched the ones he didn't recognize. He visited every unfamiliar Web site she visited and joined (under a pseudonym) every community she signed up for. But the only real secret he uncovered involved a surprise fortieth birthday party she was planning for him behind his back.

Reassuring himself that no affair was taking place, however, hardly brought him relief. Raffi's problem may have started with negative-territory self-esteem, but he was now suffering from overwhelming guilt over the sting operation he had conducted against his loving and faithful wife. How could he not trust her, and how did it become so easy for him to turn into a spy? For six whole months, he had spied on a woman who had given him no real reason for doubt. What he had done did not fit the mental image he had of himself, his wife, and his marriage, and Raffi could not forgive himself for it.

With the availability of spyware that can easily prove or disprove an act or a claim, there is less need to take a chance and trust your life or business partner. It is easy for trust, as a noble act of faith in some-one, to seem silly. The virtual world is giving us new tools to uncover unpleasantness about one another, even as it increases the likelihood of such unpleasantness occurring in the first place. Raffi, like any Web user, knows of the secrets people can hide online. Circumstances caused him to mistakenly have suspicions about his wife, and "online" was the most logical place to go looking for evidence. Inability to find it, however, did not make him happier, because the process involved a disturbing, Internet-facilitated suspension of his own moral code. Had he found it, he would have probably felt even worse.

Statistics from the general culture are, unfortunately, on the side of people who doubt what goes on behind password-protected accounts. Not just in relationships, which I will cover in more detail later, but in almost all aspects of online life. The Internet, which helps us feel bigger, more potent, and more special, also reinforces the less flattering under-side of our personality. While, certainly, we are not all active participants in dark online pursuits or downright crime, hardly anyone is spared their consequences, as these findings taken from various walks of online life suggest.

Nearly ten million Americans were victims of identity theft in 2008, as we saw in chapter 1. A good proportion of them had their private information intercepted over the course of Web transactions conducted through virus-stricken computers. Many organizations fell prey to the same kind of hacking, at a worldwide cost of $1 trillion in 2008 in lost intellectual property and expenditures to repair the damage. The U.S. government is barely more secure than your bank account: That same year, there were 5,499 known breaches of American government computers, compared to less than half that number in 2006, including an attack against the White House network where hackers obtained e-mails between government officials.

Students with the urge to plagiarize are similarly emboldened, and instructors no longer know how to combat the problem. Googling "term paper" yields 128,000,000 entries; Cramster supplies step-by-step solutions to problems in more than 200 college textbooks; and, on Web sites like eCheat and SchoolSucks, you can buy a prepackaged term paper or have an essay custom-written to meet your needs for $18.95 to $35 a page. The opportunities to "download your workload" have become too numerous for teachers to be able to police. While the urge to cheat may be ancient, the ease of "copy and paste" has made it more difficult to resist.

Gambling is another activity that is often problematic and that is encouraged by online disinhibition and a grandiose assessment of one's own talent (the talent to win, in this case). As Richard's story in chapter 1 suggested, and as I will discuss in the impulsivity chapter, online gambling has its own allure, and it is easy for the "social" gambler to become a pathological one once he starts logging on to a casino. In 2005, it was estimated that more than $100 million was wagered daily through online poker sites. Recent laws restricting access in the United States have simply shifted the industry's epicenter. PokerStars.com, the self-described "world's largest poker site," on which "you automatically become a PokerStars VIP from the moment you play your first real money poker hand," is based on the Isle of Man in the Irish Sea. Like the eleven-year-old cheating on his homework, it is difficult to localize and contain bad behavior online.

A similar argument can be made regarding online sexual content. Over 10 percent of all Web pages, 25 percent of all searches, and 35 percent of all downloads are pornographic in nature. When the sexual object is a child, potentially forgivable cyber-mischief of the sexual nature crosses the line into criminal behavior. Sadly, this is hardly an uncommon occurrence: According to one report, one in five youths has been sexually solicited online.

Finally, it is hard to become (or remain) moderate in the online climate, to find the middle ground and stay in it. Some people even leave the virtual experience radicalized. One extreme is represented by domestic hate groups that recruit online and whose open goal is to harass minorities or threaten the foundations of civil government (neo-Nazis, Skinheads, Ku Klux Klan, various militias, etc.). The number of such groups in the United States is on the rise, according to the Southern Poverty Law Center. A more disturbing extreme is the global jihadist movement. Al-Qaeda boasts a "media arm" headquartered in cyberspace—As-Sahab, Arabic for "the cloud." Its Web sites come with instructional videos and tutorials on building bombs, firing surface-to-air missiles, and sneaking into Iraq. These venues serve as virtual training grounds for terrorists, and their numbers have increased from less than 100 at the beginning of the decade to nearly 5,000 by 2007.

Reacting to data that suggest that the good guys may be losing to the bad guys online, President Barack Obama announced on May 30, 2009, the creation of a high-level cybersecurity position that would coordinate the response to cybercrime of the Pentagon, the National Security Agency, and the Department of Homeland Security. In language not usually associated with the White House East Room, the president said the goal would be to "deter, prevent, detect and defend" against cyberattacks, including "spyware and malware and spoofing and phishing and botnets"—all examples of what he termed "weapons of mass disruption." More recently, a new senate bill known as the Protecting Cyberspace as a National Asset Act has been introduced. It proposes to give the president the power to "declare a cybersecurity emergency and order the limitation or shutdown of Internet traffic . . ." It adds that the president "may order the disconnection of any Federal government or United States critical infrastructure information system or network." In other words, it would give him what some have called an "Internet kill switch" to go along with his nuclear button.

The troubling statistics, and the radical responses being considered, are evidence that the Internet is now the primary realm for "dreaming dark." Whether we are downloading our workload, engaging in risqué sexual fantasies, cyberstalking an ex, spying on a spouse, defrauding our fellow Web surfers, or even committing a crime, the Internet is today's loudest expression of people's aggressive and sometimes deviant sides. The shadowy aspect of many Internet users' e-personalities is a twenty-first-century confirmation of sorts of Sigmund Freud's theories of the id—the problematic, instinct-driven part of our psyche, which we are socialized to try to keep under tight control. It makes the grandiosity and narcissism discussed before almost seem like quirky traits. Revisiting some of Freud's ideas on personality structure conjures up interesting parallels with our current online/offline psychological split, and can help us better understand the risks of an uncontrolled virtual life.

According to Freud's model of psychological development, the id is the only component of personality present from birth. It is "the dark, inaccessible part of our personality." It is "of a negative character," and is best understood through comparisons with something awful: "we call it a chaos, a cauldron full of seething excitations." The id is undisciplined and "filled with energy reaching it from the instincts." It "has no organization" and "produces no collective will, but only a striving to bring about the satisfaction of the instinctual needs subject to the observance of the pleasure principle." It is the seat of sexual energy and a bottomless reservoir of libido. In its illogical mix of drives and urges and in the way it will not take no for an answer, it is also like a newborn's mind.

Early in life, the id has its advantages: It ensures that an uncommunicative but hungry baby will cry incessantly until he or she is fed. Immediately satisfying one's needs at all cost, however, is not always realistic, and difficulty delaying gratification, if it persists, quickly becomes problematic. "Growing up," then, must involve taming the id's self-centeredness. In Freud's view, such growth happens as the much more conscious, and conscientious, ego develops and learns how to negotiate the unacceptable impulses of the id.

If the pleasure principle drove the id's demands, the ego operates according to the reality principle. It engages with, and navigates, the real world, protecting the organism from outside threats but also from itself. The ego grows with the individual and matures over time. "[It] represents what may be called reason and common sense, in contrast to the id, which contains the passions." Far from its current meaning, which implies exaggerated personal pride or self-importance, the ego, in Freudian thinking, represents self-control, caution, and judgment. A "big ego" was rather a good thing to have.

Part of how the ego matures is through listening to the superego—the third element in the Freudian personality structure and the one that lays down the law. The superego is the voice of the authority figure within us. It reminds us of our moral obligations and sees to it that we respect societal norms and standards. In Freud's symbolic explanation of how it comes about, the superego develops when a little boy starts to develop sexual feelings for his mother, only to be faced by the father's threat of castration if the boy dares to violate that most forbidden of taboos. Freud called this moment of crisis in the child's development the Oedipus complex, a reference to *Oedipus Rex*, the Greek tragedy in which the mythical character Oedipus unknowingly kills his father and marries his own mother. In a less sexist, more relevant sense, to have, and resolve, the oedipal complex is to internalize parents' and society's proscriptions in a way that makes a moral human being—one with a conscience and a sense of right and wrong—possible.

For Freud, our natural tendencies, sexual and otherwise, tend—much like those of the precociously lustful little boy—toward aggression and transgression. Only a mature ego that has successfully incorporated the lessons of the superego can protect us from destructive impulses. Our fate, otherwise, is toward a free-for-all jungle and the very impossibility of civilization, since many of the primitive instincts Freud warns about, like violence and the overwhelming craving for sexual gratification, put the individual in direct confrontation with civilization and its need for everyone to peaceably get along. "[T]he problem before us is how to get rid of the greatest hindrance to civilization—namely the constitutional inclination of human beings to be aggressive towards one another," is how Freud sums up the challenge. The solution he advocates is the cultivation of a personal ethic that would incorporate the voice of the superego: "Ethics is . . . to be regarded as a therapeutic attempt—as an endeavor to achieve, by means of a command of the superego, something that has so far not been achieved by any other cultural activities."

If, indeed, society's only hope for progress is a civilizing process that encourages an ethical life, we may be in trouble. In "social media," the blogosphere, and on message boards, instincts run rampant and are constantly being fed and reinforced. The superego has gone AWOL. In its place, we see endless manifestations of "polymorphous perversity," another phrase from psychoanalysis originally coined to describe indiscriminate sexuality, but equally applicable across a whole range of Web activities.

Chris, who had left medical school to pursue Internet gold, was more than dreaming "big." He seemed to be dreaming "dark" as well. Beneath the inflated expectations and euphoria he showed about his startup was also a somehow less kind person than I had known. It turns out that some of what his company was doing reeked of conflict of interest:

It proposed to target retirees on limited incomes, encouraging them to funnel their savings into stocks in high-risk Internet startups, including investing in the company itself. How could the man I knew—the one who devoted his scant free time in medical school to volunteer at a free geriatric clinic—be the same man whose business model involved gambling with senior citizens' life savings? Something about his moral core seemed to have changed. The same can be said of Raffi and his ability to justify spying on his wife.

The Internet makes it easier to suspend ethical codes governing conduct and behavior. Gentleness, common courtesy, and the little niceties that announce us as well-mannered, civilized, and sociable members of the species are quickly stripped away to reveal a completely naked, often unpleasant human being. Consider the following exchange from a popular women's message board:

> janice18: I think doctors and policeman are more important than teachers and deserve to be paid more.
>
> rubyslippers: How does one become a doctor or a policeman w/o a teacher 1st? most other jobs would never be filled without teachers. everyone goes to school everyone ends up working. it's a cycle.
>
> angela47: You're an idiot. Your logic is piss poor. Just shut up.
>
> flowerchild: LOL way to make good, solid, reasonable points
>
> angela47: I did. Rubyslippers logic is piss poor. It's disjointed. It makes no sense. What's your problem?
>
> flowerchild: my "problem" is that you're an adult yet responding to a post with "IDIOT" etc.
>
> angela47: So, you have a problem with TRUTH? You're an IDIOT too.
>
> flowerchild: Ok, chill! Enough name callin.
>
> angela47: I just call 'em like I see 'em. Why are your panties all in a bunch?
>
> flowerchild: I'm not the one calling people idiot. That'd be you, sweetheart. Are you 14?
>
> angela47: No, I am 32 . . .

Note how quickly the dialogue devolves into nastiness and the ease with which the word "idiot" is thrown around. For anyone who visits message boards or chat rooms with any frequency, the tenor of this excerpt will hardly come as a surprise. Why is it that online communities, which on the surface have a big unifying interest that should theoretically hold them together, have such a hard time maintaining a minimum level of propriety online? Must people who come together under a common theme inevitably descend into scapegoating, mudslinging, or, in some cases, outright criminal behavior? Why might "anti-social media" be a better name for the social media? A group bonding and then unbonding when its members find out they can't tolerate one another is, of course, hardly unique to cyberspace, but the intensity of the infighting and the degree of negative passion displayed are. Cindy "the original Cin" Kesey, who blogs about her experiences as an avatar on Second Life, would not necessarily have been my first choice for insightful commentary into the challenges inherent to online community building, but her blog entry titled "Group Dynamics, Communities and the Mob Mentality" comes from the heart and from the trenches, not from a sociologist's academic perch. As such, it might be more relevant:

> Second Life communities . . . seem to function much like our own circles of friends in the real world. . . . Often, these groups or communities center around similar tastes or experiences, like music, art, politics, or sex. Some revolve around proximity, as in groups of neighbors. . . . And I suppose some just grow organically from the seeds of mutual attraction. This is the part where I admit that I haven't had great luck cultivating my own community experiences in SL. . . . [F]rom what I've seen of them, many SL communities tend to magnify some of the good but mostly the bad and the ugly characteristics of group dynamics. They are often ripe with rotten relationship triangles or cheating friends and lovers. Many include the he-said-she-said back-and-forth I thought we all tried to leave behind in middle school. And, sadly, some even include the gang-ups

and hang-ups of mob mentality. Why is this? Why do people . . . seem to create levels of never-before-achieved drama . . . ? Is there something left of our Darwinian evolution from animals where we work to mate and then ascend to the top of the social spectrum of the pack? . . . I think I know why in SL these group games seem so much more pronounced: because we can hide behind a veil of anonymity that we think shields us from the guilt and blame that should accompany bad behavior. In the Buddhist sense, however, we're never anonymous; our karma follows us far beyond this second, real, or any other life we might live. So why not make the most of this opportunity and try to push our evolutionary story even further? Move beyond forming Survivor-style alliances and bring our very best selves to the groups to which we belong. This might mean zipping our lips at times or finding forgiveness when we don't want to. But what else is evolution for than to move beyond the behaviors that hold us back as a society?

Protected by anonymity, bound only by how quickly they can type the next insult, members of online communities often feel empowered to engage in cruel outbursts that would violate their sense of decency in the real world. Though perhaps not as commonly, e-mail exchanges can also be marked by this blatant lack of courtesy and respect, even if we are models of etiquette and good behavior in the real world. How many of us have friends who curse more frequently in e-mail or never include a warm greeting or sign-off? Their "coldness" is not triggered by anonymity—we know who they are. They just don't think warmth and manners are necessary or even advisable in cyberspace.

Though important, anonymity is neither necessary nor sufficient for people's less flattering side to surface online. If there were an online community in which anonymity should *not* serve to encourage members to be meaner than they are in real life, where karma should be sufficient for people to self-police, it would be Flickr. The members who make up the "social photography" site are hardly anonymous: They have posted nearly three billion images that document in great detail their weddings, babies, pets, colleagues, and vacations. They are much more recognizable than a Second Life resident with a made-up persona. Because of that, one might expect personalities on Flickr to be more like a digital photograph: the good aspects highlighted, the unflattering ones touched up or cropped off. Instead, the exchanges that their snapshots elicit can be just as vociferous as those triggered by the moving and talking images of YouTube. Karma, it turns out, is just as ineffectual as the superego in preventing a Web site from turning into a still-life-with-hate picture. And that's whether its members are anonymous or identifiable.

"Behavior [on Flickr] must be moderated and a communal ethos must be preserved," writes journalist Chris Colin, of the *San Francisco Chronicle*. "Total freedom . . . would sink it in a storm of lawsuits, flame wars and gridlocked cacophony." And so, in 2005, Yahoo!, which owns Flickr, hired Heather Champ to be its "Community Manager." (To drive home the point in hiring her, the announcement came with a picture of the aptly surnamed Champ flexing an impressively large bicep.) "I can't think of any successful online community where the nice, quiet, reasonable voices defeat the loud, angry ones," she told the newspaper. "The amount of time it would take for the community to self-regulate—I don't think it could sustain itself in the meantime. . . . The computer somehow nullifies the social contract." And, absent a social contract, we are roaming, a little bit militia-style, in a sort of id fest or war zone. "There are no IEDs or snipers in this place, but it's hard not to conclude Flickr's conducting a kind of nation-building," Colin writes. Who knew Flickr could conjure up Freud or Afghanistan?

On Flickr and elsewhere, the "liberating" effects of the Internet separate individuals from the common values and ethical norms they adhere to in the real world. There is an important moral dimension to the Lewis and Clark metaphor, used earlier to illustrate the great potential of the World Wide Web: The Internet allows us to justify, in the name of exploration and progress, the guilt-free extermination of Indian tribes we encounter along the way. In other words, in the online jungle, the goal often justifies the means in a way that, in offline transactions, might make us recoil with remorse or other shaming sentiment. Just as "ordinary everyday psychosis" powers the reality-suspension of our wilder profiles, there is also an "ordinary everyday viciousness" that is operating and that seems to pervade many people's online lives. Its end result, as we will see, can be a desensitization to violence and cruelty.

Stories from the broader Internet culture regularly reinforce this idea, although reports generally eschew any discussion of the morality-transforming power of the Internet. Instead, most journalists report on the ugly cybercrime without discussing how the "unlikely" perpetrator became a likely one. The so-called MySpace Suicide Hoax is a case in point. As described in the *New York Times* in November 2007 and in the *New Yorker* in January 2008, Megan Meier, a thirteen-year-old girl who lived with her parents in Dardenne Prairie, a leafy suburb of St. Louis, Missouri, died believing that Josh Evans, the cutest boyfriend she ever had, really, really hated her. After weeks of flirting with her, telling her she was "sexi," and leading her on with his big blue eyes, cut features, "trillian" CDs, and the picture of a bare-chested teenage boy with tousled brown hair, Josh launched a barrage of insults that culminated in a lethal, "You're a shitty person, and the world would be a better place without you." Later that day, Megan's mother found her hanging from her closet organizer.

"Josh," it turned out, was a hoax fabricated by Lori Drew, the neighbor who lived four houses down the street. The deception was perfectly tailored to exploit the insecurities and dreams of a teenage girl whom the Drews knew well—they had taken Megan on many family vacations with their own daughter. Relative newcomers on the block, the Drews apparently resented the fact that they did not feel very welcome in the tight-knit community. What seemed to have upset them the most, however, was Megan's decision to distance herself from their daughter, to whom Megan had made remarks that were meant to be hurtful, such as calling her a "lesbian." Whether Lori Drew was a resentful neighbor, an overprotective mother, or both, the Internet made her fleeting dark wish toward a neighbor's kid take on a life of its own and sweep her up, along with two alleged co-conspirators—her 13-year-old daughter, Sarah, and another teenage employee of her magazine coupon business—in a diabolical three-way plot that quickly culminated in blood. In the words of a stunned neighbor, "Lori was slightly annoying, but I never saw a cruel streak." Until, that is, the virtual world helped bring it out. "The only way [Lori Drew] could harm this pretty little girl was with a computer," said U.S. Attorney Thomas O'Brien, federal prosecutor in Los Angeles, where MySpace is based and where the case was tried under a convoluted application of a computer-fraud law usually used in hacking cases. (Missouri authorities had determined there was no state law under which Drew could be tried.) "She chose to use a computer to hurt a little girl," O'Brien added, "and for four weeks, she enjoyed it."

The landmark case initially resulted in a conviction on the lesser misdemeanor offense of accessing computers without authorization; the jury failed to reach a verdict on the main charge against Drew— conspiracy. Two years later, however, a federal judge threw out the conviction, saying that if Drew were to be found guilty of illegally accessing computers without authorization, anyone who ever violated a social networking site's terms of service—and who hasn't?—would be guilty of a misdemeanor. The arguably light verdict, followed by its reversal, and the overall lack of appropriate laws to address such behaviors, belie the confusion that still surrounds cyber-harassment and other online activities that "cross the line." The legal vacuum feeds the moral vacuum, which further facilitates the emergence of people's dark tendencies.

Children are often the victims of cyber-harassment, as in the Megan Meier story, but increasingly, they are also its perpetrators, as in the growing phenomenon of cyberbullying. The most jaded and world-weary among us may no longer be shocked by the story of an adult sociopath inflicting the kind of harm Lori Drew visited upon her neighbors' daughter, or of a pedophile "friending" a youngster on Facebook. But when children go on the attack and start behaving like Lori Drew, and when we see the Internet nurturing or giving rise to a cruel streak in *them*, we have to pause and reflect on what this might portend for the future. If it is easy for a developing and supposedly still "innocent" child to turn into a cyber-monster, one has to wonder what this child will mature into and what increased offline violence he might be capable of after receiving his "training" in the virtual world. A look at cyberbullying, as carried out by children against children, helps illustrate the dangers online and, potentially, ahead.

According to Dr. Robin Kowalski, Clemson University psychologist and co-author of *Cyber Bullying: Bullying in the Digital Age*, cyberbullying occurs through e-mail, chat rooms, instant messages, video games, social networking Web sites, or digital images or messages sent via cellular phones. It is different from the traditional playground and school bus variety: "As tempting as it is to assume that our knowledge of traditional bullying carries over easily to cyber bullying," she writes, "they are distinct phenomena." Armed with data that suggest higher victimization rates for cyberbullying compared with traditional bullying—more than 50 percent of children, in some studies—Kowalski sets out to describe what makes cyberbullying much more common and in some cases more painful.

Unlike with traditional bullying, the identity of the cyberbully is often unknown (close to half of the victims did not know the identity of the perpetrator, in one study). This leads to higher levels of anxiety among victims, who don't know who their enemy is and who they should protect themselves against. Instead of their vigilance centering on a specific bully, possibly with a limited number of accomplices, cyberbullying victims are diffusingly, confusingly vigilant, unable to know who the aggressor is and where the next blow will come from. Avoiding the playground or the school bus—as problematic as those options are—and staying closer to home does not make them feel safer: Victims are now available to be attacked twenty-four hours a day, seven days a week, and there is no time when a threat or a taunt cannot be launched in their direction in the form of an e-mail or a text message. To make matters worse, complaining to parents, once a source of reassurance and support for some victims, can, from the child's perspective, backfire: Kids live in deadly fear of their cell phones being taken away or their Internet access being curtailed by a concerned parent.

The lack of access to each other's emotions during a cyberbullying episode compounds the pain. "When people tease or bully face-to-face," Kowalski writes, "they use off-record markers (winks, smiles, etc.) to indicate the intent behind their behavior" and to assess its impact. Such nonverbal cues—with the possible exception of emoticons, which I will talk about later—are largely lacking during the virtual attack. The result is that the perpetrators are more out of touch with the pain they are inflicting because it is invisible to them, and the victims cannot know if the perpetrators are truly bullying them or "just kidding." Naturally, the victims' instinct of self-preservation makes them assume the worst about the attack and the attacker and convinces them that someone is really out to get them. A host of negative consequences can then ensue, from bad grades to social withdrawal, depression, and a general suspiciousness and mistrustfulness of the world.

In part because of anonymity, "more individuals are potential cyber bullies than potential schoolyard bullies." However, it is not just the number of perpetrators that has increased but also "the magnitude of threats, taunts, and so on, that they are willing to deliver." The increased number of attackers, and the more vitriolic nature of the attacks, show how very naturally and almost automatically the dark side of children emerges online, and the real dangers attendant on that.

According to 2007 data from the National Institute on Media and the Family, 90 percent of U.S. children aged eight to sixteen play "virtual" video games, and over 90 percent of games classified as being appropriate for their age group contain violence. Further, government and industry attempts to regulate access to the most graphically violent types have been halfhearted and largely ineffective: One recent "secret shopper" study showed that attempts by underaged children to purchase a mature-rated video game from stores were successful over 80 percent of the time. It might be logical to expect that these kids will become more violent when offline and away from their computers and game consoles, but what have well-designed, scientific studies of this question actually revealed?

One of the largest studies to address this question was led by psychologist Craig A. Anderson, of the Center for the Study of Violence at Iowa State University. It included three groups taken from the United States and Japan, totaling over 1,500 participants. Subjects, whose ages ranged from nine to eighteen, were evaluated over time to assess whether repeated exposure to violent video games led to an increase in *future* physical aggression. While earlier studies had suggested the existence of such a link, most looked for an association between exposure to video game violence and physical aggression at only one point in time; for that reason, those studies could not be seen as establishing a causal relationship (if A and B are happening at the same time, then A does not necessarily lead to B; on the other hand, if A precedes B, then it might have caused it).

Participants in Anderson's study were assessed at two different points, separated by three to six months. Results showed that schoolchildren involved in habitual violent video game playing early in the school year were *twice as likely* to show aggressive tendencies later in the year as those who were not. This difference was still there even after researchers corrected for gender differences and differences in baseline aggressiveness. Furthermore, this effect was of similar magnitude in the United States and Japan.

The study offers two pieces of evidence regarding the link between aggression and habitual exposure to virtual violence: (a) It confirms the results from smaller, less well-designed studies; and (b) it demonstrates that such increases in aggression "occur in highly individualistic cultures with high societal levels of physical aggression and violence" (for example, the United States) "and in more collectivistic cultures with low levels of physical aggression and violence" (for example, Japan). In other words, the power of virtual violence to affect children's development in an aggression-prone way is not mitigated by one culture's lower overall tolerance for violence. Rather, virtual violence seems to cause a rise in violence in the entire "global village," and across cultures with very different baseline levels of aggression and different child-rearing practices. This finding contradicts one alternative hypothesis—that only children who are already aggressive (either by nature or nurture) will have problems—and points to a certain "helplessness" when it comes to the spread of violence offline, regardless of the innate characteristics of the players. As far as the less attractive side of virtual life is concerned, it would seem as though we are all more alike than different.

Finally, the study authors make the following critical observation: Virtual violence should alarm us more than other forms of media violence—TV, movie, graphic novels and so forth—whose threats to society have been debated over the years. While the increase in aggression that can happen with repeated exposure to virtual violence does recall concerns voiced about violence in other mediums, it is also unique. The *interactive* nature of virtual games—that is, "their capacity to reward and punish the player for various actions, their immersive qualities, the fact that the user is an enactor as well as an observer of aggression"— makes their violence different from that found in older forms, and potentially more contagious.

In explaining how immersing oneself in virtual violence can make a person more violent, some researchers have focused on the negative moral message communicated by the virtual medium. Dr. Vladan Starcevic, a psychiatrist at the University of Sydney in Australia, writes:

> In the virtual world of violent video games, the player may kill or injure computer-generated characters or other online gamers without any consequence, including punishment. . . . While many video games provide

a story which primes the player to kill, there is very rarely any room for moral consideration of killing, and proceeding to kill invariably benefits the player more than exercising restraint. Indeed, the players are likely to be rewarded for killing, by means of points, more powerful weapons, or their own survival.

In the top-rated Grand Theft Auto: Vice City, for example, players gain points by soliciting and then killing prostitutes. The player is "groomed as a 'virtual psychopath' with no remorse or compassion when committing acts of extreme violence." An adolescent or child who is fed this message "may learn that aggression is necessary, appropriate, desirable, rewarding, effective, and not punishable, and that victims of aggression do not deserve pity." Thus primed, it is conceivable that the virtual psychopath will then "graduate" into something that resembles a real psychopath, with the upside-down expectation that violence, at worst, goes unpunished, or, at best, is rewarded. Something similar can be said of students who grow up downloading their homework on CheatHouse. Cheating may become normalized, separated from the stigma and reproach that ought to be attached to it, almost like a standard part of conducting business or meeting a deadline.

One reason our morals change is because the virtual world can desensitize us to what is wrong. Starcevic talks about how violence no longer disgusts us to the same degree it once did. Violence, he argues, should be perceived as disgusting to be avoided. A high disgust propensity acts as an important deterrent to aggression. However, if as a result of immersion in virtual violence we become desensitized to violent content— that is, if gory Second Life scenes become "second nature"—then our inclination toward aggression might increase as what used to be uniquely repulsive now becomes almost commonplace. Less turned off by it, we will be more prone to engage in it.

That does not mean that we lose our ability to be disgusted altogether. Rather, the target shifts, and it starts taking increasingly more drastic conditions to provoke the same kind of reaction. For instance, instead of a grainy picture from a drive-by shooting nauseating us, we might start requiring high-resolution images of bloodshed to feel sick to our stomachs. This can be seen as another manifestation of how virtual life always seems to want to heighten and intensify emotions, constantly pushing the envelope by moving us away from the center of equilibrium and toward extremes in feelings and experiences. We hardly need to be a member of an online hate group for our sensitive side to become dulled from overindulgence in virtual violence.

Dr. Jeanne B. Funk, a psychologist at the University of Toledo, agrees. She writes that desensitization makes us bypass the moral centers of the brain because it robs us of our ability to empathize. Empathy, which she defines as "the capacity to understand and, to some extent, experience the feelings of others," is critical to the development of the moral individual. It "requires opportunities to view empathic models, interact with others, and experience feedback about one's behavioral choices." Discipline, as traditionally taught by parents, requires children to imagine how they would feel in the victim's shoes, and encourages the development of models for moral behavior. These "empathy-based scripts" are then automatically activated in conflict situations, where they are used to guide behavior and decision making. Yet much of virtual violence, as we have seen, involves "kill or be killed" situations, with no time to reflect on the moral dimension of our actions and no opportunity to relate to our opponents on any deep level. And how can we relate, when our virtual opponents are often portrayed in a dehumanized, cartoonish manner, lacking the subtleties that make us human? The risk is that, taken to an extreme, this process might turn automated, trigger-happy netizens into unempathic citizens, or even worse: "If the process of moral reasoning is chronically subverted, then disuse-related extinction of . . . moral reasoning may result."

In that respect, Funk finds it revealing that the U.S. Army reportedly uses similar strategies to train soldiers for war:

In actual combat situations that involve military aircraft and tanks, there is typically no direct, personal visual identification of targets. Instead, icons . . . on computerized displays that bear an uncanny resemblance to training video games lock on targets automatically. Whether by design or by chance, military training on enhanced video game systems may cause cognitive and emotional desensitization that obscures the moral implications of activating weapons from military vehicles or aircraft.

Given what the military is called upon to do, such application of virtual games may be seen as a good thing. It is hard, however, to find anything laudable about continuously circumventing the moral centers of our kids' brains and challenging their ability to learn compassion.

Of note, the military interest in the Internet predates using it for training purposes through war simulations. Some contend that the communication system that later became the Internet was born in the 1960s as an initiative by ARPANET, the Advanced Research Projects Agency Network of the U.S. Department of Defense, in part to satisfy two important military needs: create a Command and Control System that would survive a nuclear attack and reassert a post-Sputnik U.S. lead in matters of technology relevant to the military. The nuclear arms race connection that may be partially responsible for the Internet serves as a convenient metaphor when discussing the violent aspect of online life: As we have seen, a lot of what gets expressed online is more bellicose and secretive than what we are accustomed to in our offices and living rooms, and might be more at home in the operations room of a military campus. It makes some poetic sense that it is taking the Pentagon, the Department of Homeland Security, and the National Security Agency to tame this organism. The White House cybersecurity czar is, in a way, bringing us full circle.

Another way we may become desensitized to violence is by turning it into entertainment. Much of virtual violence is presented and cc'd around as something to be, if not enjoyed, then regarded as benign—a free spectacle for netizens. Videos of tragic acts of God, planes catching on fire, and unspeakable acts of violence find their way into in-boxes and onto lists of "favorite" YouTube posts. In a viral video from 2006, a scantily dressed woman, later identified as a resident of the Chinese city of Hangzhou, is seen posing with a small kitten along a scenic riverbank. At first, the woman lovingly caresses the animal's fur. Then, with no warning, she begins stomping on the kitten with her stiletto heels, crushing it into a lifeless, bloody heap. That so many can find even the littlest titillation or entertainment in such footage is disturbing. Also disturbing is that many of us with absolutely no interest in such material still end up seeing these memes, perhaps because they arrive as links in an RSS feed we subscribe to and otherwise enjoy (as was the case for me with this video), or in an e-mail from a friend with a sense of humor different from our own. What changes in our perception of violence that such inadvertent, unsolicited exposure to cruelty might eventually cause is anyone's guess.

It is a small leap from thinking of virtual violence as entertaining to thinking of it as sexy. So much of the April 2009 coverage of Philip Markoff, the twenty-three-year-old so-called Craigslist Killer, focused on his good looks, his credentials, and how much he did not fit the mold of someone who would commit the crimes he was accused of. According to the *New York Daily News*, Markoff was the "clean-cut, six-foot-tall" "brainy blond" with "no rap sheet," who lived in Quincy, a harborside town south of Boston, attended Boston University School of Medicine, and was engaged to a fellow medical student he met when the two volunteered in a local emergency room. Two months after the story broke, the preppy med student was handed an eight-count indictment, including for the April 10 violent robbery of a Las Vegas prostitute and the April 14 murder of a Manhattan woman he shot three times at close range. He was also facing assault and robbery charges in Rhode Island for attacking a stripper on April 16. Markoff had reportedly met all his victims on Craigslist, hence the moniker.

The Web made Markoff's sinister pan-geographic prowl possible, both practically and psychologically. According to attorneys general from forty states, the "erotic services" section of Craigslist routinely breaks antiprostitution laws, a fact that may have led Markoff to feel like other, more serious laws did not apply, either, or did not apply as much as they do in real life. If one can so easily get away with hiring or being a prostitute on Craigslist, maybe one can get away with murder. Easy online access to desperate victims in the lawless virtual environment facilitated a murderous spree in someone who "on paper" appeared not to have the ingredients or life trajectory of a serial killer. Stopping here, however, would make the Craigslist killer nothing more than the further depraved, male version of Lori Drew. Mrs. Drew, however, was rather universally condemned, and very appropriately so. Markoff, on the other hand, may have been too handsome for the Web to hate, and the video footage that showed him always peering into his BlackBerry may have endeared him to the wired masses—like he's "one of us."

As the coverage of the story expanded, it was revealed that the young man engaged to be married also used the Boston Craigslist site to meet men, ostensibly for sex, sharing with them nude photos of himself. "His e-mails [to other men] were very sexual and graphic, and his intentions were clear," declared the *National Enquirer*. "He led these conquests to believe he was an unattached med student—and quite a catch." Reading some Boston-area blogs to gauge the reaction to this revelation, one might expect to see only relief that no man seems to have met the fate of the Las Vegas prostitute, the Manhattan woman, or the Rhode Island stripper. Instead, one is struck by the number of commentators who wished they had . . . known the guy. Here is a sampling from one Web site:

Afrolito: "He looks like one of those Mormon boys who knock on doors
     trying to convert people. . . . I have to admit, I'd probably let him
     in . . . I have a thing for bad boys."

CM: "Me too. He is hot!!! Sick, but hot. If anyone finds those pics, let
   me know."

Ricky: "I don't care how creepy this is. But I think he's really hot! He
   kinda looks like my bf."

Lance Rockland: "Okay, I'm gonna say it: the man is hot! He's also a
   demented murderer. Oh well, nobody's perfect."

It would seem as though the offense, easier to commit online, is also easier to excuse. Less inhibitions in the virtual world mean that the threshold to act on violent impulses is lower, but so is the threshold to forgive ourselves or others such actions. Desensitizing ourselves to aggression, turning it into entertainment, into something thrilling or even "hot"—these serve to make amoral or violent online manifestations lesser deals than they ought to be. So, besides increasing someone's access to victims, online venues may also provide the person with a psychological out, convincing him that the extreme act will find an understanding audience online, one willing to absolve the perpetrator and pardon the offense.

Virtual violence need not target an external enemy; it can also be directed against oneself. In the old psychoanalytic tradition, suicide was seen as aggression turned inward, and just as the Internet is facilitating external manifestations of violence and hate, it also seems to be changing how people manage and negotiate *self*-hate. Just as it can play on people's narcissism to convince them they are godlike, it can also convince them that they are so awful they deserve to die. For the suicidal person online, it can sometimes justify and hasten death by giving it the added value of a spectacle. For the masses following such a tragedy online, too often it adds up to nothing more than a free show.

Abraham Biggs was a troubled nineteen-year-old community college student in Pembroke Pines, Florida, who saw online forums as sources of support—a substitute for therapist, friend, and kin. Message boards are "like a family to me," he once posted on his blog. However, on the

November 2008 morning when he started a thread called "Ask a guy who is gonna OD (again) tonight anything," the forum audience at bodybuilding.com where Biggs had been a regular blogger acted like anything but family. As reported in the *New York Times*, on ABCnews .com, and on the *Los Angeles Times* blogs, Biggs initiated a discussion under the alias "CandyJunkie," and linked his blog to his page on Justin .tv, a live video–streaming Web site, where the camera rolled on as he overdosed on prescription pills. "People were egging him on and saying things like 'go ahead and do it,'" said an investigator with the Broward County Medical Examiner's office. One forum participant wrote to warn Biggs that he hadn't taken enough pills to achieve his goal. "Instant Darwinism . . . ," quipped another. Other members chipped in, taking turns to call him "coward," "faggot," and a "dick." When contacted by a concerned poster, the forum's moderator reportedly said: "He's an attention whore, you should see all the posts he starts, then deletes."

After Biggs had lain curled up on his bed, facing away from his camera, for a number of hours—"Umm he hasn't moved in a long time."; "Any movement?"—an exchange ensued about whether his motionless body was an actual video or a still photograph meant as a prank. A forum member dug up a cell phone number Biggs had posted, and several people attempted to call—not everyone out of concern: "Called and went straight into voice mail," wrote one member, boasting that he left a message in which he used an anti-gay slur encouraging Biggs to "do it." Finally, "Bulker," a fellow bodybuilder and blogger, contacted the Miami police, who tracked the teen down through his computer Internet protocol (IP) address. In the live video stream, 181 viewers could see a piece of a door frame—which had splintered from the police kicking in the teen's bedroom door—hit Biggs, who lay splayed out on his bed. Reactions among viewers watching live on their computers varied from OMG to LOL to "I cannot believe what I just saw sitting at work in my cubicle!" Countless others Googled the video after the fact to view and re-view the climactic scene. Biggs was pronounced dead twelve hours after he started his suicide blog.

Regardless of his provocative act, Biggs's tragedy speaks to the degree of insensitivity some people are capable of online since they cannot give even a suicidal person the benefit of the doubt. It shows how voyeuristic our relationship with violence risks becoming and how separated we can be from the other person's pain. It is now more possible to watch someone suffer and either not be moved by his pain or find it thrilling enough to want to forward the video to our colleague two cubicles down.

Another way the Internet is changing the self-hate landscape is by rewriting the old suicide pact. Traditionally a covenant between two individuals with a deep bond, recent years have seen a "loosening" of the suicide pact into something that resembles a casual agreement between strangers who "friend" one another online, sometimes solely for the purpose of dying together. Numerous suicide-pact deaths and near-deaths have been documented in several countries. Memorable cases include the Suicide Chat Room for Young People uncovered in 2005, where depressed participants as young as twelve "paired up" with others who had access to more lethal means, and the mass suicide plan involving thirty-two individuals, which led police in 2005 to arrest an Oregon man believed to be its organizer. As they are formulated online, suicide pacts are a troubling manifestation of groupthink, defined by psychologist Irving Janis as "a mode of thinking that people engage in when they are deeply involved in a cohesive in-group," and "when the members' strivings for unanimity override their motivation to realistically appraise alternative courses of action." As such, groupthink sacrifices reasonable dissent and counterpoint in the interest of group solidarity and the single agenda.

Especially when it comes to Internet communities that coalesce around a narrow cause, as opposed to large, open communities like Second Life or Flickr, silence is often preferable to voicing an opinion deemed threatening to the group's homogeneous fabric (the community's membership privileges come with an understood pact to follow the herd). It seems that if we are not eviscerating one another on YouTube, we may be blindly agreeing, in a way that stifles debate and rational discourse. In either case, we are not really "thinking" (but more on thinking later). When the subject of our mutual agreement is a suicide plan, groupthink may be taken to a tragic extreme. Precisely when we *need* to listen to the opposing viewpoint and should absolutely consider the other perspective on the issue, it is easy to find wide agreement and avoid deliberation.

Even when they are not part of a sinister pact and are not provocatively broadcasting their actions, there seem to be limits to the kindness and help that suicidal individuals can count on finding online. (And if they can't elicit sustained, genuinely kind feelings, who can?) Indeed, the Internet may have exacerbated the suicide problem. Dr. M. David Rudd, a psychologist at Baylor University and a noted suicide expert, says that the Internet has not lived up to its potential to help as a suicide prevention tool. Instead, "most of what's available via the Internet only serves to make the problem worse," he told the *New York Times* in 2008. Scientific data seem to support this position. According to an analysis published that year in the *American Journal of Preventive Medicine*, the overall suicide rate in the United States increased by around 5 percent between 1999 and 2005. The increase was especially marked among people aged forty to sixty-four—a period in life generally thought of as one marked by relative stability and emotional security. Many factors may have contributed to this increase: a rise in pain medication abuse; heightened fear and anxiety following the 9/11 attacks; new antidepressant labeling laws that have led to a decrease in antidepressant prescribing; and a decrease in hormone replacement in menopausal women, which, while justified because of increased cancer and other risks, may have put women at increased risk for depression. However, a possible role for the Internet also deserves consideration.

In a 2008 *Journal of Clinical Psychiatry* article titled "Googling Suicide," Brown University psychiatrist Patricia R. Recupero and her research team reported on the type of information a desperate person might find through a simple Internet suicide search. Their goal was to assess the accessibility of potentially harmful resources, such as prosuicide forums. Using five popular search engines, including Google and Yahoo!, and four suicide-related search terms ("suicide," "how to commit suicide," "suicide methods," and "how to kill yourself"), they judged the search results they got as being prosuicide, antisuicide, "suicide-neutral," or "not a suicide site." The results show that prosuicide Web sites were quite numerous—41 Web pages, compared to 109 antisuicide ones. Further, prosuicide pages were easily accessible, and many contained detailed how-to instructions on how to end one's life:

> These sites often describe . . . methods that would not be known to the general population, such as gas asphyxiation or other methods that contribute to the higher rates of completed suicides among medical professionals armed with such knowledge. While in former years, laypersons would have had to research such subjects extensively in medical textbooks and reference guides in order to plan successful attempts, in recent years, several individuals have committed suicide with unusual methods that they learned online.

It is no longer that unusual for people to commit suicide by helium or ether gas inhalation, eating the roots of a poisonous plant, or injecting lighter fuel into their arms. We will discuss later the downside to the democratic dissemination of obscure, highly specialized knowledge online. For now, suffice it to say that suicide know-how, at the fingertips of someone who is both hopeless (because he is depressed) and disinhibited (because he is online), might make the person give up much sooner than he otherwise would. In light of their findings, the study authors conclude that "mental health professionals should ask patients about their Internet use." Although many of us routinely ask our depressed patients whether they own firearms, an equally relevant question might be: "Have you Googled suicide lately?"

"As a human being, you don't watch someone in trouble and sit back

and just watch," Abraham Biggs's broken father told reporters shortly
after his son's death. Unfortunately for him and his son, however, some
people seem to become a bit less human, or at least less humane, online.
It is easy to see the "other" as only a shadow of a person, not fully
realized or fully alive or fully sensitive to pain and, as such, not quite
worthy of the respect normally accorded to personhood. Even if he is
in extremis, as suicidal individuals by definition are, it is easy for his suffering to become our distraction; his pain, our lunch break pastime. If
we can dehumanize that person, it goes without saying that it would be
significantly easier to dehumanize someone who misrepresented a plate
he sold us on eBay or someone with whom we disagree on whether doctors and police officers are more important than teachers . . .

Whether it is a suicide forum, an e-mail back-and-forth, a girls-only
site like the one where rubyslippers, janice18, flowerchild, and angela47
had a catfight, or a bodybuilding chat room full of testosterone-driven
guys, being online often brings out the worst in people in a manner that
recalls the lynchings and gladiatorial blood fests of bygone and, one likes
to presume, less civilized, eras. Online, a race ensues to be meaner-than-
the-last-person-to-post-on-the-subject. This may be the inevitable next
step in the mimetic competition that fueled the grand-scale dreaming of
the Internet bubble and the meme-like propagation that creates virtual
celebrities. Nonetheless, one of the effects is to nurture, echo, and then
release into the world cruel instincts that over the course of history we
have tried to channel into healthier outlets.

Yet despite depressing facts and statistics, one should not lose sight
of the goodness we are capable of in the virtual world. For every online
store encouraging you to install keyloggers on your wife's computer,
there is a free Web site that patiently teaches her how to detect and
expunge such software. For every desperate person driven to suicide
in part because of the Internet, there is a "Bulker" trying to throw him
a lifeline. As the number of radicals recruited to hate groups rises, so
does, probably, the size of online donations to nonprofits that advo-

cate tolerance. The Internet can be, and is, a force of good, too. Law enforcement agencies can now obtain information and carry out their duties much more efficiently because of it. Crime mapping, protection-through-awareness campaigns, and response to emergencies have all improved, and many a criminal is behind bars because of the ability to pinpoint his location using the IP address obtained from his e-mails or texting device. Some individuals even react to the darkness they see in the virtual world by taking it on, transforming themselves into their own version of a cybersecurity sheriff intent on maintaining order and detecting abusers. As an episode on National Public Radio's *This American Life* showed, Internet scammers, for example, find their equal in vigilantes who are out to get them just as scammers are out to get the rest of the world. The episode featured three men, "Professor So and So," "Jojobean," and "YeaWhatever," who spent part of each day tracking Nigerian con men, motivated by nothing other than implementing justice and protecting little old ladies who might fall for this ruse and e-mail them their credit card numbers. One particularly complex plan they carried out involved sending a notorious Nigerian spammer/scammer 1,400 miles away from home—to the border with Darfur—to teach him a lesson. Unfortunately, however, I, like many people, still get about an e-mail a day from princes, finance ministers, and estate executors headquartered in Nigeria . . . Despite undeniable and very noble manifestations of online benevolence, the bad guys seem to always have the upper hand in the cyber wars, perhaps because a lot more people act worse than better online.

The World Wide Web has become a playground for the id. Online, we are free to express negative passions and urges, with little fear of retribution, let alone castration, by the superego or any other authority, and no clear legal or moral boundaries to help rein us in. Psychoanalytic theory holds that the superego uses its strict voice to contain the id. We seem to need for our real-life personality to exert a moderating, ethics-minded, superego-like influence over its reckless online cousin. We need it to advocate restraint, reflection, and analysis in the face of the anti-social and aggressive leanings of our e-personality. However, with the endless opportunities to misbehave online, it is unclear whether most people's "real I" is up to the task. Our job, like the cybersecurity czar's, is daunting.

Still, it behooves us to honestly and diligently try. According to psychoanalytic theory, ignoring the id's instincts leads to a whole range of pathological symptoms, from depression to psychosis. Likewise, pretending our e-personality goes to sleep when our computer goes to sleep would be naive. The negativity we display online does come back to haunt us, because of karma, or because the majority of us simply aren't as good at compartmentalizing as we would like to think. Psychoanalysts have traditionally tried to bring about symptom resolution by familiarizing patients with the disturbing content of their id—that is, by making the unconscious conscious. One principle way they have done so is through careful analysis of people's dreams. But because the Internet now serves as the repository for our dark impulses and secrets, it, not our dream life, is the best window we have into our modern frustrations and our oedipal and other complexes. In order to fully comprehend those, we must look for their manifestations online. Indeed, the modern-day version of the classic Freudian question *What did you dream about last night?* is *Where did you go online after your wife went to bed?* So to preserve our civility and sanity—the very things the virtual world seems to compromise—a process by which our "dark side," as manifested online, is brought into consciousness and explored under the light of day would seem like a worthwhile exercise.

_CHAPTER 5

IMPULSIVITY

No one can accuse Google of not having its users' best interests in mind. In 2008, the company unveiled Mail Goggles, a service intended to make sure you count to three, almost literally, before you use its e-mail program to send a message you may be better off not sending. Here is the blog announcing the new product, by Gmail engineer Jon Perlow:

> Sometimes I send messages I shouldn't send. Like the time I told that girl I had a crush on her over text message. Or the time I sent that late night email to my ex-girlfriend that we should get back together. Gmail can't always prevent you from sending messages you might later regret, but today we're launching a new feature . . . which may help.

> When you enable Mail Goggles, it will check that you're really sure you want to send that late night Friday email. And what better way to check than by making you solve a few simple math problems . . . to verify you're in the right state of mind?

When you click "send," Google throws up five math problems on the screen and specifies the amount of time you have to produce the answers. If you have the focus and wherewithal to solve the equations correctly, your composition cannot be considered impulsive and is free to go to its destination. Here is a sample Goggles pop-up box; compute accurately within forty-three seconds and you are compos mentis enough to tell your boss off or let an ex-lover know how much you are still not over that relationship:

Gmail aims to help you in many ways. Are you sure you want to send this? Answer some simple math problems to verify.

69 − 38

11 x 2

37 + 19

2 x 5

48 − 38

By default, Goggles is only active between 10:00 PM and 4:00 AM on Friday and Saturday nights, when alcohol-related disinhibition compounds Internet-related disinhibition, increasing the likelihood that regrettable e-mails will be sent. Fortunately, one can go to Gmail's general settings and extend the service well beyond weekend nights.

It would probably behoove many of us to do that. Even the most diplomatic and image-conscious among us can benefit from taking a deep breath and double-checking what we are writing and whom we are addressing it to. In 2005, no lesser a communicator than Alastair Campbell, the director of communications at the British prime minister's office, used his BlackBerry to send an e-mail to the BBC nightly news crew, expressing his disdain for the corporation's election coverage. "Fuck off and cover something important you twats!" his message read, rather shocking the nation. Campbell later explained that he had actually intended the missive for a colleague—it is not entirely clear why he would be addressing a colleague with the words "you twats"— and blamed the incident on the fact that he was "not very good at this email . . . malarkey." Malarkey or not, not even a spin doctor trained in the trenches of Iraq diplomacy could explain the mishap as anything other than an impulsive outburst made possible by the new world of virtual communications, where it is easier than ever to slip publicly, with potentially irreparable consequences.

Would that online impulsivity, that other e-personality trait, were limited to e mail banter and to the "send" command. It seems as though the equivalent of Goggles is required to protect us from clicking on the "buy now," "make a bet," and "meet me" icons, among other daily online functions that in more ordinary circumstances would be subjected to further cognitive processing and deliberation. Our increased risk tolerance when it comes to e-mail is matched only by our mouse-happy approach to online shopping, gambling, and sexual relating. Taken together, it would seem as though one major consequence of the virtual age and our online personality is a more impulsive humanity.

Chapter 1 touched on impulse control disorders through the stories of Liz and Richard. That family of conditions may be expanding both in the number of diagnoses it comprises and the number of patients affected. That is what psychiatrists and impulsivity researchers Eric Hollander and Dan Stein conclude. "With the development of the Internet and its unlimited access to sex, gambling, shopping, and stock trading, there has been a subsequent rise in impulsive behavior and even new forms of impulsive behavior," they write, in *Clinical Manual of Impulse Control Disorders*. They define impulsivity as "the failure to resist an impulse, drive, or temptation that is potentially harmful to oneself or others." It is characterized by "carelessness, an underestimated sense of harm . . . impatience, including the inability to delay gratification, and a tendency toward risk-taking, pleasure, and sensation-seeking." Neuroscientists Samuel Chamberlain and Barbara Sahakian, of the University of Cambridge, agree. Impulsivity, they say, manifests with a set of behaviors that are "poorly conceived, premature, inappropriate, and that frequently result in unwanted or deleterious outcomes." Uncontrolled impulsivity can affect us by impairing three crucial areas of healthy functioning: "reflection," or the ability to "collect and evaluate information before reaching decisions"; "deferment of reward," or the ability to "opt for larger delayed rewards over smaller more immediate [ones]"; and "motor impulsivity," or the ability to suppress ingrained motor movements that can get us in trouble, such as repeatedly pulling the lever on a traditional slot machine.

As a clinical concept, impulsivity is hardly new. In 1915, the German psychiatrist Emil Kraepelin, a forefather of modern psychiatry, called impulsive buyers "oniomaniacs," borrowing from the Greek roots for "buying maniacs." Swiss psychiatrist Eugen Bleuler elaborated on the concept in 1930 in his *Lehrbuch der Psychiatrie* (Textbook of Psychiatry). Here, he describes the phenomenon of otherwise normal individuals who are overtaken by irresistible impulses to buy. It remains one of the best descriptions of an impulse-ridden life:

> The particular element is impulsiveness; they cannot help it, which sometimes expresses itself in the fact that notwithstanding a good school intelligence, the patients are absolutely incapable to think differently and to conceive the senseless consequences of their act, and the possibilities of not doing it. They do not even feel the impulse, but they act out their nature like the caterpillar which devours the leaf.

When they are more or less in check, impulses can be a benign feature of a healthy personality. Chamberlain and Sahakian remind us that "we all engage from time to time in impulsive acts, such as blurting out critical comments without thinking, or buying [something] on the spur of the moment." We can probably all relate to the example of standing in line at the grocery store behind a woman who has just unloaded her shopping cart onto the conveyor belt. She is patiently watching as the cashier scans each item. All of a sudden, we see her turn to the right, grab a bag of M&Ms from the candy display to her side, and quickly add it to the goods on the belt. We can almost bet that the woman did not plan on buying M&Ms; that they were not on her shopping list. She acted on an impulse.

Most of us are often similarly tempted, but we try to build a metaphorical wall between us and the candy stand staring us in the face. Something tells us to try to distinguish between a product we simply want and one we really need. Yet evidence suggests that, increasingly, we are becoming that shopper, acting in a rash and nondeliberative way on the urge to buy things that we can live—and live rather well—without, and at prices that far exceed the cost of a bag of candy. The same seems to apply to other impulses, too.

Impulsive behavior can cross the threshold of what may be considered healthy to become a clinical condition. Too many M&M bags consumed in a single sitting with no sense of control over the behavior, and one starts approaching the *DSM* definition of a binge episode. Impulses become pathological when they are repetitive and hard to resist and when they seriously affect quality of life, including relationships, work, or school performance. This is what impulsivity "looks like" in a number of established psychiatric conditions, including binge eating disorder, alcohol and substance abuse, and, of course, the impulse control disorders. The latter group deserves special attention, as it might offer the best proof of an increase in the number of pathologically impulsive individuals among us.

Unlike psychiatric conditions where impulsivity is but one of several features that together make up the diagnosis, impulse control disorders are all about the impulse and its negative consequences. Examples include sexual compulsions (to be discussed later), compulsive shopping, and pathological gambling. Despite how strikingly different the "outward" impulse appears to the world, all three share a common basic mechanism: the person feels a repetitive, anxiety-laden urge to perform an act that is thrilling in the moment but leads to long-term dysfunction and guilt.

Let us start with the impulse to buy, since most of us have an Amazon or eBay account (and many of us have authorized these Web sites to store our credit card information to allow for an even speedier checkout next time). In a comprehensive review of compulsive shopping disorder, written for a book I coedited with my Stanford colleague Dr. Lorrin Koran, University of Iowa psychiatrist Dr. Donald Black starts by evoking the simultaneously colorful and sad history of some famous profligate spenders: Marie Antoinette, queen of France, whose extravagance before the revolution may well have cost her and her husband their lives; Mary Todd Lincoln, wife of President Abraham Lincoln, who had "spending binges that greatly distressed her husband"; publishing magnate William Randolph Hearst, whose "insatiable appetite for arts and antiques" nearly drove him to bankruptcy during the Great Depression; Jacqueline Kennedy Onassis, whose personal charm belied an "obsessive" shopping habit that "dismayed both of her husbands;" and, finally, the late Princess Diana, who was known to have an "intense interest in shopping and spending," and who died tragically while on a date with the scion of Harrods, London's top department store. One might add to this list Imelda Marcos, notorious couture and accessory collector and wife of deposed Philippines dictator Ferdinand Marcos, who memorably told the BBC, "They went into my closets looking for skeletons, but thank God, all they found were shoes, beautiful shoes." The collections of these famous figures may have defined taste and material beauty for their time, but Dr. Black is struck by how "their episodes of excessive and sometimes senseless spending" contributed to their problems and, in some cases, to their tragic demise.

While these individuals went on spending sprees from positions of privilege and power, research into compulsive buying disorder convincingly shows that it is an equal-opportunity affliction not limited to individuals of superior means. "Income has relatively little to do with compulsive buying disorder," writes Black, "because persons with a low income can be as preoccupied with shopping and spending as wealthier individuals." It is just that "level of income may lead one person to shop at a consignment shop, while the other shops at a high-end boutique." Still, being rich does shield the individual for a while from the effects of overshopping, in some cases giving him or her a let-them-eat-brioche callousness that can justify continued spending, come what may. For the average Joes and, more like it, average Janes (for most, but not all, studies have shown the problem to be more common in women), there is no cushioning of wealth to help soften the fall. Yet, like the famous examples we cited, they, too, are victims of conspicuous consumption, living embodiments of "shop till you drop." And they seem to be increasing in number, according to studies of compulsive shopping disorder.

The Compulsive Buying Scale is a brief questionnaire developed by researchers Ronald Faber and Thomas O'Guinn in 1992 to distinguish normal from pathological buyers. It is the most widely used research tool to help identify compulsive shoppers and track the severity of their symptoms. Individuals being screened are asked to rate on a five-point scale feelings and behaviors associated with five different aspects of the shopping experience:

- *need to spend money*: "If I have any money at the end of the pay period, I just have to spend it," and "I feel anxious on days when I don't go shopping";
- *awareness that the spending behavior is excessive*: "I feel others will be horrified if they knew my spending habits";
- *loss of control over spending*: "I have bought things though I can't afford them," and "I wrote a check when I knew I didn't have enough money to cover it";
- *buying things to improve one's mood*: "I feel anxious on days I don't go shopping";
- *probable negative financial problems*: "I make only the minimum payments on my credit cards."

The respondents' answers are tallied into a score, and predetermined cutoffs separate the pathological shoppers from "normal" ones who "can take it or leave it." Using questionnaires such as this to assess the prevalence of compulsive shopping, surveys conducted over the last two decades have yielded rates that have generally been under 10 percent. That is why the rate of 44 percent seen in a study of British adolescents commanded real attention. The 2005 survey was conducted by Helga Dittmar, of the University of Sussex, an expert on consumer attitudes, and published in the *British Journal of Psychology*. Dittmar's sample consisted of 195 sixteen- to eighteen-year-olds from two schools in the UK who completed shopping questionnaires during class time. Compared to similar studies she conducted in adults at around the same time, "age proved to be a significant predictor of compulsive buying," with younger shoppers much more likely to be affected. Her results suggested that problematic shopping and spending habits are extremely widespread among teenagers. This is an inauspicious finding given that the troubled adolescent shoppers of today will be the full-fledged consumers of tomorrow. Further, "the greater prominence of compulsive buying among younger respondents was accounted for, at least in part, by their stronger endorsement of materialistic values." This was reflected in their answers to the Materialistic Values Scale, a separate questionnaire where they endorsed much more heavily than adults did statements like: "My life would be better off if I owned certain things I don't have," "I like a lot of luxury in my life," and "I admire people who own expensive homes, cars and clothes."

Dittmar's teenage subjects are also the so-called digital natives who have had access to the new communication technologies since a very young age, and who have the highest rates of Internet access of all groups: 93 percent for twelve- to seventeen-year-olds in the United States and 89 percent for eighteen- to twenty-four-year-olds, according to 2008 data from the Pew Internet and American Life Project. (Data from the UK, where Dittmar's study was conducted, shows a similar age distribution pattern.) As a group, digital natives constitute a particularly computer- and Internet-savvy population, and Dittmar's data suggest they are also the most reckless of shoppers. While we cannot see the staggering 44 percent rate of pathological shopping among them as a direct effect of a very active virtual life (the study didn't address that link directly), it is worth considering whether the standards and values, including materialism, that the Internet encourages, the traits that it brings out, and the access that it gives to marketers might all be contributing to this phenomenon. Another study, also conducted by Dittmar and to be discussed below, suggests that this might indeed be the case.

Although longitudinal data are lacking on how the rates of compulsive shopping in the United States may have risen over time, we are, sadly, drowning in evidence for the financial ruin that has befallen us at all levels—the individual, the family unit, the local community, and the nation as a whole. Even if we spare ourselves extreme statistics from the economic meltdown of 2008 and 2009 (I cited some in chapter 2), and insert ourselves in the relative boom years that preceded them, we find that our financial health was already depressing enough:

- In 2005, 2006, and 2007, an average of six billion credit card offers went out to the 300 million residents of the United States—or some twenty offers per year to every man, woman, and child, as cited by April Benson, founder of Stopping Overshopping.
- In 2007, the average credit card debt per household was $7,430, or nearly 150 percent more than in 1990, according to Americans for Fairness in Lending.
- In the same year, consumer debt reached an all-time high of $2.55 trillion, almost double what it was a decade earlier, according to the Federal Reserve.

These figures reflect how, as a culture, we are bleeding red ink, and how "buy now, pay later" seems to have become our mantra. Could it be in part because materialism has found its perfect outlet in Buy .com? In an age when "stuff," like information, is instantly accessible, can a depleted bank account really still hold anyone back? How might something like Amazon's "one-click option," which further facilitates buying by essentially eliminating the checkout process, and the online psychological transformations we talked about, be contributing to our collective bankruptcy? Can out-of-touchness with money come from out-of-touchness with who we are in the virtual world?

Helga Dittmar attempted to answer some of these questions in a 2007 study, published in the *Journal of Social and Clinical Psychology*. Her research group recruited 126 University of Sussex students—58 women and 68 men—who had purchased something online at least once. Their average age was twenty-two. Using the Compulsive Buying Scale to find the dysfunctional Internet shoppers among them, they determined that nearly 10 percent met criteria for compulsive online shopping. The researchers then asked questions to understand specifically what prompted the pathological shoppers' online sprees. Was it the *economic benefit* made possible through the ease of price comparisons online? Was it the *efficiency* and convenience of not having to go to the store? Was it the *mood enhancement* provided by a dose of online "retail therapy"? Or was it *identity gains* and the possibility of feeling grander than one's old self through buying goods online?

Perhaps contrary to expectations, the results showed that economic benefit and efficiency did not trigger compulsive online buying—people didn't shop compulsively online because it was easier and less time-consuming than going to the store, or in order to save money. In contrast, psychological motives and identity gains were clear triggers for compulsive buying online, in that compulsive shoppers tended to shop online specifically in order to feel better about themselves and because they thought it got them closer to an ideal image that they were chasing. Their reasons for online shopping "are concerned with a 'better self,'" the authors conclude, and not so much with saving money or avoiding the inconvenience of a trip to the mall. "Individuals appear motivated by self-improvement and self-repair in the sense that they are seeking enjoyment, mood regulation, self-expression, and moving closer to an identity ideal." The Internet, which, as we have seen, helps us create a better version of ourselves, also gives us the illusion that Amazon is our shortcut to it. The problem is that "the more individuals believe that the acquisition of material goods will bring them happiness—improved emotions and mood—the more they should be motivated to buy goods in order to obtain these emotional benefits. The same should hold for beliefs that material goods bring social status and self-definition: the more individuals endorse such materialistic beliefs, the more they should seek social and personal identity gains when they buy goods."

"I shop, therefore I am" is, of course, an old slogan. Consumers have used material goods as a way to become someone, or something, they are not for a long time. But in the context of the virtual experience and of the endless illusion of personal reinvention that the Internet sells us, shopping as a self-transformative act takes on a larger (and costlier) role. The idea that we can "become" this other person if we buy a particular item feels much more achievable online than in the mall. And the consequences seem much less near and tangible. With our grandiose and narcissistic sides, it is easier, online, to feel as potent and as immune to repercussions as a Marie Antoinette or a Marcos—and to shop accordingly. Keeping up with the Joneses may have been the goal of the last few decades. Today, we are busy trying to keep up with our e-selves and our alter egos.

"What would Plato do?" one might be tempted to ask. We have no way of knowing, but Dittmar and her colleagues advocate that as a society we increase awareness into the psychological and financial pitfalls of impulsive online buying, through education and consumer advice and, for some, through psychotherapy. "Individuals seem most vulnerable to compulsive buying tendencies online, and would therefore benefit most from such intervention when they believe that a better self is only a button click away."

Psychotherapy for your e-tail therapy? It wasn't supposed to turn out that way. A decade ago, it was thought that the Internet would encourage responsible buying by helping consumers avoid the marketing distractions of traditional stores, facilitating price and product comparisons, and freeing us from time pressure. This myth has been punctured. Instead, we find ourselves in a virtual bazaar where we have our alter ego to contend with and where "the buying transaction is so remote from handing over cash that it does not really feel like spending money." And so we spend more.

Still, one cannot blame the "one-click option" for 2009's credit default swaps miasma . . . The reasons for our fiscal predicament are not agreed upon by economists and Great Depression scholars, let alone compulsive shopping researchers or impulsivity neuroscientists. But the idea that the Internet might be contributing by making money virtual and more abstract than ever before deserves serious consideration. After all, as I suggested before, the obscene living-beyond-our-means that has characterized the credit and mortgage bubble is an experience in unreality that may have more in common with Second Life and its official currency, the Linden dollar, than any sustainable economic model.

Another example of an impulse control condition seemingly on the rise is pathological gambling disorder. Unlike compulsive shopping disorder, pathological gambling is included in the *DSM*, reflecting wider acceptance of the diagnosis in the psychiatric community. Reliable statistics on how the Internet has changed the gambling landscape are difficult to come by, and researchers hunting them down will find themselves sending e-mails to Antigua, Gibraltar, and the Dominican Republic, among other offshore casino havens. Still, by 2001, enough evidence had accumulated about an increase in gambling rates in the United States that the American Psychiatric Association (APA) issued an advisory highlighting the risks. Studies had already established that the spread of gaming institutions (such as Indian and floating casinos) was leading to more cases of pathological gambling. So, with the exponential increase in the number of virtual casinos, the APA feared that pathological gambling might become an epidemic, especially among younger individuals, which prompted its advisory:

> Research has shown a correlation between the availability of legal gambling in an individual state and the proportion of that state's population reporting gambling problems. In virtually all studies of the rates of gambling problems at various ages, high school and college-aged individuals show the highest problem rates. In recent years there has been an explosive growth of gambling opportunities and activities on the Internet. . . . [W]hile in 1997 there were approximately 6.9 million potential Internet gamblers and a revenue of about $300 million from this activity, just one year later there were 14.5 million potential Internet gamblers and a revenue of $651 million. And last year, there were more than 1,300 of these online sites.

The advisory goes on to enumerate the ways in which Internet gambling differs from traditional gambling, and how these differences can make it potentially riskier:

- Internet gambling, unlike other types of gambling, is a "solitary activity." People can gamble undetected and uninterrupted for potentially unlimited periods of time.
- There are no fail-safes that would protect underage individuals or prevent people from gambling while intoxicated or gambling at work.
- Since most virtual casinos operate from servers located outside the Unites States, Internet gambling is more difficult to challenge—an unscrupulous operator can close down a site or move its base to another country if confronted.
- Few regulations are in place to assure the fairness of the games.
- Hackers can potentially interfere with the process by manipulating online games, or steal funds by accessing credit card information.

Much anecdotal evidence, and at least two research studies, have since then confirmed the APA's fears. A 2007 British survey of 9,003 individuals aged sixteen and over, found that 72 percent of the population had gambled in the twelve months before the survey. The venues included national lottery participation, sports betting, online gaming, and playing slot machines. Although a large majority of the group had gambled, the overall rate of *pathological* gambling—repetitive gambling that is experienced as irresistible and that negatively affects the gambler, was only 0.6 percent. However, when researchers compared the number of pathological gamblers among those who gambled online versus the rest of the group, the rate in the online group was much higher—5 percent. Also, online gamblers were more likely to be young (defined by the study as under thirty-four) than traditional gamblers. The results led the authors to conclude that the "medium of the Internet may be more likely to contribute to problem gambling than gambling in offline environments."

An American study published in 2002 in the journal *Psychology of Addictive Behaviors* points to a similar phenomenon. Researchers at the University of Connecticut Health Center evaluated gambling behavior, including Internet gambling, among 389 patients receiving subsidized medical or dental care in the university clinics. Ninety percent had gambled in the twelve months before being interviewed for the study. The most common forms of gambling were lottery, slot machines, and scratch tickets. Internet gambling was reported by only 8 percent of participants. However, Internet gamblers were much more likely than non-Internet, "traditional" gamblers to show signs of pathological gambling—74 percent versus 26 percent. As in the British study, Internet gamblers were more likely to be younger.

Because it was conducted in a medical setting and involved individuals who don't have health insurance, this study is not reflective of the U.S. population at large. This can bias the results, because gambling problems may be what caused these patients to have financial difficulties and lose their jobs and health insurance in the first place. For that reason, the rates of pathological gambling the study arrived at seem artificially high. Still, the difference between the two groups is striking enough to allow the authors to make the following point: With the expansion of Internet gambling, "a rise in disordered gambling may be inevitable as individuals gain easier access to gambling opportunities." "We're not seeing a lot of recreational gambling on the Internet," Dr. Nancy Petry, a psychiatrist and one of the study researchers, said in an interview. Her results support that opinion: There is little that is "recreational" about a 74 percent rate of pathological gambling among people who gamble online.

By increasing access, dissolving inhibitions, and falsely empowering people with notions of their invincibility and special talent for winning, the Internet seems to be increasing the rates of disordered gambling. This magnifies the offline costs to society, since, by definition, disordered gambling is associated with severe impairment, and a rate of 74 percent of pathological gambling disorder among online gamblers (or whatever the "real" rate actually is) means that that proportion of online gamblers exhibit one or more serious signs of offline trouble as defined in the *DSM* diagnosis:

- the person has committed illegal acts to finance gambling;
- the person lies to family members, therapists, or close friends to conceal the extent of gambling;
- the person has jeopardized or lost a significant relationship or opportunity because of gambling; and
- the person relies on others to provide money to relieve a desperate financial situation.

That gambling-related problems have increased is also reflected in the fact that the twenty-four-hour helpline operated by the National Council on Problem Gambling has seen its call volume from persons seeking help, information, or referrals more than double between 2000 and 2008.

Fearing that the socioeconomic consequences of online gambling were ruining more lives, a Republican-led Congress moved quickly in 2006 to pass the Unlawful Internet Gambling Enforcement Act, or UIGEA. (Cynics say that scandal-wary lawmakers were in reality acting to distance themselves from disgraced gaming lobbyist Jack Abramoff.) The UIGEA attempts to interdict Internet gambling by prohibiting financial institutions such as credit card companies from approving transactions between U.S.-based customers and offshore gambling merchants. It struck an immediate blow to the bottom line of many Web casinos that rely on American gamblers, but ambiguous language in the bill, creative interpretation of its content, and the fundamental ungovernability of the Web have all made oversight complicated and assured the survival of online gambling as a potentially abusable Internet pastime. (Some in the gaming industry have expressed hope that the UIGEA may now be reversed altogether; they are betting that President Obama, a self-declared "pretty good poker player," will be more sensitive to their cause.)

It remains to be seen how effective policy alone can be in controlling this problem, so harm reduction efforts have also focused on increasing gamblers' own self-control. Safeguards against impulsivity are offered by some gambling Web sites. Those limit the amount of money users can wager, thus temporarily getting in the way of a gambler acting on the urge to gamble. This is the virtual cousin of the "self-exclusion" programs that are offered by some land-based casinos, and which some problem-gamblers utilize to help regulate their visits. According to a Harvard study published in 2008 in the *Journal of Gambling Studies*, such interventions may be worth considering in cyberspace, too. The study involved *bwin*, a European sports betting service that offers subscribers the option to impose monthly self-limits on the amount of money they wager online. Over eighteen months, researchers followed the gambling patterns of 47,000 bwin subscribers, checking how many of them chose to impose self-limits and whether those limits changed their gambling behavior. Among subscribers who took advantage of this service, the self-limit values ranged from $12 to $5,680. But the overall results were decidedly mixed: While the behavior of "self-limiters" after imposing the self-limits moved in the direction of fewer bets and less money wagered, only 1.2 percent of subscribers chose to take advantage of that option—a very small percentage when one considers the potential for online gambling abuse as suggested by the prior studies. Even when tools that might enhance our impulse control are made available online, few people seem to avail themselves of those services. Limits and filters are okay when we are concerned about our kids' virtual whereabouts, but most of us like our Internet experience unfiltered, thank you. We seem to trust in our ability for online self-discipline more than is warranted.

Taken together, the studies in online gambling and shopping point to decreased self-control and to an intensification of urges as these old activities are carried out in the virtual casino or virtual marketplace. By severely compressing or obliterating the steps that separate us from goals like buying another green pressed-glass plate on eBay to add to our collection, or betting a lot of money on the outcome of a basketball game, the Internet makes it more difficult for our higher cognitive functions to intervene and put the brakes on potentially problematic behaviors before they occur. Acting in a stepwise fashion gives our higher functions the opportunity to analyze facts, consider pros and cons, and intervene to abort a process if, as a result of careful deliberation, the outcome is seen as more bad than good. By making many goals only a click of the mouse away, however, the Internet often turns this deliberative process into nothing but an annoying set of inconvenient roadblocks that separate us from what we "really" want. Whereas the average person in the pre-Internet age could flirt with bankruptcy and live dangerously close to the credit card limit, it was easier for common sense to prevail at some point in the complex, multistep process involved in making a trip to the antique store or to the casino. But with the Internet making gambling and the acquisition of superfluous products effortless and automatic, we no longer have the opportunity to "talk ourselves out of it." As a result, we have to work significantly harder to resist temptation, and we are living in a more impulsive, impatient, and immediate-gratification-oriented world, one in which it is harder to control a whole range of impulses.

As I mentioned in the first chapter, when behaviors like gambling, shopping, or sex seeking become disabling, some clinical treatments exist to help control them. Those include some medications that have been shown to work, and some forms of individual and family psychotherapy. For the rest of us, however, these behaviors have a negative effect on our lives without being debilitating or rising to the level of a clinical disorder. Our "treatment" might as well consist of some external controls that will make us pause and think as we give the urge a chance to dissipate. In that sense, the Gmail Goggles program may be on the right track. But in order to make a meaningful difference and create a real obstacle to online impulse-driven behavior, the arithmetic may have to be a bit more challenging. (And the program may have to be mandatory.) On a CNET blog discussing the launch of Goggles, hidden among entries that recommended extending it to cell phones and other texting devices, an interjection from a certain "Beta_Delta" caught my eye. The blogger is either a math whiz or someone who has suffered unspeakably as a result of online impulsivity, for here is what he had to say:

i think the five math problems should be like this:

82 x 62 =

13 x 9 =

890 x 999 =

98765432 / 8 =

I think "Beta_Delta" is on to something.

_CHAPTER 6

INFANTILE REGRESSION AND
THE TYRANNY OF THE EMOTICON

AFTER GRANDIOSITY, narcissism, a penchant for mischief, and impulsivity, the next building block of e-personality is the easiest one to acquire, and requires little effort or planning. The person, online, simply relives a less complicated phase of life, when responsibility and maturity were but distant developmental milestones to be achieved in due time, no rush. He or she then lingers there, unperturbed and unperturbable, and forgets to grow back up. Ah, the carefree joys of childhood.

In many cases, infantile regression dominates e-mail, texting exchanges, social networking sites, and the blogosphere. The Internet has become, in some sense, a place to regress, as many immaturities not permissible offline—petulance, evasion of responsibility, and a certain spoiled attitude—become less impermissible online. In the virtual world, many adults have found a convenient way to avoid the complexities of life and act like children again. One obvious indicator of that, and a good place to start, is the dramatic rise in the popularity of video, computer, and online games. Because the demarcation lines among the various platforms have become blurred, and because most games now have online capabilities, I will, from here onward, refer to them collectively as virtual games.

Several of these games seem designed with the clear aim of helping adults unleash the child within—in one case, crayons in hand. As reported by Winda Benedetti, msnbc.com's "Citizen Gamer," Crayon Physics, the winner of the 2008 Independent Games Festival grand prize, "looks like it was plucked from a 5-year-old's coloring book." It is "a world of crinkled notebook paper and crayon scribbles . . . a place where castles and dinosaurs and rockets look like they've been scrawled into existence by immature hands." The virtual game that seemed to turn the most adult heads in 2009 and generate the most "mature" buzz has a rather modest objective: "There is a ball over here and there is a star over there. You must move the ball to the star by using [virtual] crayons to draw the physical objects that make it possible to transport the ball to its goal. . . . It's like a kindergartner's dream come true: The objects you've conjured in your imagination spring to life before your eyes, imbued with their own weight, beholden to gravity and momentum . . . and to your whims."

Transporting the ball over to the star is big business, it turns out. From $2.6 billion at the dawn of the Internet revolution in 1996, virtual game sales grew to 9.5 billion in 2007, and, according to a 2008 survey of 1,200 households by the Entertainment Software Association, 65 percent were "gaming households." Moreover,

- Three quarters of regular game players are over eighteen, and a quarter are over fifty.
- The average age of the regular gamer is thirty (not fourteen!).
- The average age of the most frequent household game purchaser is forty.
- Perhaps contrary to expectations, a full 40 percent of virtual game players are female. In fact, a lot more women over eighteen play virtual games than boys under seventeen.

Data from other surveys suggest that parents may even be outgaming their kids. In a 2008 survey by the Pew Internet & American Life Project,

66 percent of parents of children under seventeen said they played computer games, but not because the offspring dragged Mom and Dad to the gaming console—only 31 percent of parents said they played with their kids; the majority played alone. Finally, 45 percent of adult game players specifically prefer online games to games that don't involve going online, according to a 2006 Associated Press/America Online poll. They also spend more time and money doing it than non-online players.

The cost of these games is hardly limited to how much money is spent buying or subscribing to them, or the number of hours killed playing them. Virtual games are not just a regressive activity that can bite into one's discretionary income or downtime. The indirect cost is the precious time they take away from more adult activities and responsibilities. The price of not meeting these expectations because we are tethered to World of Warcraft, Sims 2, or Call of Duty 4—all recent top sellers—is incalculable.

The road from an innocent virtual pastime to serious consequences is more linear and direct than it might appear. Virtual games are more lifelike than ever, stimulate all our senses, and engulf us in an all-engaging experience. As the life-simulating aspect becomes more sophisticated and convincing, it becomes easier for some to think that what is permissible in a virtual game might also pass offline—something I explored in chapter 3. It also becomes easier to lose perspective on one's divergent priorities: the need to perform well as a favorite game character or as an accomplished player versus the need to function as a responsible adult. It's all one big life with one big "cumulative" score, the faulty justification goes, and if we are breaking records in an online game, we may feel, in aggregate, responsible and productive enough, and thus allow for some gross negligence elsewhere in life. A look at two very popular virtual games—Sims 2 and World of Warcraft—further highlights the pull that such computer games can exert on people and the potential real-life consequences.

In April 2008, the Sims 2 Web site celebrated 100 million copies of the Sims series sold. "Create Sims, design their homes, and bring their stories to life! Will your Sims lead privileged lives and live happily ever after or will there be a shocking twist at the end? It's entirely up to you." That is how the official Web site entices you to try the popular product, very much in the spirit of Second Life, and playing on the same e-personality tendencies that have made that Web site popular (and problematic), namely a desire to self-perfect and to control one's fate and that of others.

During the game, Sim characters progress through six stages of development: baby, toddler, child, teen, adult, and elder. Characters have "needs" that drive them and that vary with their age. Those include "Bladder" (the need to urinate), "Energy" (the need to sleep), "Hunger" (the need to eat), and "Social" (the need to make human contact). The degree of any need is communicated through a meter that changes color from green (full) to yellow (low) to red (desperation). A total measure of a Sim's met and unmet needs is clearly displayed as a diamond that hovers over the character's head and that serves as a convenient contentment index (such a handy barometer of global well-being, if it became available in real life, would make the practice of psychiatry much more scientific!). Part of the game involves the player addressing the Sims' various clearly expressed needs. Otherwise, a Sim with an empty Energy meter will pass out; a Sim with an empty Hunger meter will die; and should a Sim adult fail to care for a baby Sim by failing to meet its needs, a Social Worker will materialize and whisk the baby off the family lot. Of course, an "expansion pack," available for extra cost, allows one to "Plead with the Social Worker." However, in another clash with reality, my experience with my tough-as-nails social worker colleagues suggests that there is no "pleading" with social workers when they smell child abuse.

Other mechanisms still, besides the watchful social worker, are in place to protect younger Sims, especially, and make them tamper-proof. For example, built-in features prevent a deranged parent character from hurting them. Sims babies, toddlers, and children are designed to be fireproof and will not die of hunger, hard as a homicidal parent might try to harm them with these methods.

If these protections worked, we might wish real life were more like a Sims 2 game and came with similar survival-guaranteeing features. But, alas, none of the safety measures designed to keep virtual games wholesome, clean, and family-oriented seem to succeed. Instead, much of the pleasure that players find in these games appears to lie in circumventing the parameters of the games in ways that too often involve breaking as many real-life taboos as possible. Through clever "cheats" that players discover and then disseminate online or post on the game's "wiki," every game rule is questioned, challenged, and ultimately rewritten to make unthinkable acts like burning one's child or killing one's babies entirely possible. As with other games, a large cottage industry of Sims 2 cheats proliferates with the aim of helping players take their game to another level—lazier and more disturbing. Call it playing with fire; call it a G-rated Medea; or call it *Sins 2*. As a quick tour of one message board dedicated to Sims cheats indicates, easy step-by-step instructions exist to allow you to:

- *Torture your Sims:* "To torture your sims (kill them), first make them walk into an empty room with nothing in it. Go into buy mode and delete the door. (Note: you can not delete the door if it is open) If the door is open make your sim walk out of the room and try again. If your door is gone then they can not get out of the room and they will DIE! Have fun!"
- *Age your babies so you don't have to raise them:* "Well, all you have to do is to perform the L & D Tombstone Cheat. Click 'spawn' and keep clicking 'more' until you see AGE BABY to the left. Click that, choose your baby, and wa-lah! Baby no more!!"
- *Potty-train your toddler in one session:* "When ur potty training a toddler just enter boolProp TestingCheatsEnabled true which lets u move the needs, skills, and, other things on a sim. in order to drag the

needs and skills and relationships, you still need to type the cheat TWICE in neighborhood view or mode before you enter the home. Well after u enter the cheat make an adult potty train a toddler an when there doing there bussiness before the bladder need goes fully green pause the game an drag bak to red the toddler will remain an the skill will increse keep doing this until the toddler ir fully potty train an also pause an raise all the needs of the adult so they wont starve to death or pass out while potty training the toddler. This will help a lot"

- *Get fit without working out:* "What you do is type in BoolProp Testingcheatsenabled true to get the cheat bar up type shift+Ctrl and C then a white bar should appear at the top of the screen.
Then hold shift and click on the sim you want to be fit/muscly.
It should come up with *Change fit
Click on that and then it should say get thin or get fat
Click on get thin and then your sim should be muscly
P.s: Make sure that your sim isn't doing anything at the same time you click cos it might not work.
Happy Simming! Xoxo"

- *Get a teenager pregnant:* "To get a teenager pregnant all you have to do is press shift+Ctrl and c and type in 'boolprop testingcheatsenabled true' but without speechmarks then shift click on the teen you want to be pregnant got to spawn then tombstone of L and D. Then click on the gravestone with the teenager as the selected sim and then choose make me pregnant.
HAPPY SIMMING BABES!!"

- *Get a man pregnant:* "to get your man pregant get the cheat code up then type in boolprop testingcheatsenabeled true then click on the gravestone of L&D then click on the man and then on the grave stone go to spawn then click on the person you want a baby with the if u want him to have the baby faster click speed my pregance then the bump will get bigger and bigger then he will have the baby not the woman!!!"

Two broad categories of virtual behaviors emerge from an analysis of these and similar cheats: the deviant (torture your Sims, get a teenager pregnant, get a man pregnant) and the idle (age your babies so you don't have to raise them, potty-train your toddler in one session, get fit without working out). The former could easily have been included in chapter 3, alongside the malware and cyber-harassment statistics. Virtual games can degenerate to the point where they highlight the same disturbing tendencies, only here the process unfolds in a childlike, playful guise. The dark content is made less creepy because it is harbored by cool, lazy avatars operating within the dreamlike contours of a fantasy land. But it remains dark nonetheless, and it would be a mistake to think of the regression that goes hand in hand with it as simply a recapturing of a certain lost childhood innocence. Rather, the childlike aspects have more to do with style than substance—a veneer that has the effect of making the other content less threatening and less obvious. This is also true of World of Warcraft, also known by its cutesy diminutive, WoW.

World of Warcraft is an example of a "massively multiplayer online role playing game," or MMORPG, in which a large number of players interact in a virtual world. The most popular of all MMORPGs, World of Warcraft counted more than 11.5 million worldwide subscribers in December 2008. As with other MMORPGs, players control an avatar within the virtual game world. Avatars here are created with a variety of colorful attributes, before players can start exploring, battling, and "questing" in the fantasy setting of Azeroth. Indeed, much of World of Warcraft centers around questing—a string of quests, or missions, that reward the player with experience points, items, or in-game money, and that commonly involve killing a creature, finding a difficult-to-locate object, visiting specific locations, or delivering an item from one place to another. Quests are usually linked by a common theme, with one completed quest triggering the next, thus forming a quest chain through which the story of the game is told.

World of Warcraft is painless to get into, according to the reviewers at GameSpot.com, the popular game resource ranked among the two hundred most trafficked sites on the Web: "You can go from your desktop to being in-game in just seconds, and it's virtually just one great, big, seamless world." Although it can be an enormous time sink, the player apparently never leaves feeling wasteful or unrewarded. GameSpot explains why:

> For one, World of Warcraft has a nice, brisk pace to it, and the fast-loading, seamless world obviously has a lot to do with this. But, in addition, recovery times between battles are minimal, as even those characters without healing spells can still easily recover from their wounds by using bandages, eating a quick meal, or just from natural healing.

Even that most dreaded game outcome, player death, need not slow the gamer down or make him feel like a failure:

> Death in this game really is nothing to get bent out of shape about, so when you get killed, don't worry. Previous games of this type have made it a point of penalizing the player upon death (death should be very bad, right?), directly resulting in a sense of failure and wasted time. . . . World of Warcraft all but eliminates the sense of penalty altogether—which turns out to be a great thing. Here, death mostly just puts you out of the action for a bit, which is undesirable enough as it is. . . . In all, the game's death penalty feels just right, in that it's consequential without being frustrating.

The lack, or at least considerable softening, of penalty and "consequences" attached to player incompetence contributes, then, to the wild success of World of Warcraft, where players have a way to escape, relatively easily, the punishment and suffering they might expect in a nonvirtual world. Error is much better tolerated in Azeroth than in the context of one's marriage or one's workplace, just as it was better tolerated in childhood, where the threshold for triggering serious retribution was significantly higher. Of course, "traditional" toys and games are free of consequence, too: For decades, army action figures have died and resurrected themselves; Barbie dolls have lost their heads and respawned; and trains have collided head-on, then got right back on track. But, except for a few isolated collectors, those games never really appealed to adults or made them yearn to relive their childhoods. For the most part, they were tools we used to distract and entertain our kids, not ourselves. Virtual games, on the other hand, are quite appealing to a significant proportion of the adult population, and seem to be triggering in many of us nostalgia for a consequence-free state; one that allows us to reproduce, over the course of a WoW quest or a Sims session, a long-lost phase of early development.

Children may have led the curve on virtual games, but adults, as we have seen, have caught the bug, too, and seem to be just as engrossed. The same applies to social networking sites, where 35 percent of adults now have at least one profile, according to a 2009 Pew Research Center analysis. This represents a quadrupling in the number of adults on MySpace, Facebook, and the like since 2005. Among them, 51 percent have two or more profiles. ("Move over, kiddos," is how *USA Today* opened an article on the topic, titled "A Few Wrinkles Are Etching Facebook.") As with MySpace, Facebook, and virtual games, activities that began as an addictive pastime for teenagers have now gotten many a mature adult addicted. It seems as though, with some things, the Internet and related technologies are helping facilitate a reversal in how habits and behaviors have normally been taught and transmitted: More and more in the virtual world, parents seem to be emulating their children rather than the other way around, in a sort of very curious reverse parenting.

One could argue that there is also a positive side to parents coming together with their children around activities that children are known to enjoy; that this facilitates the "my mom is my best friend" or "my son is my best friend" notion that our culture increasingly values. I know some parents who would love nothing better than for their teenage off-spring to describe them as their BFF (best friend forever) on Facebook. Being BFFs and having more interests in common can help break down generational barriers that make conversations awkward and can lead to more open and honest discourse, not just about WoW strategy or how to update your Facebook profile, but perhaps also about grades, drugs, sexually transmitted diseases, pregnancy, and so forth. Under that light, what I am describing as regression might be seen by some as "bonding," and it is not so bad that the game console may have replaced the din-ner table. While this is a valid position to take, I hold the opposite view, not out of old-fashioned adherence to dinner table conversations and rigid intergenerational hierarchy, but because immaturity tends to breed immaturity, and it is hard for parents to play their role as parents—to model, teach, and inspire mature behavior—if they are going out of their way to act very young.

This is perhaps more obvious yet when it comes to our online rela-tionship with language. So much of our virtual interactions are con-ducted in a language that is extremely far from the one we learned over the course of our lives and our education. Games and other childlike pursuits that flourish in cyberspace are made to look even more innocu-ous by the use of a *certain kind* of language. On Facebook, apparently, "totes," "probs," and "dorbs" stand for totally, probably, and adorable, respectively. In World of Warcraft, to "rez" a player is to bring him back to life, or resurrect him, and to "mez" him is to mesmerize him; a "griefer" is a player who intentionally tries to annoy or distract another player—that is, someone who causes you grief (I admit a strong likeness for this word); "spi" and "sta" signify spirit and stamina, respectively; and "OOM" is a serious cry for help, signifying "out of mana," a situa-tion you never want to be in because mana is magical power sought by "casters" to cast their spells.

Likewise, the tour of the Sims 2 cheats message board was made all the more painful because of the linguistic regression that marked the posters' language. ("click on the person you want a baby with the if u want him to have the baby faster click speed my pregance then the bump will get bigger and bigger then he will have the baby not the woman!!!") Still, poorly written as those tips were, they were more language-like than how Sims themselves talk to one another during the game—using "Simlish," a system of communication that consists of gibberish words, sometimes enhanced with clues provided through paralinguistic cues and tone of voice, but where the meaning is largely left to the fecund imagination of the player. Indeed, well beyond virtual games and Facebook Wall posts, many of our online communications are only a few small developmental steps above Simlish on the maturity scale. Although the regression is hardly only linguistic, how language is devolving is probably the best symptom of the overall devolution that marks e-personality. Analyzing it in more detail should offer a good window into those other regressions.

Plenty of resources are available on the Web to alert parents to the shorthand lingo used by their children in chat room conversations. The Internet dictionary NetLingo conveniently compiles a popular list of "Top 50 Internet Acronyms Parents Need to Know." "143," parents are warned, stands for "I love you"—each digit representing the number of letters in each word—and "182" means "I hate you." "KPC" stands for "keeping parents clueless," "PAL" for "parents are listening," and "MOS" for "mom over shoulder." "8," we are told, somehow signifies oral sex, while "420" refers to marijuana. More ominously, perhaps, "LMIRL" means "let's meet in real life." Directed at parents, however, these warnings can imply that adults themselves are above such hieroglyphic means of communicating: "Now you're ready to learn cyberlingo, the secret language that children use while in Internet chat rooms or while using instant messaging," announces one Web site. What "lingo," exactly, does the Web site think most adults use these days in their e-mails and text messages? Chaucer's? A visit to the Sims 2 or WoW chat rooms frequented by many adults, or simply a random sampling of the average adult's in-box, reveals that e-language has taken over many of our communications and that, with the help of netspeak, many adults are writing, and, it would follow, acting, like children again.

According to Brazilian linguist Sérgio Costa, much of the communicating that happens online is in a childlike language. Just as children who do not master the conventions of language write in abbreviated code, rich in neologisms and pictorial characters, adults in their e-mails, blogs, and text messages adopt these less sophisticated forms of communication, willfully using lowercase when capitalization is indicated, and freely shortening and conflating words. The use of the emoticon represents an equally simple substitute for complex communication—who needs to carefully process feelings and logically organize thoughts before finally communicating a state of mind, when a simple hieroglyphic can convey everything and . . . nothing?

Some linguists, including Nigel J. Ross, of the Milan Institute for Interpreters and Translators, have likened the information age to the advent of printing in the fifteenth century, when profound changes in language and in society's management and control of information occurred. David Crystal, author of *Language and the Internet* and *The Cambridge Encyclopedia of the English Language*, says that prophets of doom, just as they did in the fifteenth century, now complain about the deterioration in language caused by the overly casual nature of Internet communications and the absence of any "quality control" over what gets published online. He agrees that "resources for the expression of informality in writing have hugely increased—something which has not been seen in English since the Middle Ages," but he sees this as a net gain, not a giant step in the wrong direction.

For Crystal, instant messaging and the phone texting craze it has spawned are partly a "game." The player's exciting challenge is to fit a semi-meaningful message within some predetermined constraints that include the number of bytes and characters allowed. (Twitter has taken the same game to a new extreme, as we will discuss later.) That gives rise to colorful solutions as texters try to get their ideas across concisely, such as by using g2g for "good to go" or brb for "be right back." In Crystal's view, this is a *creative* game, much like writing an Elizabethan sonnet within the confines of the fourteen-line poem was a creative exercise. His argument rests on a belief, shared by many linguists, that naturally occurring changes in language are never bad—just interesting. People who text, many linguists argue, often know well how to write; they are simply *choosing* to use "u" for "you" to partake in an old linguistic process that has been unfolding since people shortened "I am" to "I'm" three centuries ago or, more recently, compressed "for your information" to FYI and "répondez s'il vous plaît" to RSVP. There is nothing to fear in the contractions, abbreviations, and initialisms of netspeak, we are reassured. We can no more complain about lol (laughing out loud) than about PS (postscript). These shortcuts are only proof that our language is organic, dynamic, and alive—something that should fill our hearts with joy and warm feelings. "Netspeak is a development of millennial significance," glows Crystal. "A new medium of linguistic communication does not arrive very often in the history of the race." We should be so lucky. Still, it is hard to rejoice, given the rise in sloppiness and confusion that netspeak, instant messaging, and texting are bringing about. I would argue that as communication methods, these "games" are much more regressive than progressive. And that is just imho (in my humble opinion).

It is hard not to see texting, specifically, as "a giant leap backward in the science of communication," as Louis Menand wrote in a 2008 *New Yorker* piece. Referring to the number of text messages that fly across the ether every year, Menand writes, "A trillion of anything has to make some change in cultural weather patterns." And he predicts bad weather ahead. Rather than a technology-empowered step toward a future of more efficient and more *scientific* communicating, Menand sees texting as backward-looking, "primitive and improvisational—like the way prisoners speak to each other by tapping on the walls of their cells in *Darkness at Noon.*" Why would "F?" (what my eleven-year-old niece uses for "are we still friends?") be any more advanced or mature than "73" (Morse code for "best regards")? Rather than a naturally unfolding linguistic process that will enrich and expand our vocabulary, Menand worries that texting may be severely contracting it: "C. K. Ogden's *Basic English* had a vocabulary of eight hundred and fifty words. Most texters probably make do with far fewer than that."

Other features of the new language are also worth noting: Texting and, more broadly, netspeak are making us speed-obsessed in our interactions with others, and disembodying our words by separating what we are trying to say from our body language. More than any other value contained within our communications system, netspeak and its texting "dialect" focus disproportionately on speed. The one mortal sin in the world of texting is to ignore a text message you have received. "To delay is to disrespect," Menand warns. "In fact, [it] is the only disrespect." Everything else is forgiven, or can be cleared up with a few more hastily exchanged messages. "You can be sloppy and you can be blunt, but you have to be fast," seems to be the dictum. That might explain why the most frequently texted message is also the speediest, most economical one we can type, containing nothing but a single letter—"k." But it is a pregnant "k," signifying, according to Menand, "I have nothing to say but God forbid you should think I am ignoring your message." And that brings us to the pregnant pause, for which we no longer have any patience or room in today's fast-paced communication style. Speechless moments and reflective uh-, er-, ah- moments—breaks in speech that point to cognitive deliberation and a process, called thinking, taking place somewhere in the cortex—have been deleted. As the late William Safire wrote in On Language, his *New York Times* column: "The 'pregnant' pause has been digitally aborted."

Indeed, at times it seems that there is little that is golden about silence in the new language, and a portion of the exchanges that take place seem to be invested in filling it up, with the help of multiple language short-cuts that end up shortchanging the language. Those include initialisms, contractions, and abbreviations, as we have seen, and the most child-ish of all time and space fillers, the tyrannous emoticons. What are *they* pregnant with, and what do they tell us about our real age and about our current state as communicative creatures?

The word emoticon is a portmanteau (from the French word for a suitcase containing two separate hinged compartments) of "emotion" and "icon," much like brunch is an amalgamation of breakfast and lunch. They are meant to convey, pictorially, emotional content on the Web. The first documented use of the emoticons :-) and :- (for commu-nicating happiness and sadness, respectively, was by artificial intelligence researcher Scott Fahlman in 1982, on the Carnegie Mellon computer science message board. Fahlman had apparently gotten tired of humor-less scientists never getting the joke, so he offered to help separate the serious posts from the jokes with some original iconography that he designed:

```
19-Sep-82   11:44   Scott E. Fahlman
From: Scott E Fahlman


I propose that the following character sequence for joke markers:


:-)


Read it sideways. Actually, it is probably more economical to mark
things that are NOT jokes, given current trends. For this, use


:-(
```

Because words cast into cyberspace lack the context usually pro-vided by body language, intonation, and facial expression, and because we are too rushed to provide such context the old-fashioned way—that is, through exposition—a simple drawing is invoked to help the disembodied word reconnect with the body that launched it and with the state of mind of the writer. Today's repertoire of emoticons is much expanded from Fahlman's days on the Carnegie Mellon computer science message board—Geocities' Canonical Smiley List counts 2,231, and some even come with a maddening feature that makes them dance on your screen. They continue, however, to serve the same objective early smiley and frowny users originally intended for them: to graphically narrate the mood state behind out-of-context, speedy words. Yet despite their significantly increased breadth, emoticons are still not very good at emoting.

Forty-three individual muscles in the human face contract and relax in different combinations to produce facial expression (with frowning apparently requiring more muscles—more work—than smiling). The Facial Action Coding System, or FACS, is a system developed in the 1970s by psychologist Paul Ekman, of the University of California, San Francisco, with the goal of codifying the whole range of human facial expression based on a detailed understanding of musculature. For example, it can help reliably distinguish a genuine, involuntary smile (achieved by contraction of the zygomatic major muscle and the inferior part of the orbicularis oculi) from a fake, voluntary smile (only requires contraction of the zygomatic major). A FACS coder dissects an observed expression, breaking it down into the various "action units"—those individual visible changes from the neutral face—that produced it, and notes the duration, intensity, and symmetry or asymmetry of each movement. The resulting "FACS score" is a precise calculation of expressed emotion that can then be translated into psychologically meaningful information with the help of an interpretation system database available to researchers.

Since its introduction, FACS has become a popular method for reading facial movements, used by the FBI, the CIA, and animators, as well as by psychotherapists and interviewers interested in interpreting the subtlest facial microexpression. To read some of the FACS research literature—and to see pictures of some of the more expressive study subjects' faces featured in it—is to appreciate the infinite spectrum of emotion those forty-three muscles are capable of combining into. In comparison, emoticons possess a much narrower range, like FACS on Botox. And even when we force them to convey a complex, more "adult" sentiment, they still manage to look baby-faced and one-dimensional, like something pulled out of a toddler's dream sequence or bubble bath.

That emoticons are childish and have limited range when compared to the human face are, of course, obvious points. Less obvious is the price we pay for relying on them and, in a more general sense, on netspeak. That price is confusion, a sort of e-babel in cyberspace. As we lose complexity and maturity in language, as we speed it up, squeeze it down, and make it dance, literally, on our screens, we may also be taking away the function of words to communicate, clearly and unambiguously, specific states of mind. Writing is a science, much like calculating a FACS score to quantify a complex facial expression can be considered a science. Emoticons and other building blocks of netspeak, on the other hand, are shots in the dark—fluid and equivocal and endlessly open to interpretation.

Increased online confusion is the natural consequence, and has been borne out in well-designed research studies. According to experiments led by Justin Kruger at New York University's Leonard N. Stern School of Business, e-mail communication, which by definition lacks "the benefit of paralinguistic cues such as gesture, emphasis, and intonation," is more easily misunderstood than verbal communication, especially when users are trying to express subtleties like sarcasm and humor. In one of Kruger's studies, participants were given a list of ten different topics (including parties, art, dating, sports, television, food, family, and politics) and asked to e-mail two one-sentence statements on each subject. They were instructed to make one sentence sarcastic and the other earnest, and to indicate whether they thought the receiver would be able to correctly identify the nature of each. Participants receiving the e-mails were also asked to evaluate the nature of the statements. The results, published in 2005 in the *Journal of Personality and Social Psychology*, strongly suggest that people are "overconfident in their ability to communicate sarcasm, seriousness, anger, and sadness over e-mail." Other experiments published in the same paper indicate that people are also overconfident in their ability to *detect* such emotions in e-mail. By adopting e-mail, let alone instant messaging or texting, as our prime modes of communication, we are compromising our ability to express ourselves precisely, forthrightly, and with nuance. Sarcasm and earnestness are mature, "adult" sentiments. Losing the ability to accurately communicate or "read" them significantly diminishes our repertoire of developed emotion and our expressive bandwidth. While predicting that the end of language as we know it is premature, research like Kruger's indicates that netspeak represents a largely inadequate mode of communication, one characterized by informality to the point of sloppiness, curtness to the point of rudeness, and a childlike avoidance of complex ideas that cannot be reduced to monosyllabic words or frownies or smilies.

Graver consequences than confusion may result, too. As with virtual games, there seems to be a misestimation of risk when it comes to netspeak. That is most tragically reflected in the phenomenon of texting while driving. The extent of the problem was brought to light in September 2008, when texting was implicated in the Los Angeles commuter-train crash that killed 25 and injured over 130. The train engineer, Robert M. Sanchez, did not heed a red light and crashed into another train. The investigation revealed that Sanchez had multiple texting relationships with teenage rail enthusiasts and had sent forty-three text messages the day of the crash. One message, sent to a rail buff whom Sanchez had apparently allowed to control the train before, read: "this time I'm taking a picture of you @ da throttle!!!" The last text message, sent to another "friend" only minutes before the crash, read:

"I'm gonna do all the radio talkin' . . . ur gonna run the locomotive & I'm gonna tell u how to do it."

Texting while on the move is hardly a fringe lunacy: A full 47 percent of all texting adults in the United States say they text while driving, according to a 2010 survey by the Pew Research Center's Internet & American Life Project. That compares with "only" 34 percent of sixteen- and seventeen-year-olds, according to a 2009 survey conducted by the same organization. Also, when it comes to the total number of text messages sent, adults are quickly catching up with teenagers, who, on average, sent or received 1,742 text messages a month in 2008, according to the *New York Times* (four in ten also said they could text while blindfolded).

It has been calculated that those who text and drive face a twenty-three times greater risk of crash or near crash. That has prompted organizations ranging from NASCAR to emergency room physicians' associations to warn about the behavior, and several states to enact laws that formally ban it. U.S. adults send and receive more text messages than phone calls, according to 2008 data from consumer research company Nielsen Mobile, making texting while driving more likely to happen as people increasingly rely on it over other methods of staying in touch.

The 47 percent of texting adults who engage in this behavior should, of course, know the risks involved, yet they choose to pursue an activity that is as potentially lethal as it is regressive. One way to try to understand how this abdication of responsibility and common sense may come about is to think of the process as being facilitated by an innocent, childlike language: one that looks like the last thing in the world that would harm a human being, let alone result in a fatal crash. How can sending one more smiley face before focusing on the road ever hurt anyone? How can it be a bad idea to install a browser on your dashboard, as several automakers taking part in the 2010 Consumer Electronics Show in Las Vegas announced they were planning to do? Let's hope no adult takes up the challenge of driving while texting *and* blindfolded.

The inner child that comes alive online or on the iPhone or Black-Berry keypad acquires a "voice" that is playful and orthographically challenged like a kid's, but calculating and potentially dangerous, like an adult's. It is this toxic mix of dark desires that tend to emerge in the virtual world and the immature, barely oral phase to which many adults regress online that is partially to blame for the number of adults masquerading as children in online communities frequented by young people. First, they meet their "peers" through Web sites such as MySpace; then they see them face-to-face to "consummate" the friendship; and, finally, they end up the object of sex-with-a-minor probes wherein their unpunctuated, third-grade-level e-mails serve as damning evidence in obtusely written official court documents. Formal language triumphs— one may even say exacts revenge—in the end.

Talking like their underage victims makes the chilling content of what many child predators are proposing seem less scary to their unsuspecting victims and probably to them, too. In May 2006, *Wired News* senior editor and hacker extraordinaire Kevin Poulsen carried out an automated search of MySpace's 100-million-plus membership rolls for 385,932 registered sex offenders from 46 states, culled from the Department of Justice's National Sex Offender Registry. Limiting his results to a five-mile radius of the offender's registered zip code, Poulsen searched by first and last name, then manually checked his matches against age, picture, and other identifying characteristics. Sifting through the data in this manner, Poulsen was able to confirm 744 sex offenders on MySpace, 497 of whom were registered for crimes against children. One match, a thirty-three-year-old man who had served eighteen months for molesting a child in 1994, gave his MySpace motto as "Love knows not age." Another, a thirty-nine-year-old with an even more disturbing rap sheet, was on MySpace recruiting (very) underage boys only months after serving a nine-year prison term. To one teenager who had just added him as a "friend," he wrote, "Thanks for the ass, I mean add." To another "friend," a fourteen-year-old boy who lived a six-hour drive away, he wrote: "Damn it's a shame you don't live close by boy the things we can do." To a fake teen, an undercover cop tipped by Poulsen, the man wrote, "u into hair? like hary [*sic*] men?"

Embarrassed by Poulsen's findings, but also in response to calls by state attorneys general, MySpace subsequently conducted its own purge of its Web site, netting some 29,000 sex offenders. I bet none of them minded his grammar. (This is, of course, not intended to imply that adults who relax their grammar rules online are likely to be sexual predators! Rather, it is that antigrammatical, innocent-looking, childlike language makes it easier for deviant impulses to sneak in, relatively undetected.)

It is perhaps telling that the closest historical kin to e-language is probably the "automatic writing" of psychoanalysis. This form of rapid-fire, unfiltered writing of whatever is on the person's mind, without letting the rational, linguistically or politically correct mind sugarcoat or organize its content in any way, was, along with the interpretation of dreams discussed earlier, a favored technique among Freudian therapists for making the unconscious conscious and for exploring repressed urges and conflicts. Bringing these hidden forces to the surface, analyzing them, and seeing how they inform the patient's behaviors constituted the meat of the treatment and, presumably, helped bring about symptom resolution. Comparing this old "healing technique" to the use of online language reveals some interesting parallels and points of divergence, and can help us better understand the function of netspeak in our lives today.

Psychologist Pierre Janet (1859–1947) was among the first clinical researchers to specialize in trauma and its effects on people's psyches. Janet theorized that overwhelming stress can lead to the development of two discrete layers of consciousness. (Recall the earlier point regarding how severe stress was thought to lead to multiple personality disorder.) Janet used the now largely abandoned term "hysteria" to describe the resulting condition. In his 1894 work *The Mental State of Hystericals*, Janet carefully describes the clinical symptoms of a long list of patients (Bertha, Celestine, Isabelle, Justine, Léonie, Lucie, Marcelle, Margaret, and Maria, as though men are immune to the consciousness-splitting effects of extreme stress) and the therapeutic tools, including automatic writing, that helped him diagnose and treat their illness. Janet's discoveries about distinct layers of consciousness would later deeply influence Freud's concept of the unconscious, leading some to describe Janet as the "true father of psychoanalysis."

For Janet and psychoanalysts after him, automatic writing was a tool to bridge two states of awareness, allowing patients to express feelings they would not be able to access otherwise. Janet even employed an elaborate writing apparatus, invented by neurologist Jean Charcot, to facilitate the release of "automatic" information from his patients: "It is first of all a long stem, suspended . . . and movable in every direction. The subject holds the stem by the middle as he would hold a penholder." The subject then looks away, allowing the hand to take over as an independent, autonomous, and automatic entity, one that is "disembodied" from the writer who is actively trying to ignore it.

What the hand pens in this state was considered to hold clues to key unconscious processes unfolding in the patient's mind. Here is the subjective experience as described by Bertha, one of Janet's patients:

> When I want to write, I find that I have nothing to say; my head is empty, I must let my hand write what it pleases; it thus fills four pages: I cannot help it if it is all absurd trash. . . . My ideas are no longer comprehensible to myself; they come of themselves; one might say that they are written on a big roll which unrolls before me. . . . I am nothing more than a puppet held by a string; everything leaves me; I am here to stand for something.

Bertha is a shell allowing her unconscious content to flow out and, one hopes, purging her demons along the way in a sort of psychiatric exorcism.

Compare the stem contraption, compare Bertha's description of writing, to the deliberate, intentional, and conscious act of *normal* writing, a process that is well controlled by the agency and authority of the author, like other willful acts tend to be. Normal writing originates in the individual who started it, can decide when to end it, and can save a memory of it in his mind when done. Here is how Janet describes it:

> It is I, we say, who, before executing it, have foreseen this act; it is I who, at the moment of accomplishing it, feel that I am performing this action; it is again I who later keep the remembrance of it. I connect it in every respect with my character, with my sentiments and with my ideas; I consider it henceforth as an integral part of my personality.

Netspeak and textspeak, in their lack of any serious editing and their focus on speed before any other consideration and symbols that are open to interpretation, share more with automatic than normal writing. They defy the rational, "aware" mind and cannot be considered an "integral part" of our personality as we have always known it. They are, however, the way our e-personality speaks and its perfect conduit. It is as though the virtual world is serving, this time through e-language, as today's psychoanalyst, giving some people carte blanche to express, in automatic, broken English (or French or Korean or Arabic), regressive tendencies and repressed impulses that are often better off unexpressed. Indeed, some people (men and women) seem to approach the Internet the way Bertha, Celestine, Isabelle, Justine, Léonie, Lucie, Marcelle, Margaret, and Maria may have approached Charcot's writing apparatus—desperate to purge themselves of whatever is on their minds, with limited self-control over what comes out or concern over how un-pretty it might look or whether it should stay private.

Psychoanalysts, at least, saw therapeutic value in unlocking a patient's mind through the use of automatic writing. Janet wrote: "[T]he automatic writing . . . will help us to verify those sensations, remembrances, and reflections whose existence we had heretofore merely supposed. . . . It will reply to our questions and reveal to us a thousand innermost thoughts which the subject would not confide to us or of which even she was completely ignorant." It is less clear what the salutary effects of net-speak are, despite how endlessly fascinating and creative some linguists may find it. Instead of healing, a language that is both impoverished and childlike runs the risk of encouraging impoverished and childlike behaviors, as many people seem to retreat to the virtual world to play, throw a tantrum, or be lazy, rather than to be proactive or work toward a purposeful goal: Did I look for another job after the tense meeting with my boss this morning, or did I just send a nasty e-mail about her to my colleagues? Did I sign up for Weight Watchers after overstuffing myself this weekend, or did I simply blog the pounds away at blogawaythepounds.com? Did I do my homework, or did I download it?

Also, unlike the automatic writing of psychoanalysis, e-language is not limited to the confidential relationship with a trusted therapist and the well-guarded psychiatric record. Rather, it is "out there" for the whole world to see (and cc, and bcc). E-language evidence does not die with the psychoanalyst's death or go away with the shredding of the medical chart. As I will explore in more detail later, like much of what is on the Web, online transcripts, and the immaturity that they can bear witness to, might never be completely deleted from one's online history.

Further, it is easy for the kind of unfiltered online communication that makes up netspeak to escape the virtual world and create informality, confusion, and tension in our real-life relationships and other business. If one sends and receives 1,742 text messages a month, and "I" is spelled "i" in each one of them, the lowercase first-person pronoun will sooner or later invade offline grammar. Think back to Jill, the schoolteacher I introduced in the first chapter. Having drastically simplified her vocabulary in her e-mails to her boyfriend, she started using similar language in the comments she would leave in the margins of her students' papers, often adding the familiar smiley or sad emoticon to reflect the general "mood" of what she was reading, but also the occasional "Gr8" next to a particularly strong paragraph or the yawning emoticon (;-O) when the student went on a bit too long. E-language is gradually replacing other, more standard forms of communication, even gaining credence in such heavily formal arenas as the courtroom, in the form of e-mail exchanges, now considered perfectly acceptable evidence. In fact, more than half of e-mail users surveyed in the 2008 Digital Future Project had contacted either a teacher or a government official using e-mail. Without a doubt, that can be entirely normal and healthy and is certainly convenient, but it can also be the vehicle that makes offline life look like online life.

Aspects of life that lie well beyond our day-to-day vocabulary and orthography are being transformed. The ultimate effect of e-language can be to bring into the real world the childlike, impatient, and immediate-gratification-oriented style of transacting and of conducting oneself that it mediates so well in cyberspace. When Junior sees no problem sending an e-mail to Mrs. Wilson that is similar in its tone and informality to something he would post on MySpace, he is also at increased risk of showing disrespect to her in the classroom. When our boss is accustomed to blasting orders into our BlackBerrys—no hi, please, or thank you required—he is at risk for treating us the same way when we cross paths in the hallway (and we are at risk of thinking of ourselves as undeserving of anything better). When we "ping" someone on Yahoo! as we simultaneously chat with someone else on Facebook, it becomes more natural to text a co-worker from our iPhone in the middle of a special anniversary dinner with our spouse. Finally, when we cannot imagine ourselves typing pleasantries in a texted message or an e-mail, we may, with practice and time, start thinking of those as a perfect waste of precious time in our face-to-face encounters as well.

Indeed, our e-personality—whether it is infantile, inflated, narcissistic, immoral, or impulsive—can be destructive, not just in the virtual world but in reality as well. Worse than having an e-personality with some troubling traits is that those traits can get unconsciously incorporated into our real personality—just as netspeak can get unconsciously incorporated into our daily speak—fundamentally changing us and the world we live in. This is evident in how our relationships, knowledge base, and memory, among other crucial functions of offline living, are being reconfigured. This reconfiguring of our offline psychology in the image of our e-personality is the subject of the remainder of the book.

CHAPTER 7

LOVE AND SEX RECALIBRATED

A SIX-MONTH subscription to Match.com comes with a warranty: Find someone special or you get six additional months free. Given the Web site's more than fifteen million subscribers, it should be statistically unlikely not to find somebody. Multiply that number by two to account for subscribers' e-personalities, and you suddenly have thirty million identities to choose from—it is now downright embarrassing not to be able to find your match. As Plentyoffish.com, the "fastest growing relationship site on the Web," reminds us, there are, indeed, plenty of fish in the sea. One does not even need to do the fishing: eHarmony's "patented Compatibility Matching System®" narrows the field down from millions of candidates to a select group of singles who are compatible with you, based on "29 Dimensions™ of personality that are scientifically-based predictors of long-term relationship success." If this does not sound evidence-based enough, Chemistry.com boasts about enlisting Dr. Helen Fisher as its "chief scientific advisor" and "biological anthropologist": someone who "spent the last three decades figuring out why love makes us go weak in the knees and causes our hearts to skip a beat." With love databases as exhaustive as these, and with the likes of Dr. Fisher at the service of relationship alchemy, how come so many people remain single and frustrated?

Online dating venues such as Chemistry, eHarmony, Plenty Of Fish, and Match, highlight the promise of online romance, a promise so big it is only rivaled by the degree of disappointment one feels at failing the online love challenge. How can such a gold mine of romantic opportunity sometimes turn into such an emotional minefield? How do the previously discussed psychological transformations that happen online coalesce in the already anxiety-laden territory of love and lovemaking? Think back to Alex, my twentysomething patient who was spending long hours surfing the Internet, and who had so thoroughly embraced virtual life, especially virtual love. His story and another one like it, while extreme, can help shed some light on these questions.

Leaving his fiancée would not necessarily have been a "big deal" if Alex were a man who left one woman for another, but, of course, there was more to the story. He had become hooked on an online virtual community where couples can lead "complete" virtual existences, picnicking, playing volley ball, philosophizing, and making love, all in the virtual realm, with no expectation of bringing their relationships into the real world. There, Alex met Nadia, then perfected her features to better suit his tastes. And, the more time he spent online working on Nadia or being with her, the less attractive real-life love became.

I would have been less surprised by the course of events in Alex's life had I first read the story carried by several news outlets in 2008, involving a Second Life love triangle. The story involved Dave Pollard, a forty-year-old, six foot tall, 350-pound unemployed man from Cornwall, England (Second Life avatar: Dave Barmy, midtwenties, six foot four, 182-pound nightclub owner); his wife, Amy Taylor, a twenty-eight-year-old, five foot four, 224-pound former waitress from London (avatar: Lauren Skye, midtwenties, six feet, 112 pounds); and the "other woman," a fifty-five-year-old American divorcée logging in from Arkansas.

According to media reports, Amy Taylor had already caught her husband in flagrante delicto on Second Life once before: "I looked at the computer screen and could see his character having sex with a female character," she said of the first witnessed episode of conjugal betrayal. "I went mad. I was so hurt. I just couldn't believe what he'd done. It's cheating as far as I'm concerned." Still, Amy was able to find it in herself to forgive her husband, and the couple managed to patch the relationship up. Several months later, however, Amy caught her husband's avatar in another compromising position, this time cuddling with a woman on a sofa. "It looked really affectionate," she said of their embrace. When Amy demanded to look at his chat history with the woman, her husband "turned off the computer so the history was all deleted." Although David had not met the women outside the game, Amy was devastated by what she saw as her husband's pattern of cheating on her with virtual women. She filed for divorce from her husband of three years the following day, citing "unreasonable behavior."

It was soon revealed that the home wrecker in the story was Linda Brinkley, a significantly older, twice-divorced Arkansas woman who was the mother of four children, aged fifteen to thirty-five. Brinkley, in real life, was apparently interested in religious studies and hoped to become a missionary someday. Those pious aspirations might have inspired her Second Life name, Modesty McDonnell. It is unclear what inspired her Second Life professions—she played a prostitute and a half-naked hostess at Dave's virtual nightclub. Regardless, Brinkley seemed invested in making clear that Modesty was not to blame for Dave's real-life divorce: "He's told me that his relationship with his wife was over way before I came along and he's been very honest with me so I take his word for that."

Still, despite hard feelings, mutual accusations, and much dirty laundry broadcast from all sides in the press, a swift and happy denouement was soon at hand for all involved, as perhaps can only happen in a virtual fairy tale. Dave Pollard and Linda Brinkley's avatars got married on Second Life in an intimate ceremony, and the couple were planning to meet and get married in their "first" life as well. ("It's amazing that we've found each other across so many miles and we love each other very much. . . . I haven't had much luck with men until now.") No tears need to be shed for the jilted wife, either. Amy Taylor has a new love in her life, too. "I have met somebody new, and we are living together," she told London's *Daily Mail*. "I am very happy." The couple met playing World of Warcraft shortly after Amy's separation. "I know it all sounds pretty strange, but it works for me." Good for her.

While most of us neither subscribe to Second Life nor allow our virtual relationships to detach us so radically from reality, the behavior of Alex, Dave, Amy and Linda sheds light on how the Internet is changing social mores and the age-old rules for relating, communing, mating, and loving. Having reshaped Nadia as a knockout, Alex no longer found Natalie as physically attractive as he once did. Similarly, Dave Pollard found in Modesty, the leggy brunette he met at a "fancy dress night" on Second Life, a sexy, radical departure from his five foot four, 224-pound wife. Why settle for Natalie when you can pretend to be with Nadia— someone whose name alone evokes a dreamy *Swan Lake* ballerina, not to mention her many other talents and perfection? Why spend time with plain Amy when you can be making out on a Second Life couch with anything-but-modest Modesty? Plus, there was this important added advantage: Just as one can be, virtually, with a perfect woman, one can, I imagine, "delete" her if she becomes too needy, or if the relationship becomes too real-like.

Second Life and similar Web sites—IMVU, Active Worlds, Kaneva, There—may represent the "next generation" in the virtual experience, romantic or otherwise, where all pretense of being anchored in reality is finally dropped. Self-aggrandizement, extreme behavior, dark thoughts, regression, and impulsivity, all of which I have described as largely unconscious forces shaping our online experience and in need of taming, are now being openly and proudly embraced. On these Web sites, it is no longer *implicit* that people are lying about their age, weight, or other defining characteristics—they are exulting in those lies. Nadia's profile, which Alex fell in love with, was not a new and improved version of a real-life person; it was entirely fabricated. So were Dave's, Amy's, and Linda's. This is pretense for pretense's sake, Match.com on steroids. While the ever-tighter embrace of pretense in our electronic lives is evident in nonromantic arenas as well—think of Sims 2 and compare it to the old Tetris, for instance—its costs are perhaps more glaring when it comes to how people's offline love and relationship maps are being redrawn. Somehow, developing the capability to fall in love with, and have erotic feelings for, a picture is more portentous for our future than the notion of getting hooked on a virtual game.

Still, far fewer people play Second Life than post personals online, "poke" people on Facebook, or simply use virtual communication as a normal part of day-to-day functioning. How are *their* relationships and love lives affected? Are middle-aged couples who are in fulfilling relationships and have never heard of Match, let alone of avatars, "safe," or do some of the same tendencies apply to them as well? Is anyone immune to the message—overt, hidden, semeiotic, or subliminal—being communicated by JPEG file after JPEG file of overly beautiful and impossibly sexy people?

The answer, unfortunately, is no. When we begin subscribing to difficult-to-meet criteria based on the images and ideals we are being fed online, what used to be perfectly "good enough," maybe even attractive, somehow becomes less so. When people exaggerate and misrepresent themselves online—think back to "sales-rep" Jill and "Doctor" Chris; think back to Ron and his inferiority complex—our standards of beauty and sexiness change. What used to be clearly above average is downgraded to "so-so," and what used to be average becomes subpar.

It is estimated that 12 billion spam e-mails, of which around 2.5 billion are pornographic, land in people's in-boxes daily, bringing electronic Viagra and weight loss ads into every living room and office to a degree simply unimaginable before the advent of the Web. Even if we try to tune out these sorts of ads, and the overwhelming majority of us do, they can still infiltrate the culture and spread the message that ever-ready virility and hourglass femininity are the norm—and that, best of all, they are only a click of the mouse away. With time, this can cause one's standards to shift and one's expectations to readjust. Without your wanting it, it can make the love of the last thirty years of your life seem rather boring. That is, of course, if you are already happily married or stably partnered and not flirting online. It is arguably worse if you are actively "looking," for you may find yourself chronically dissatisfied by what the real world has to offer. Everyone can suddenly seem too fat or too short—all in all, much more "not" than "hot" (a reference to hotornot.com, the "#1 Social Entertainment Network," where people rate the attractiveness of subjects of photos submitted by others, with a matchmaking function available as well). And the further away beauty ideals move from what is natural and normal, the less attractive and romantically desirable people feel themselves to be, too.

Marketing is key here: It is not just the message embedded in so much of what we see online that makes us want to fit the new standards of beauty and sex appeal. It is also the blatant and relentless "selling" of that message through online advertising—a 22-billion-dollar industry according to 2007 U.S. figures, not a small portion of which aims to help us improve our sexual desirability by improving our looks and bodies. (This refers only to commercial marketing. The dollar value of the self-marketing that takes place on vanity and social networking sites is, as they say, priceless.) In a sense, it is a two-pronged approach to shaking people's self-esteem, and its effect is to turn many of us into easy victims for claims like: "FatFoe™, kiss calorie counting and sweaty exercising good-bye"; "six pack abs for everyone"; "BountiFul® breast pills: no surgery, no recovery, results guaranteed"; and "be proud to change your underwear in public."

In people's desperation to fit that extreme model, to be "hot" in the new love bazaar and on the new social (media) scene in general, many will go to extreme lengths, including seeking sometimes unnecessary surgical transformations or starving themselves. The question has not been formally studied, but one has to wonder what role the Internet, and the new "ideal body" that it is promoting, may be playing in the increased popularity of plastic surgery and the increased prevalence of eating disorders such as anorexia nervosa. Nearly 11.7 million cosmetic procedures were performed in the United States in 2007, according to statistics from the American Society for Aesthetic Plastic Surgery. That represents a 457 percent increase since 1997, when the systematic collection of statistics began. The numbers also reveal an increase in procedures among nontraditional consumers of these services: Aesthetic procedures on men increased by 17 percent between 2006 and 2007, and one in five procedures in 2007 was performed on ethnic minority patients.

Also related to unhealthy body image, anorexia nervosa seems to be increasing in prevalence according to some studies, and its age of onset seems to be decreasing. It is unclear what is contributing to this sad phenomenon of "pro-Anna" (for pro-anorexic) Web sites, described as "a disturbing growth industry" by the *New York Times*. These are essentially chat rooms where young women go to find "thinspiration." Similarly, "pro-Mia" groups exist to teach people how to be "better" bulimics. But one hardly has to have a formal, "clinical" eating disorder like anorexia or bulimia to feel overweight and to be dealing with undue pressure to lose a few pounds. Writing in *Newsweek* under the title "The Internet Makes Me Feel Fat," Helen A. S. Popkin says:

> In the Internet age with its endless playground for reinvention and resources for human understanding, it's painfully clear just how hung up we are on appearances. Even in a world—heck, especially in a world— where computers control our illusions, nobody wants to feel like—let alone be seen as—anything less than an "8." The deluge of cyberspace images and social cues is making us more self-conscious than ever.

Anxiety focused on body image pervades our culture. While no one can blame the Internet, solely, for this anxiety, the Internet does intensify it, then reflects it back to the real world, bigger and fatter than it would have been. Like TV and other media, the Internet promotes an image of difficult-to-attain perfection. Much more so than TV and other media, however, the Internet also promotes the notion—self-empowering on the surface—that we can in fact attain perfection relatively easily. In essence, the Internet is selling us two dreams: The first is that, online, we can pretend to be much more than we really are, as the chapters on narcissism and grandiose thinking tried to show; the second is that it is easy to close the gap between what we are in the virtual world and what we are in reality, through services that are easily available on the Web and that only require logging on and a credit card number. It is partially because these dreams are often "just that" that many people seem to feel less comfortable in their skin than ever before, and significantly less sexy.

Beauty standards are, of course, dynamic, and indirectly play into our concept of the perfect mate. The Victorian and Edwardian female ideal was physically opulent, and came with a full bosom, smallish waist, and wide hips (thin women were advised to hide their "angles"). This, in the pre–World War I era and into the 1920s, gave way to the "boyish" woman with smaller breasts and slimmer hips. Her beauty queen reign ended with the return of the voluptuous figure in the 1930s, followed by a thin look comeback in the 1960s, best captured in Twiggy, the world's first supermodel, memorably described as "an X-ray, not a picture." Several variations on thin have captivated us since, but our current physical ideals seem to be the least realistic and most uncomfortable to fit into yet. They have less in common with real people than with avatars like Dave Barmy and Lauren Skye: a "ripped" young man and a striking young woman with the perfect waist-to-hip ratio of 0.70. From the male perspective, not looking like him in real life can make a man feel like he does not have enough to offer, and not finding a woman like her can make him feel like he is settling for less. For the guy who falls prey to this, one of two negative consequences may ensue: His self-esteem may be affected to the point where he may start avoiding real-life relationships and pursuing online interactions or online pornography instead; alternatively, he may "settle," but is plagued by the thought that he "could do so much better," and so remains on the lookout, especially online, for better opportunities.

For living with the suspicion that you may have "settled" is becoming increasingly uncomfortable. A 2010 survey commissioned by Match .com indicates that one in five relationships, and one in six marriages, now start online. There is no reason to doubt these impressive statistics or the long-lasting happiness many of these couples will find. Still, it might be more telling to scientifically study the longevity of relationships among individuals who believe that love is easy to find online. Will they still want to work hard to better the relationships they already have, or will they give up much more easily because 15 million other subscribers await on Match?

Whether it is a grossly exaggerated Second Life profile, a Craigslist post that takes too much poetic license, or a Viagra or Bountiful pop-up that makes people wonder about their masculinity or femininity, it is difficult to completely shield ourselves from the lure of online misrepresentation, in part because it often inspires awe and desire, rather than resentment and wariness. As we have seen before, many consumers of online information are quick to suspend disbelief and to accept what they are reading and seeing as the truth, rather than question its inherent lies and exaggerations. In other words, the reader of the online ad is often more impressed than suspicious, and before the person stops to challenge the accuracy of what is being said, he or she has already hit the reply button. The same process unfolds whether we are buying a sweater we desire but don't really need or responding to an online personal where the profile, "come to think of it," contained some clear red flags that should have given us serious pause. Yet the toll the process can take on people's love and sex lives, in particular, is the heaviest, maybe because that is the arena in which self-doubt and vulnerability tend to express themselves most loudly.

Unfortunately, hitting the reply button out of infatuation with a touched-up, Photoshopped-to-death online picture can carry real risks, as suggested by a 2007 study of the online sexual behavior of gay youths published in the *American Journal of Public Health*. Of course, to many young gay men, the Internet has come as a godsend, relieving much of the isolation that marked previous generations. But this godsend comes at a significant cost. Beyond increasing these young adults' ability to socialize with like-minded people, the Internet is facilitating random sexual encounters among those not yet fully competent to appreciate what is at stake. Because this is all happening in the age of AIDS, what is at stake here can be their lives.

The 2007 study, conducted by Robert Garofalo, MD, of Northwestern University, was the first to demonstrate that the Internet is an important venue for forming sexual networks among young gay men aged twenty-four and under. Of the 270 gay youths interviewed, 48 percent reported having had sex with someone they met online. What is concerning is that only 53 percent of those reported using safe sex practices. Given that this was higher than the rate of unprotected sex seen in the young population offline, the authors, at the end of their article, ask the unavoidable question: Is the Internet simply a tool for taking risks or is it an *independent* source of risk—that is, is there something about the medium itself that encourages risk taking in a way that goes beyond what we would see if the same two individuals became intimate after meeting offline?

I would argue that the Internet is an independent risk factor, and that the conflation of delusions made possible by the Internet and familiar to the reader at this point—godlike invincibility, a false sense of perfection, impulsivity—naturally leads to increased risk taking in the romantic sphere, and to acts that normally would be stopped or slowed down by the interference of common sense or the fear factor. When the victims are vulnerable, socially isolated youths who are just beginning to learn how to be intimate, the real-life costs can be staggering.

That the risks are real, even though the profiles may not be, has also been shown in studies of adult gay men as well as straight men and women. In research published in 2000 in the *Journal of the American Medical Association* and led by Dr. Jeffrey D. Klausner, scientists report on a fascinating investigation of a syphilis outbreak that occurred in San Francisco in the summer of 1999. Two cases of gay men with early-stage syphilis, a sexually transmitted disease once considered almost eradicated in the United States, were initially reported to the San Francisco Department of Public Health, raising researchers' concern and suspicion, especially since interviews with both men revealed that they had met their sexual partners in an Internet chat room (San Francisco M4M). The two patients could only give the chat room screen names as identifiers for their online sexual partners, not a first name or phone number or physical address. With the cooperation of the Web site's Internet service provider, the San Francisco Department of Health initiated an e-mail campaign targeting those screen names and faxed a syphilis alert to physicians and clinics that catered to the city's gay population. As a result, a cluster of seven cases of syphilis, all linked to the San Francisco M4M chat room, was eventually identified. The patients' average age was thirty-seven—significantly older than in the preceding study of gay youths, but not necessarily wiser or better able to exert self-control when it came to protecting themselves from the Web's temptations.

To further confirm the role of the Internet in the risk of acquiring a sexually transmitted disease, the same researchers conducted a study to measure the frequency of Internet use for the purposes of meeting sexual partners among syphilis patients (who were not necessarily part of the outbreak cluster), compared to controls who did not have syphilis, but who were otherwise similar in such key demographic characteristics as sexual orientation, age, and race. The results revealed that 67 percent of patients with syphilis compared with only 19 percent of healthy controls had met their sexual partners online, a finding that strengthens the link between online hunting for sex and offline STDs.

Lest one think that this was a "gay thing" or a "guy thing," that testosterone is solely to blame, and that men were the only group at risk of catching a bug in a chat room and bringing it home, a much larger study, focusing on adult women this time, was conducted and published in 2007 in the journal *Sexuality Research and Social Policy*. The study, led by Paige M. Padgett, PhD, of the University of Texas School of Public Health, examined the impact of the Internet on the safety of women who met men through online ads. Of the 740 women who completed the survey, 568 reported having met in person with a man who had answered their online personal ad. Their ages varied widely—from eighteen to seventy-eight, with an average age of thirty-eight.

The results showed that women relied heavily on online communication before the face-to-face meeting to negotiate issues of safety and ascertain respect for their boundaries. Representative statements from study participants include: "I told him I would say how fast we moved, not him," and "I let him know that sex wasn't going to be part of our first meeting." Some explicitly prioritized relationships with their interlocutors so as not to raise the men's hope of a sexual encounter happening right away: "We talked about the fact that I was not going to have sex with anyone until I took the time to build a relationship with them first," and "We were going to meet to explore a potential serious relationship, not to have sex on the first meeting." To prevent surprises and misunderstandings, expectations were typically clearly spelled out: "Very specifically, we discussed our expectations and what we both wanted to get out of the encounter." No topic was off-limit in the often detailed pre-meeting negotiations: Sexual likes and dislikes, history of STDs, condom use—all were broached by many study participants. Some women went further in screening would-be dates, performing the requisite Google search and requesting the men's photographs, of course, but also analyzing small-talk inconsistencies, calling workplace phone numbers to verify employment, even running criminal background checks in some cases. Final precautions before the first face-to-face meeting included arranging to meet the men in public places, providing their own transportation, and giving the man's name to a friend "just in case." So how did the encounters that the women showed so much caution about finally go?

It depends who you talk to. Despite the weariness and self-preservation that the women in the the study demonstrated in screening and triaging potential mates, the final results point to a rather reckless increase in risk tolerance among them: 30 percent engaged in sexual activity in their first face-to-face meeting, and 77 percent did not use condoms.

The women in the study were not necessarily looking to meet for casual sex; many were specifically looking for serious relationships. Still, for a significant percentage of them, it was easy to drop the "third-date rule" and other such offline reference points that generally preach that playing hard-to-get might be worthwhile if one wants to maximize a relationship's long-term success potential. Old-school anxieties that in a different time and place would have delayed sexual intimacy—such as how to convince your new partner that you do not always do this and that you are not as promiscuous as your behavior may have suggested—were not on the forefront of the women's minds. They seemed less concerned about what human sexuality author Yvonne Fulbright calls the "scarlet letter factor": the notion that, for those ruled by social definitions of proper sexual behavior, "the mere stigma of having a partner who was willing to put out prematurely can eat away at them," and doom the relationship by making them not want to see again someone whose sexual behaviors are socially frowned upon. (Padgett does not tell us how many women had second dates.)

More alarming, however, is that the majority of women in the study—77 percent—threw caution to the wind when it came to safe sex practices, and did not use protection during their first sexual encounter with someone they met online. While studies suggest that condom use does indeed decrease after several sexual encounters as people become more comfortable with each other, the Internet speeds up the process, breaking through people's guardedness and softening their inhibitions. "The anonymous environment of the Internet and the high frequency of communication both encourage disclosure of personal intimate information at an earlier stage than in other types of relating," Padgett writes. "Online relating becomes hyperpersonal; relational partners tend toward greater feelings of intimacy than they might have experienced in face-to-face communication." So much so that by the first date they know, or think they know, virtually everything. They have seen the pictures, researched the company, Googled the ex-wife, and gotten a sense of the man's health history; little is left but to have sex.

The women in Padgett's study felt that they knew the men quite well, and that they had an Internet relationship with them already, so "they [did] not seem to see these in-person sexual encounters as one-night stands." They relied heavily on instinct, intuition, and gut feeling, and felt overly confident of their reading of the men. They thought they could sense whether a man was safe to meet by analyzing how he communicated via e-mail: "He gave off a very honest and 'normal' vibe, and I felt like I knew him already"; "It sounds stupid but he gave me a 'safe' feeling"; and "I just went with my gut feelings I guess and numerous conversations on e-mail with him . . . probably not the smartest thing I have done." As is often the case, but perhaps more dramatically than it would be in real life, it was after the sex that the regrets surfaced. Because they were lulled into a sense of "virtual intimacy" mediated by the Web, otherwise cautious women seem to have engaged in premature, potentially dangerous sex.

The breathless, hyperpersonal e-mails that many single people exchange are, then, today's equivalent of a series of dates, and the first face-to-face encounter is the physical culmination—finally!—of a long process, and more like the natural conclusion to something old than a new beginning. That "something" can be compared to foreplay, unfolding electronically in cyberspace, and the first meeting is the point when things expect to come to some kind of resolution. Many people no longer date; they "power-date" at the speed of light.

Not only is dating sped up online, but so, apparently, is the all-important and already speedy enough "first impression." Considered a quick assessment based on difficult-to-articulate vibes and the mysterious flow of pheremonal chi, the first impression no longer requires a true "impression." A poor choice of tagline or e mail address may often suffice. A good friend who was experimenting with a popular online dating service related to me over e-mail how she "immediately pressed delete" when contacted by someone whose profile carried the headline, "The Ennui and the Ecstasy." "OMG," she wrote, "Ennui is not putting your best foot forward. It's like saying, hi I'm depressed. Shame because he was cute and obviously smart, but that's way too pretentious for first impression . . ." While I can understand my friend's reaction, I hope she did not pass up on the next Lord Byron based on a first micro impression.

If, as Padgett's study and my friend's anecdote suggest, adult women are finding it confusing to navigate between the online and offline worlds, how are teen girls and younger adults in general faring? Studies are scarce, but they point to a young generation growing up feeling unprecedentedly casual about sex. Facebook, their huge pastime, features the "poke," a term that was formerly avoided for its sexual connotations, but which teenagers have now embraced as one of the bread-and-butter activities on the site, without completely dropping its undercurrent of sexual mischief. A Facebook poke can simply be an attention getter from someone who wants to say hi but is too busy to write an e-mail, or a way to communicate "I think you're really hot," or both. It's often hard to tell—which is precisely the point. A poke's meaning is contextual and in the eye of the beholder, and teenagers seem to be relishing the ambiguity and sexual double entendres that poking conjures up. (Apparently, a popular Facebook group is called "Enough with the Poking, Lets Just Have Sex.") Then there is the Facebook "superpoke," with its orgiastic overtones, but I will not go there . . . If one wanted to see all this sexual informality in a positive light, one might say that today's teens do not have the previous generation's complexes and "hang-ups" about sex. But one shouldn't. They face other serious challenges as a result: challenges so novel and foreign, their mothers and fathers (and social workers and therapists and sex ed teachers) are ill equipped to help them confront.

A 2008 survey of 1,280 participants, commissioned by the National Campaign to Prevent Teen and Unplanned Pregnancy, helps illustrate this point. According to the survey, electronic exchange of sexual content, a process that has been termed *sexting* when conducted over a cell phone, has become very common among teenagers and young adults. Twenty-two percent of all teenage girls surveyed said they have posted online, e-mailed, or sexted nude or seminude images of themselves. Likewise, 18 percent of teen boys reported posting or sending such pictures of themselves. Young adults from the ages of twenty to twenty-six are even more likely than teens to have done so: 36 percent of women and 31 percent of men in that age group admitted to the behavior.

The racy exchange often starts innocently enough. Here is how sixteen-year-old Megan described her experience on the *Today* show: "I was with my friend and we were busy texting a couple of boys we were friends with at the time," she recalled. "And they sent us a picture of them without their shirts on, and we just kind of decided to send one back." The picture that the then-fourteen-year-olds responded with showed them with their shirts pulled up, revealing their bras. For Megan and her friend, the downside to the electronic baring of themselves quickly became apparent. The boys, being boys, could not resist sharing the pictures, causing the girls much guilt and shame. "They didn't think it was a big deal, they just kept sending it to other people."

What motivates Megan and girls like her to post or text sexually suggestive pictures of themselves? According to the same survey, two-thirds said they did it to be "fun or flirtatious"; half as a "sexy present" for their boyfriends; and 40 percent as a "joke." These motivators are, of course, as old as the sexual dance itself, and have for generations pushed people with any soupçon of libidinal interest in someone into all manner of embarrassing acts. Yet, when played out in the virtual world, they take on new risks. For Megan and her friend, the consequence was a painful violation of an old-fashioned expectation of privacy that is not applicable in the virtual age, something I will explore further in chapter 10. It would not console them, but they are hardly alone in having their private information circulated: A third of teen boys in the same survey, and 40 percent of young men, say they have seen sexually suggestive images intended for someone else, as have about a quarter of teenage girls and young women. It is as though our virtual bodies are meant to be shared.

Another real danger of the new sexual culture increasingly seems to be legal. In Greensburg, Pennsylvania, six teenagers were facing charges of child pornography in January 2009 as a result of nude pictures sent via a cell phone. Three girls, ages fourteen and fifteen, sent naked photos of themselves to three boys, ages sixteen and seventeen. A school administrator found the photos on a cell phone during class and confiscated the phone. According to police, both the senders and the recipients were at fault, because child pornography laws encompass both the distribution and the possession of images of underage children, regardless of the distributor's or possessor's age. If convicted, the teens would have to register as sex offenders and could end up in prison. Similar cases have been prosecuted in Texas, Michigan, and Ohio.

Much more likely than an arrest, however, is the effect on offline sexual behavior of the sexually charged virtual banter. As with the older women in Padgett's study, the pressure to bring matters to sexual consummation builds up quickly online for the younger demographic as well. In the National Campaign to Prevent Teen and Unplanned Pregnancy survey, nearly one-quarter of teens admitted that technology makes them "more forward and aggressive," and more than one-third agreed that exchanging sexy content makes real-life sex "more likely."

Further, nearly one-third believed that those exchanging sexually explicit content are "expected" to date or, more appropriately for their generation, "hook up," offline. "Things get hot and heavy pretty quick over text," is how a college sophomore recently described to me his experience flirting via his iPhone.

That the National Campaign to Prevent Teen and Unplanned Pregnancy should take a keen interest in the online sex lives of teens and young adults is an indication of another real-life outcome of virtual sex—pregnancy. Add this to the other risks of electronically mediated teenage sex and you have a host of problems spilling from Facebook Wall posts into the family kitchen, and many tense and awkward conversations around the dinner table. Especially when it comes to sex, what happens online does not tend to stay online.

When it comes to the early development of the Internet, sex is absolutely foundational. It has been said that lust motivates technology. Indeed, many everyday online functions owe their start to the entrepreneurship and resourcefulness of cyberpornography sites and their users. Web adult businesses led the way in developing secure online credit card transactions, for example, and have been at the forefront of database management. *Playboy* was among the first companies to introduce digital watermarking. Virtual Dreams, a company that provided online striptease shows, pioneered the use of videoconferencing. Streaming audio, peer-to-peer file sharing, and the current platform for "mainstream" online dating Web sites also came into being to support adult pursuits. Even though these functions are no longer limited to pornography, and "sex" is no longer the most Googled word (it has been dethroned by "Facebook" and "YouTube"), the World Wide Web is still a playground for temptations and sexual exploration. To say that it is easy to find sex online would grossly understate things; cyberspace is suffused with it. If the sexual revolution of the 1960s began when "The Pill" helped separate recreational aspects of sex from procreation, Craigslist and the Internet in general might be its apotheosis.

In a 2008 Harris Interactive survey, 2,119 U.S. adults were asked whether they would be more willing to forgo sex or the Internet for two weeks. Forty-six percent of women and 30 percent of men said they would rather abstain from sex rather than lose their Internet connection. But this is hardly the Hobbesian choice the researchers presented it to be: Participants who chose the Internet over sex were, in a sense, choosing "the best of both worlds," since for many people being online hardly means abstaining from having a "sex life," even if it doesn't always result in real-life physical contact. This is, at least, what the following 2005–2006 data from comScore and Family Safe Media suggest:

- The average Internet user spends a quarter of an hour a day viewing pornography;
- One in five men view pornography online at work;
- More than a third of all downloads are pornographic;
- A quarter of all search engine requests are pornographic; and,
- More than a third of Internet users report unwanted exposure to sexual material.

Not only are people's interactions with someone they are interested in typically more sexual in nature—something that, as we have seen, can lead to ill-considered, potentially unsafe encounters—but the average person's virtual life will necessarily expose him or her to significant sexual content, whether or not he or she is actively seeking it out. Such exposure is much higher if the person is seeking companionship and decides to consult the personals section of a favorite Web site. Here are three rather representative specimens from Craigslist, a mainstream Web site. Their language has been cleansed of overly vulgar content and of the kind of creepy netspeak innocence discussed earlier, which in this context can make the ads read like they had been written by children soliciting sex from other children:

- "Are you tired of the BS and need a good . . . ?
  Hey ladies. I'm off today and looking for a female that wanted to

hook up this morning or early afternoon and have some adult fun. I'm drug/disease free and clean cut. It can be a one time thing, or maybe lead to something regular. I don't care if you're married and just creeping, have a boyfriend, or just curious. I just want to have a good time and expect you to bring that same energy and excitement. Pics are required, and I enjoy women of all shapes and sizes. Let's do this and it shouldn't take more than a few e-mails." (From the Norfolk, Virginia, "Men for Women" Craigslist Web site)

• "A site to behold, and want to hold you.
I always thought Craigslist chicks were desperate, that is until I played myself . . . Fun, fun! Truth or dare? Reply with a question for me and I'll give you the truth or take the dare. My life is way too hectic for anything serious. Again please don't think I'm looking for a boyfriend. I want no strings, that's it. I'd rather meet in a public place first, hope you understand. Come and be wild with me." (From the San Francisco "Women for Men" Craigslist Web page)

• "Hook up now!
I am heading up 400 within the next 10 minutes looking for somewhere to stop off and have a hot time 25 6'2" 180 blonde blue eyes lets do this in two e-mails." (From the Atlanta "Men for Men" Craigslist Web page)

These ads, selected from listings by a straight man, a straight woman, and a gay man, respectively, and originating in very different locations across the United States, are hardly unusual. Thousands like them get posted daily on hundreds of sites, blanketing the entire country. It takes a certain kind of courage to post a sexually provocative ad, but it can take more courage not to respond. It requires commitment and self-control that are in short supply in today's world not to drown in all this overabundance of sex; not to Google a derivative of the word "sex"; not to log on, for free, to AdultFriendFinder.com, where men and women can "meet real sex partners tonight" from the site's repertoire of over twenty million subscribers. Some sex-based Web sites are even designed to mouse-trap the visitor, a trick that allows the site to take control of the browser, making it impossible for the visitor to escape by pressing the back button or closing the browser window; nothing but a computer reboot can stop the flood of X-rated pop-ups. Regardless of this malicious feature, however, many people are already *psychologically* mouse-trapped, and feeling the negative effects of their online sexual pursuits on their real-life relationships, but unable to break free.

Another effect of the overabundance of Internet sex is to make "dating," defined as a series of rendezvous meant to test the romantic waters between two individuals who share a mutual attraction, a high-rope maneuver that is becoming more difficult to execute. Getting to know the other person, and assessing over a few dates the prospects of the match, may now require turning a blind eye to Web offerings such as these that many find rather tempting. As the postings illustrate, sex, for some, can be as easy to find as a couple of hastily exchanged e-mails. Any effort beyond that can start feeling like a waste of time. Courting someone; impressing that person over a few dinners, maybe with roses, your witty conversation, sense of humor, or knowledge of the world; perhaps suffering a bit as you wait in hopes of a bigger reward in the near future all this can start feeling like too much work and too much uncertainty and too much delay in gratification. How to, and why, wait when you can have, off the 400 on your way home, what you were patiently awaiting to have after the third date?

The cost, then, of the "conflation of delusions" described earlier— one that manifests itself across sexual orientations, age groups, and genders—is a skewing of the already tenuous equilibrium between love and sex. For much of history, love has survived in part through the deliberate control of indiscriminate sexual activity. Fidelity within the committed couple was understood to be crucial to the survival of love and to the sustenance that people need to find in a relationship. Self-discipline, religion, societal pressures, and mores—all joined together to bolster sexual exclusiveness inside loving relationships. But another important deterrent to promiscuous, random sex was the relative lack, for much of our civilization, of easy access to a willing partner. That dearth helped ensure that the potentially problematic urge had a chance to dissipate or be confronted, before the person had an opportunity to act on it. However, by saturating people's lives with temptation, sexual imagery, and sexual access, the Internet has changed the equation. And the more accessible sex is, the more complicated love can become.

With the Internet, sex can be turned into a straightforward, simple transaction. Arranged online, it can be a mostly devoid-of-feelings pleasurable exchange of something, with no future-oriented expectation for long-term anything. Bam. Wham. Thanks. L8R. In her paper on the risks facing women who meet men online, Paige Padgett describes highly sexualized personal ads as examples of a screenplay or "sexual script," one that specifies in painful detail:

(a) what the individual wants to do,

(b) how she or he wants to do it, and

(c) who she or he wants to do it with.

The script clearly identifies "the actors, the situation, and the plot for the sexual 'performance.'" The problem with scripts, of course—their raison d'être—is that they demand to be acted out. This is how they become templates for real life. "The script for the interactions in which individuals engage over the Internet may set the stage for their actual encounters," Padgett writes. Indeed, the impatient, raw, and cut-to-the-chase manner of transacting around issues of sexuality gets played out beyond Craigslist, causing tension and tipping the balance, in real life, away from love or romance or dating and toward a sex-focused business affair; one that is primarily "business" and only secondarily "affair," at least in the connected, "liaison" sense of the word. This was the crux of my patient Paul's struggle.

Paul first came to see me to ask for a Prozac prescription. He had heard that SSRIs, the family of drugs to which Prozac belongs, had the side effect of diminishing a person's sexual appetite. Paul had developed the compulsion of cruising the Internet for quick sex, both free and on a "fee-for-service" basis. The ease of finding sexual mates online only reinforced Paul's compulsion: He swore that every time he went online, he could meet someone "within thirty minutes of logging on." When Alan, his best friend, doubted his truthfulness, Paul challenged him to a bet. He logged on with Alan sitting at his side, and, twenty minutes later, Paul had given his address to a "part time escort." Paul had won the bet.

However, instead of taking Paul out to lunch as he had promised, Alan offered to pay for his psychiatric consultation. For Alan could remember the days when Paul was happily, and monogamously, married. That was before Paul's sexual compulsion took over—and before his wife left him after finding one too many suspicious e-mails on the family computer. Paul agreed to see me, as he could understand how his expectation to find immediate sexual gratification had imposed itself onto his real life, first by causing his wife to leave, then by rendering him unable to tolerate the gratification-delaying nature of the multistep courting process. On his attempts at dating, Paul found himself treating all women like the "masseuses" and "escorts" of the online ads, unconsciously directing the conversation toward quick sexual consummation rather than a meaningful connection with his date. I did end up prescribing Prozac for Paul, but not because it caused a decrease in libido as one of its side effects. Rather, Paul's inability to have a true relationship led to severe social isolation and a sense of failure in his romantic life, all of which resulted in a deep depression. So while the Internet facilitated quick sexual hookups for Paul, it ultimately left him emotionally bereft.

Yet genuine romantic feelings are certainly possible in the virtual world. How strong and meaningful that intimacy is, and how it compares with what develops between two people meeting offline, are questions that defy quantification and scientific pinpointing—it is easier to inquire about the rate of adherence to safe sex practices than to ask about shades of love and fulfillment or "how much" it hurts because you miss someone terribly. Such measures of longing and attachment cannot be easily plotted on a graph or subjected to regression analysis (not a reference to the e-personality trait, but a statistical tool used to investigate the relationship between variables in a scientific study). Still, this has not stopped researchers from trying (somewhat awkwardly) to put numbers on this feeling. In 1970, Harvard social psychologist Zick Rubin pioneered the measurement of love with his "love scale," a thirteen-item questionnaire that was the first to quantify love. (The original study also made a point of distinguishing "love" from "like," for which Rubin developed a separate liking scale.)

The love scale was statistically validated in a population of college students and is still used to track, as objectively as can be expected, this most mercurial of emotions, through questions such as: "If I could never be with _____, I would feel miserable"; "I would forgive _____ for practically anything"; "I feel very possessive toward _____"; "I find it easy to ignore _____'s faults"; and "I would do almost anything for _____." Each item on the questionnaire is scored one to nine—nine being the maximal positive end of the spectrum—which makes 117 ($= 13 \times 9$) the number representing the utmost in lovesickness. Talk about going weak in the knees!

Fast-forward to 2006 and to research conducted by psychologist Maria J. Lavooy, of the University of Central Florida, to compare the level of intimacy in online versus offline relationships, as determined in part by Rubin's love scale. The survey included 546 men and women aged eighteen to fifty-nine, and compared "virtual relators" (individuals who had pursued online and offline relationships) to "traditional relators" (those who had had only face-to-face relationships). The study also compared the degree of intimacy virtual relators achieved in their online relationships to what they had experienced offline.

The results show that virtual relators had significantly lower intimacy in their virtual relationships than in their face-to-face relationships: The average Rubin love scale score for the subjects' face-to-face relationships was 83, compared to a virtual relationship average of only 62—a difference that is considered statistically significant. Moreover, virtual relators had less intimacy in their face-to-face relationships than traditional relators, suggesting that individuals who have trouble with face-to-face relationships may turn to online relating as an alternative. Unfortunately, however, "they are, statistically speaking, not likely to obtain greater intimacy online than they did face to face," as the 83 versus 62 spread in their scores suggests. In general, the authors conclude, "the potential theorized benefits of computer-mediated communication—including greater self-disclosure, increased access to each other, and the possibility of sexual attraction developing out of genuine emotional connectedness rather than from superficial, physical attraction—did not translate into increased reported intimacy in the participants' online, virtual relationships." Instead, online relationships, while capable of being intimate and romantic, were less so than offline ones. Certainly no "perfect 117" Rubin love score seemed within reach! (Not that this feat is easy to achieve offline . . . Only a bit easier to conceive of, statistically speaking.)

It would seem, based on the research and anecdotes presented so far, that love in the digital age may be more elusive, and that many people are stumbling as they try to learn the new etiquette and evolving equilibrium of relationships. How are people negotiating their way through this unfamiliar new world? Many compromise. Too embarrassed to admit their online exploits, but too "plugged-in" to say they still date, many, instead, "hook up." This is the new offline reality, a meet-me-in-the middle settlement people can live with between Internet sex-on-demand and the dating of yesteryear. It neutralizes the "ick" factor associated with random sex by making what goes on look not too overtly sexual, while avoiding the "D" word now dreaded by anyone under thirty as a sign of being seriously behind the times. "The paradigm has shifted," writes *New York Times* columnist Charles M. Blow, in response to a report that found that more high school students said they never dated than said they dated frequently. "Dating is dated. Hooking up is here to stay," Blow writes. "Under the old model, you dated a few times and, if you liked the person, you might consider having sex. Under the new model, you hook up a few times and, if you really like the person, you might consider going on a date." These are not the high school and college days most of us remember.

It can be argued that real relationships among college students do not exist anymore; that, instead, they live in a world of virtual pokes, super-pokes, and poke wars—and their corresponding offline hookups. The same word best describes many adults' liaisons as well. Adults may be learning from teenagers how to love, just as they learned from them how to love texting. For adults, too, much is the opposite of what it used to be. Their virtual quest for romantic fulfillment is fraught with a range of hurdles for which they have received no training, which may be putting them at risk for a whole spectrum of unattractive consequences, from alienation to divorce, from increased loneliness to low self-esteem, and from a weakness for multiple surgical enhancement to a susceptibility to eating disorders and the like.

In simpler times, Oscar Wilde wrote that "life imitates art far more than art imitates life." Increasingly, life also imitates *online* life. The real-life rules people have loved and courted by are being rewritten on Facebook Wall posts, in Craigslist personals, and through easy voluntary and involuntary access to pornography. This creates confusion, which intensifies the insecurity many people already feel as a result of tighter, more impossible standards for what constitutes sexy. The heartbreaking truth is that our e-personality is getting many of us in trouble with Cupid, and the renegotiation we are having to do of the old rules and parameters is not making it any easier to find everlasting love, Match.com's warranty notwithstanding. There are, indeed, plenty of fish in the sea. The problem, seemingly more than before, is the sharks.

_CHAPTER 8
THE ILLUSION OF KNOWLEDGE

IN A SENSE, the previous chapter addressed romantic literacy—the struggle to understand the new relationship paradigm and the challenges we face in the age of the hookup in getting to truly know someone. Part of why some of us may feel romantically "illiterate" is that much of the online search for the right mate is *horizontal* in nature, and involves jumping from Wall post to Wall post on Facebook, skimming through personal ads on Yahoo!, or bouncing among parallel accounts on Chemistry, JDate and Match. Yet getting to know someone and building a future-oriented relationship with that person require patience and a certain degree of exclusive attention focused on that one individual. As a process, it is more vertical than horizontal or superficial, and aims at understanding the person's core values and beliefs and discovering his or her innermost thoughts and feelings.

The same lack of probing is hindering other "literacies" and other aspects of knowing as well. Just as our romantic life can suffer from breezily zipping through possible matches, calling the behavior hooking up or power-dating, so can our larger cognitive life and our ability to learn about, retain, teach—in a word, *know* the world.

One central pillar of knowing is reading. It is how we extend our horizons toward new scenarios of being. The lessons that we absorb from books, the characters that mark us, the mental notes that we take—all get stored in an inner library that we transport with us wherever we go. Then, when we need a reminder of them, they leap out of our brain to give us sustenance, just as they leapt out of the page when they first touched us. We talked about the abuses inflicted on the written word by the Internet, instant messaging, and texting. Not surprisingly, reading has radically changed, too. And as the nature of reading changes, so does this internal library; so does our ability to carry it around with us; and so do the nurturing and beauty we are able to find in words. Words: We have lost patience for their complexity; do not find them worth supporting financially or in other ways; and do not think of them as something to capture and hold on to anymore.

For some, today's personal library is gleaned off the Internet rather than built book by book, and it accumulates very differently because we read very differently. According to a 2008 study commissioned by the British Library, 89 percent of college students use search engines such as Google to begin looking for information. Only 2 percent start from a library Web site, let alone an actual library. Once they find what they are looking for online, their behavior bears little resemblance to how they might handle a printed page. The British Library report describes today's reader, based on an analysis of five years of digital trails left by millions of e-book and e-journal readers.

Online readers are "promiscuous, diverse and volatile," says the report. Their information-seeking behavior is "horizontal, bouncing, checking and viewing in nature." They spend an average of only four minutes reading an e-book, then drop it for better opportunities, also online. They "scan, flick and 'power browse' their way through digital content, developing new forms of online reading on the way that we do not yet fully understand or, in many cases, even recognize."

"Serious" scholars—professors, lecturers, doctors—consulting research articles on academic sites aren't any more patient, faithful, or probing. Roughly 60 percent of them view no more than three pages of an e-journal, and 65 percent never return to take a second look or delve deeper. Overall, they display "a form of skimming activity, where [they] view just one or two pages from an academic site and then 'bounce' out . . ."

Regardless of age group or background, and across a host of information goals, people seem to be clicking and flicking their way through the virtual stacks of cyberspace, searching horizontally rather than vertically, and spending more time circuitously looking for answers than actually reading them. Their quest for hidden knowledge and the quality of much of what they read along the way brings to mind Bassanio's description of Gratiano's brain in Shakespeare's *Merchant of Venice*: "His reasons are as two grains of wheat hid in two bushels of chaff: you shall seek all day ere you find them, and when you have them, they are not worth the search." This reading method, which propels the reader from search to search until something, related or unrelated, catches the attention, does not constitute true reading. It constitutes *evasion* of reading. According to the British Library report, "It is clear that users are not reading online in the traditional sense." In fact, "it almost seems that they go online to avoid reading . . ."

As early as 1997, Jakob Nielsen, an early authority on Web page "usability," showed that 79 percent of online readers scan, rather than read word-for-word, Web content. One simple reason, Nielsen explained, is that reading from computer screens is more tiring than reading from a paper page, because it is "about twenty-five percent slower" (a shortcoming that improvements in technology and screen resolution since then have not completely corrected). The more interesting reason, however, may be attitudinal: According to Nielsen, Web users approach the Internet wanting to be in the driver's seat. They want to decide what to read and how to read it, and resent being at the mercy of an omniscient author who will take them on a meandering, circuitous path, before delivering, maybe, the nugget of information they are after. Online readers want their nugget now, and will scan a couple of paragraphs quickly for it, then forever desert the page if the initial glance yields nothing promising.

At the same time, intense competition, in the form of other possible sources of information and totally irrelevant Web offerings vying for our attention, works to distract the reader from focusing and actually reading. Much like the one hundred other personals we are skimming, and which keep us from being patient with a particular person if we perceive any "red flag," the same applies to our quest to know something online. Online readers are "selfish, lazy, and ruthless," writes Nielsen. They don't cut you, the writer, any slack. They are slippery, peripatetic, and forever on the lookout. "[They] don't know whether this page is the one they need or whether some other page would be better: they are not willing to commit to the investment of reading the page in the hope that it will be good. . . . Experience encourages them to rely on information foraging. Instead of spending a lot of time on a single page, users move between many pages and try to pick the most tasty segments of each." In the thickets of online information, we become hunters and gatherers (talk about regression!), going after the easiest prey first and the lowest-hanging fruit.

Like the study commissioned by the British Library, research by Nielsen and others is fine-tuning our understanding of what online reading consists of. One high-yield experiment involves the use of eye-tracking equipment to record how our eyes take in a Web page: where they pause to register information, and what they choose to overlook. The data collected from a large group of viewers in an eye-tracking experiment can be combined to generate a composite eye-tracking "heat map"—a graded color scheme that shows the hot spots on the Web page where most people fixated their attention, and what parts of the page most people avoided. Such research increasingly drives online marketing decisions. It can, for example, inform a Web designer about to announce a sale where the most strategic location is for that "50% off" sign, so we are less likely to miss it.

In an eye-tracking study involving 232 subjects and thousands of viewed Web pages, Nielsen's group found that users' online reading behavior was rather consistent across many different sites, and did not progress in any familiar or logical way—not carefully, from left to right as, I hope, you are reading this text; not right to left, either, as one might read Hebrew or Arabic; and not in a top-down fashion and progressing in organized columns from right to left, as one might read Chinese. Instead, online reading seems to unfold like a giant-font letter *F* superimposed on the virtual page. Users first read in a horizontal movement across the upper part of the content area (the *F*'s top bar). Next, they move toward the bottom of the page and read across in a second horizontal movement that covers a shorter span than the first one (the *F*'s lower bar). Finally, users scan the page's left side in a quick vertical glance (the *F*'s stem). "F for fast," Nielsen says of online reading, based on his eye-tracking results. For "fickle," too, no doubt. "That's how users read your precious content," he says, advising Web designers: "In a few seconds, their eyes move at amazing speeds across your website's words in a pattern that's very different from what you learned in school." It turns out that our online reading is just as curious as our online writing.

Inspired by Nielsen's work, Michael Agger succinctly sums up the characteristics that make an online text more attractive to online readers. He should know. Agger is senior editor of the heavily trafficked and highly readable *Slate*. Here is his bulleted list of an online article's most important features:

- Bulleted list
- Occasional use of bold to prevent skimming
- Short sentence fragments
- Explanatory subheads
- No puns
- Did I mention lists?

Other helpful tips Agger shares include: Limit yourself to one idea per paragraph; give the illusion of a well-referenced document with copious hypertext links ("Keep things short for the masses, but offer links for the type A's"); and, finally, as a rule of thumb, always aim for half the word count of "conventional writing." But fret not about curbing your verbose impulses. Agger quotes Nielsen's comforting assertion that "a good editor should be able to cut 40% of the word count while removing only 30% of an article's value." *Only* 30 percent? It seems as though the expectation is that most of us will accept an almost one-third reduction in the value of what we are reading as a reasonable price to pay for speeding up our reading, or whatever one wants to call taking in a Web page in patterns of *F*.

As with instant messaging and texting, speed is of the essence when it comes to online reading and supersedes any other consideration. We should be able to view the information quickly, then minimize the page and go check e-mail or update our Facebook status to inform people of what we just read. This tendency has been successfully exploited by Twitter, the microblogging service where information is squeezed, compressed, anything-superfluous-wrung-out, so that it can be made to fit within the 140-character limit that the site imposes on entries. "It's not too many words, but that makes it great," announces Twitter's homepage. "Twitter means you do not ever have to read long messages." Here is the 140-keystroke description of Twitter by Michael Liedtke, of the Associated Press: "It's a potluck of pithy self-expression simmering with whimsy, narcissism, voyeurism, hucksterism, tedium, and sometimes useful information." Its name is as appropriate as Google's and encapsulates the service perfectly, in that to "twitter," according to Dictionary .com, is to "talk lightly and rapidly, especially of trivial matters."

But nontrivial subjects can be broached, too, such as "Working on term paper. Any good links on the founding fathers?" and "Anyone lose weight on Wellbutrin?" One can even distill masterworks of world literature to their absolute essences, like a much speedier and more efficient

CliffsNotes, then "tweet" those, as the National Public Radio program *Wait Wait . . . Don't Tell Me* recently did with three classic novels:

> *Grapes of Wrath*: Times are hard. Sister breastfeeding homeless guy. I'm SO outta here.

> *Pride and Prejudice*: I hate that guy. But actually, he's kinda hot.

> *Lolita*: (Message removed for violating terms of service.)

Your "followers"—and you can have thousands of them—simultaneously receive your quips and queries, and quickly provide you with their microreactions and microanswers. Not unlike Facebook's friend counter, and with similar implications for one's ego, the number of followers one has is prominently displayed. The more of them you have, the more popular you are and, presumably, the more knowledgeable and better informed.

If blogging, by liberating people from the need to patiently and logically build an argument, dumbed down intelligent debate, microblogging might be the proverbial last nail. Because of the near impossibility of a sophisticated exchange within the confines that Twitter or texting forces on us, the nontrivial is necessarily trivialized, robbed of the weight and gravitas it may have possessed. As though the early Internet didn't challenge our attention spans and communication skills enough, virtual life, through Web sites like Twitter, is moving to further accentuate the process—and the losses. E-mail, already speedy and informal enough, is being replaced by texting, a system of communication even less suited for discussing big ideas and complex issues. Somebody please tweet, "Where will it all end?"

With Twitter, as with online love, we take a drive-through approach. In our relationship with words, as in our online relationships, the Internet allows us to cut corners and cut to the chase. We "tweet" like we hook up and power-read like we power-date. And just as this can present real challenges to our romantic lives, it can also upset our long-standing relationships with words and books and overall cognition. In "Is Google Making Us Stupid?" Nicholas Carr writes eloquently of the plight of someone (all of us) who has spent too much time reading online, texting, or tweeting. Carr relates how he has felt his thought processes inexorably alter:

> Over the past few years I've had an uncomfortable sense that someone, or something, has been tinkering with my brain, remapping the neural circuitry, reprogramming the memory. My mind isn't going—so far as I can tell—but it's changing. I'm not thinking the way I used to think. I can feel it most strongly when I'm reading. Immersing myself in a book or a lengthy article used to be easy. My mind would get caught up in the narrative or the turns of the argument, and I'd spend hours strolling through long stretches of prose. That's rarely the case anymore. Now my concentration often starts to drift after two or three pages. I get fidgety, lose the thread, begin looking for something else to do. I feel as if I'm always dragging my wayward brain back to the text. The deep reading that used to come naturally has become a struggle.

Carr's difficulty concentrating will resonate with anyone who has wasted precious time going in circles on or around Facebook, flirting, reconnecting with old acquaintances, or trying to make new friends. Cognitively speaking, many users feel enslaved to the Web site, unable to focus their attention elsewhere for any meaningful duration. In a year-end review of what she sees as regrettable cultural trends, Martha Brockenbrough writes:

> For many, 2008 was the year that passed in a blue-and-white blur of Facebook status updates, inane friend comparisons and awkward "poking" situations with complete strangers. We spent hours throwing cup-

cakes at people we barely spoke to in high school. We compared our
taste in movies with that of our ex-boyfriends' new girlfriends. We let
everyone know we were fans of Starbucks, "Battlestar Galactica" and
pants. Worse, where we used to just send e-mail messages, now we send
the messages through Facebook. Then Facebook sends our recipients
e-mail that our friends then use to then log in to Facebook so they can
see what we've written. Then they send their replies to our Facebook
accounts, which send us e-mail, which prompts us to log back in.

As the sun is to the solar system, Facebook is to many of our lives.
It is the center about which many of us revolve, sucking us in, diverting
us from other social and informational pursuits, and giving us the illusion that updates and cupcakes are, anymore, how people meet, learn,
and know. All this mindless typing and reading take their toll, and Carr
can sense a reconfiguration of the reading and attention neurons in his
brain happening as a result. The wordsmith has diagnosed himself with
a neuropsychiatric malady fatal for an author: Complex words now bore
him to distraction. Having described his illness and its symptoms, Carr
has no difficulty pinpointing the cause: "I think I know what's going
on. . . . My mind now expects to take in information the way the Net
distributes it: in a swiftly moving stream of particles. Once I was a scuba
diver in the sea of words. Now I zip along the surface like a guy on a Jet
Ski." What neither Carr nor anyone else can give us, however, is a practical cure: a dose of something that will make us probe again rather than
skim, and think vertically rather than browse. With every status update
we read, with every tweet we type à la "Ach . . . fridge is empty. dunno
what to have for dinner," our library stacks feel dustier and more and
more like a claustrophobe's worst nightmare. Fresh air used to come in
the form of a new book by a favorite author. Now we hope somebody
pokes us on Facebook.

Still, there can be no doubt that the Web represents a tremendous
wellspring of information. Who among us hasn't checked on the poten-

tial side effects of a new prescribed medication? Who hasn't brushed up on a piece of world history that escaped his or her notice? Who hasn't explored activities to engage in while in a foreign city, or decided on what destination to visit in the first place, based on media reports, visitor reviews, climate patterns, government data, or scholarly articles—all found online? Who hasn't double-checked the meaning of a word on Dictionary.com or used Google's built-in spell checker to avoid making an error (the nifty "did you mean *knowledgeable*" prompt, for example, if you enter *knowledgable* in the search engine)? With all of this information at our fingerprints—information that previous generations would have had to work very hard to track down—many of us feel informed in a diverse range of fields, or at the very least capable of quickly *becoming* informed in the time it takes to do a few Google searches. But the surfeit of false information circulating online, from the extreme (conspiracy theories on 9/11) to the subtle (the misspelling of a historical figure's name), can make it difficult to separate truth from lies, fact from opinion. In fact, the Internet bestows on many of us a false mastery of knowledge as it convinces us that we are more qualified, educated, or mature than we truly are. In doing so, it facilitates a potentially dangerous social phenomenon—the dissolution of offline hierarchical relationships when it comes to information, be they child-parent, student-teacher, patient-doctor, or layman-expert.

Hailed by many as the "great equalizer," the Internet is a societal leveler the likes of which humankind has never seen before. In the way it spreads information, the Internet evens out the playing field by bringing together people whose lives would otherwise never intersect and whose voices in almost any other setting would carry differential weight, in proportion to their class, race, profession, or age. Here is the analogy that early Internet proponent Howard Rheingold used in 1991 to describe the promise of emerging e-mail technology: "Just as the advent of the Colt .45 revolver during the taming of the West equalized the balance between a small person and a larger one, telecommunications, properly used, can equalize the balance of power between citizens and power brokers." Computer-mediated communications were at long last going to peaceably erase unwarranted privilege, bringing us closer in class and stature to one another than ever before, thereby boosting our democratic system of governance and way of life.

Almost twenty years later, however, one can say that there has been a downside to this "Athens without slaves," as Rheingold called it. A lack of boundaries between groups online has led to situations that challenge the utopian version of democracy, as everybody feels equally informed and qualified. The free flow of information, open access to knowledge, and glut of data can be seen, paradoxically, as threatening our democratic ideals. The life experiences of a fifty-year-old mother, for instance, ideally should help inform decisions made by her fourteen-year-old daughter, particularly in matters on which parents and children may disagree: choice of school, dress code, alcohol, drugs, and sex. Similarly, in matters of health, the medical opinion of a board-certified physician should carry more weight than the smattering of information gleaned, either from Internet sites or by exposure to drug companies' direct-consumer marketing, by a layperson. However, the daughter and the layperson may nurse the illusion, fostered by the Internet, that their opinion is as valid as the mother's or the doctor's, a phenomenon that can impede the efforts of the parent or the doctor to have seasoned, evidence-based advice accepted. An example from my practice helps illustrate the limits of "one man, one vote" in the virtual era.

Ashley, a sixteen-old ballet student, was brought in by her mother to see me for a consultation. Ashley had already decided to prescribe to herself the antidepressant Wellbutrin, ostensibly for depression, and was on the verge of ordering it online from an overseas supplier when her mother insisted on making the appointment. "I'm sure Wellbutrin would help," she told her daughter, avoiding a fight that might have made Ashley reluctant to see a doctor. "But let's at least have a specialist prescribe it. This way we know we're getting the real thing."

Ashley's mother, a medical social worker, had used her maternal and clinical instincts to accurately diagnose her child's problem: not depression but a serious case of anorexia nervosa that required immediate medical attention. Objective signs for the disorder abounded: the smell of vomit in the bathroom shortly after the family's meals, the weight loss and accompanying arrest in menstruation, the obsessive calorie counting, and the number of bookmarked nutrition Web sites on the family computer.

It didn't take long during my first meeting with Ashley to agree with her mother that she was not depressed. Ashley was social, enjoyed ballet, was doing relatively well in school, and smiled broadly when a text message from a friend arrived to her cell phone during the meeting. Yet she quickly blurted out, "Insomnia, poor concentration, poor energy, and anhedonia" in describing to me how she was doing. When I asked her to explain what she meant by anhedonia, a formal clinical term with a Greek pedigree, Ashley grew nervous and impatient. It was obvious that whatever Web site she had consulted to memorize the symptoms of clinical depression apparently did not explain what anhedonia was. (She could have looked up the term on Wikipedia, where it is accurately defined as the "inability to experience pleasure from normally pleasurable life events such as eating, exercise, and social or sexual interaction.") I told Ashley that given her very low weight Wellbutrin was a poor choice for antidepressant, as it could cause serious seizures in underweight people and might lead to further weight loss. That had little effect on Ashley, however, who threatened to buy the medication on the Web if I did not write her a prescription for something she "knew would work for her."

Wellbutrin, I had learned from other patients with anorexia, had a reputation in online eating disorders circles for being an appetite suppressant and is commonly sought out by anorexics to help them lose weight. Just as Ashley learned online how to more effectively induce vomiting ("stick the bottom of a toothbrush down your throat, itll all come out," according to funadvice.com), she also learned how to manipulate her mother and doctor into prescribing the last medication she needed.

Still, I did not completely close the door on the possibility of prescribing this medication at some point in the future for Ashley, in part to keep her in my clinic and to encourage her to join an eating disorders therapy group. Unfortunately, Ashley barely lasted for two meetings before the psychologist running the group, a colleague of mine, had to ask her to leave. She could not handle Ashley's constant defiance and the distorted, partial knowledge clearly gleaned online that Ashley would use to refute every fact the group leader was trying to communicate—how, for instance, the human race did not evolve to eat 2,000 calories a day; how the research showing that the brain of anorexics shrinks as the disease progresses was "seriously flawed" because it "didn't include a control group"; and how most religions of the world have incorporated some element of fasting into their rituals, so how bad can it be? In addition, Ashley would blurt things out, drown out other participants, and speak out of turn. "She acted like she was in a chat room!" my exasperated colleague commented. "She wouldn't let me do my job of moderating the group."

It is easy to see how children and teenagers like Ashley can pretend to be adults and make adultlike decisions about their health and other important matters without being equipped, experience-wise, to be making those decisions. It is also easy to see why people like Ashley have a hard time accepting the fact that, in real life, one person's voice sometimes *should* carry more weight than another's—this is not the case online, where everyone's opinion is equal. Increasingly, whenever their half-facts are challenged, people are quick to accuse others of dismissing the vast knowledge and equal status they have earned through hours of . . . surfing.

Many of us swear by TripAdvisor and would not consider reserving a hotel room before checking the average rating generated from other patrons who visited the hotel before us and reviewed it for the site. A friend who is a big fan of TripAdvisor swears he can even tell the multiple rave reviews written by the hotel owners themselves, to prop up their scores, from honest ones contributed by real visitors. (One clue: Different entries by the same poster tend to repeat the same grammatical errors and follow the same sentence structure.) He does not let the few "bad apples" mar his experience of the TripAdvisor democracy and does not question the wisdom of a big enough pool of reviewers. Instead, he calculates what he calls the "real rating," leaving out of the equation what he suspects are fake reviews. He then confidently books his room and rarely ever regrets his choice.

Similarly, many of us go to Epicurious for culinary inspiration, and sometimes have had the experience of being turned off an interesting recipe by a reviewer's tepid two-fork rating (out of a maximum of four). Taking time to read the actual review, however, may reveal something: The author, who is trying to reduce his fat intake, used only half the amount of butter that the recipe called for and substituted skim milk for half and half. Yet his two forks imply that he actually followed the step-by-step instructions and was disappointed with the results. Similarly, a vegetarian may give one fork to a pot roast recipe "on principle." The boldness of reviewers who judge recipes they didn't even try is striking, but an intelligent consumer of online information would read the fine print and know to "delete" their ratings when deciding whether to attempt a recipe, essentially doing what my friend does with TripAdvisor. Doing so would put him well on his way to tasting the best pot roast he ever had because its recipe simply has to be online. This is one way to make the Web's wealth of democratically generated data work to inform us—who said democracy had to be perfect? But it takes analysis and patience and reading between the lines, all of which go against the Web experience as we have become accustomed to it. Online, it is easier and more natural not to probe, and, for many people, the prominently displayed picture of one or two forks is all it takes to dismiss an otherwise promising recipe and jump to the next one.

In their paper titled "From Movable Type to Data Deluge," John

Gehl and Suzanne Douglas, publishers of the education journal *Educom Review*, offer a potential mechanism for understanding many Internet users' exaggerated self-confidence about how much they really know. They argue that there is a fundamental shift taking place in our relationship to information and the knowledge it brings us: "Whereas books, newspapers, radio, and television are all essentially 'one to many' broadcast media (i.e., one source transmitting to many readers, listeners, or viewers), the Internet allows a surfer to exercise complete control over what is now an 'interaction with' rather than a 'reception of' news or information." As they see it, receptivity in the passive, absorptive, open-to-what-you-may-have-to-teach-me sense is a dated stance toward information. Active, especially *inter*active, is what is "in," and we are all, together and equally competently, creating, disseminating, and exchanging information online, in the form of "content." "Whereas the communication process has in the past typically implied an assumption that the message sender had more information than the message receiver, now the relationship is effectively reversed," Gehl and Douglas write. "The one with the control is not the one with the message but the one with the mouse."

Weaned on Facebook, my patient Ashley's generation finds it hard to see a distinction between information producers and information consumers. The same blurring exists for older Internet users as well. Everyone is an "iReporter" or a "citizen journalist" these days, whether reporting from the frontlines in Anbar province or riffing in his underwear. The shift away from apportioning relative weight to different voices as a function of knowledge and experience is painfully reflected in how people increasingly find absurd the idea of having to pay for information. Newspapers are feeling the effects most fatally, with traditional book and magazine publishers closely behind. The *New York Times*'s experience with TimesSelect provides a good illustration of how much our value system has changed when it comes to weighing information quality.

Facing a precipitous drop in advertising sales and in paying subscribers as more readers migrate to the Web, U.S. newspapers are feeling the pressure to increase online revenue. Arguably more popular than ever (because more people are reading them online, and much of the blogosphere and online news sources are piggybacking on their reporting and "cutting and pasting" from their articles), newspapers are nonetheless bleeding money, because fewer and fewer people are willing to pay to support them. Our expectation is that their news should be made available online, gratis, as most online information is; that the 1,000-plus members of the editorial staff of the *New York Times* should continue to feed news to *Huffpo*'s less than 30. This is as untenable as it is unreasonable. Here is how *New Yorker* writer James Surowiecki summarizes traditional journalism's predicament with us, its entitled online readers, and what's at stake: "We want access to everything, we want it now, and we want it for free. That's a consumer's dream, but eventually it's going to collide with reality: if newspapers' profits vanish, so will their product."

Trying to avoid that dire fate, the *Times* introduced TimesSelect in 2005, an experiment to make online content pay for the Baghdad bureau and other non-optional accessories of first-rate reporting. For a fee that was less than it would cost to subscribe to the print edition, online readers could have access to 23 news and opinion columnists unavailable to nonsubscribers, the entire *Times* archive of over 16 million articles dating back to 1851, and several tools that can be used to customize the Web site. The idea was abandoned two years later when it became amply clear that the project had failed: TimesSelect attracted only about 227,000 paying subscribers, when at the beginning of the experiment the site was registering over 500 million page views monthly. The Web edition may have contained all the news that's fit to post, but the overwhelming majority of its online visitors didn't find it worth $7.95 a month.

Scott Karp, the creator of Publishing 2.0, a blog about technology and the media, sees the demise of TimesSelect as a sign of how "the fundamental economics of content in the digital media age . . . may soon put the final nail in the coffin of paid content." No one, not even the *Times*, and certainly not the late *Gourmet*, that grande dame of food magazines, can claim a monopoly on information in this age, because "anyone can create and distribute content on a meaningful scale." The ability to charge for content in nondigital media like newspapers and magazines was based on a limited supply of content and monopoly control of distribution. However, by providing an "overabundance of content," the Web has "utterly destroyed" that model. Another explanation, besides information surplus, might be something else we talked about: Our narcissistic side now insists that the *New York Times* be available at our fingertips free of charge at all times. If its publishers fail to oblige, then they don't deserve our "business."

So what's a venerable, but broke newspaper to do? Craigslist's Craig Newmark, who by taking the highly profitable classifieds to his Web site may be the one person most responsible for journalism's woes, has some ideas. His suggestions, expressed on a blog hosted by the *Times*, include a recommendation to go "hyperlocal." Since most people go online to obtain local information—local store hours, local restaurant reviews, local movie theater offerings, and so forth—newspapers, he suggests, are more likely to survive and successfully charge for content if they cover local zoning board meetings and Little League games. Author and Internet critic Andrew Keen agrees. "Local information is potentially the most valuable product in the new knowledge economy," he writes on the same blog. Ironically, the Internet, which has the potential to extend our knowledge transgeographically like no other medium before it could, is only worth paying for if it can deliver to us our local grocer's phone number. We like to think that we live in a global village, and sing its praises at every chance, but please don't put it on my credit card!

The problem with the ultraneighborhoody focus, of course, is that while it may pay the newspapers' bills, it will not cover Putin, the Middle East peace process, macroeconomics, or global warming. Those would have to be left largely to armchair bloggers with no credentials or press passes. It is hard not to see this approach to journalism and information in general as diminishing our collective fund of knowledge and our democracy.

Another solution that Newmark, among others, has proposed, is the "philanthropic model for news," by which is meant that a newspaper would give up altogether on the notion of profitability, and would survive, instead, off the kindness of benefactors, as a sort of endowed, nonprofit museum of knowledge. Note to the *Times* board: Google.org, Google.com's philanthropic arm, is known to sit on huge cash reserves, and had, as of September 2008, committed $100 million to further the charitable fund's five adopted "initiatives," one of which is a commitment to "Inform" and "Empower." Check. Check.

Yet a third strategy that some financially strapped publications are implementing to make people pay for information is to be "more Internet" than the Internet. Facing a plunge in circulation and advertising, *Newsweek* announced a major restructuring of its pages. As part of the makeover, the last page of the weekly would feature "The Bluffer's Guide," a tip sheet for readers on how to sound as if they are knowledgeable on a current topic, whether they are or not. It is a tongue-in-cheek move for sure, and one hopes it will help keep the award-winning magazine in business for another seventy-five years, but it does smack of desperation and risks producing a mutant cross between Answers.com and Twitter. Call it another example of offline life imitating online life.

It is unclear, reviewing these and similar strategies, how or in what form the one-to-many model of imparting knowledge will survive, where the "one" is a professional voice attuned to certain principles and standards, and the "many" is an audience hungry to be accurately informed. We should hope for the survival of that system. Otherwise, we are faced with the possibility that intelligent debate will be replaced with a muddle of facts and outsized online personalities. Because of the grandiosity and narcissism that can glut cyberspace, and the anonymity and casualness of the medium, it is tempting for people to think of themselves as simply too good to need a teacher, a professional editor, or an obsessive fact-checker. They may be quick to elevate a personal musing to something that resembles a "last word" on a topic, and may present their mere opinions as unquestionable truths. They may then disseminate, gratuitously, their authoritative content for the edification of their many followers. As a *Time* magazine article put it, "every time a news source dies and an online opinion site rises up, we move a little closer to the fact-starved day when the loudmouths have only themselves to talk about."

The end result may be what Andrew Keen calls a "democratic swamp of crowd-generated content," one that people looking for honest information on a topic are expected to waddle through or surf right over. And what an appropriate word—surfing—to capture the horizontal process of gaining knowledge on the Web. (The word "browsing" is equally beautiful.) One glides, barely scratching the surface, atop mountains of information, with no easy way to sift the good from the bad, often finding amid the detritus whatever evidence one needs to confirm a preconceived opinion already made. To the extent that there is directionality to our quest, something that might be conceived of as "depth," often it is the order in which we consult our search results—an order dictated by Google. We trust the search engine to present information in the right hierarchy of importance and relevance, and we often proceed through the results from first to second to third, blinded to any motives Google might have for assigning its rankings. Independent sifting, like independent thinking, takes a backseat.

Regardless, much of the information search engines yield is not "news" in the true sense, tends to be more homogeneous than one would expect, and does not inspire us to commit it to memory. "If what you want is real information, you may have a problem," Educom's John Gehl and Suzanne Douglas warn, "because the ubiquity, immediacy, and relentless repetition of media communication have resulted in the decline of the very commodity all these media purport to be selling:

news." What we have, instead, is a hyperaccelerated news cycle given to "breaking stories" and drama, with the likes of *Politico*, the *Drudge Report*, and *Huffington Post* in a mad race with each other and with the Associated Press to be first, sometimes making a victim of accuracy in the process. News, in the surprise sense of the word, has become rare. Very little surprises us anymore, or if something does, then it is not for long; another event is sure to steal our attention, even before we have had a chance to process and analyze the last one. "There is less and less surprise in the 'global village,'" Gehl and Douglas write. We have become desensitized to surprise, that is to news, by the unstoppable online stream of it.

Further, much of the news that people read is homogenized. Newspaper consolidation, a direct effect of the decrease in subscribers and in advertising revenue, is shrinking the pool of original reporting. To cite but a few, five newspapers in New York and New Jersey formed the Northeast Consortium in 2009 to enable the sharing of stories, graphics, and photos. Around that time, eight Ohio, five Maine, and three South Florida newspapers merged. Two formerly bitter rivals, the *Dallas Morning News* and the *Forth Worth Star-Telegram*, also came together and now share concert reviews, sports sections, and coverage of local meetings. The lack of diversity in voices and opinions that these mergers have produced, and the recycled feel of the news, give readers further reason not to subscribe.

Homogenization can take other forms, too. Many Web sites make a point of highlighting their "most read" and "most e-mailed" stories. Many of us will choose to read those over others in order to stay current with what Topic A for the day seems to be, and because of how strategically positioned the links to them are on the Web page. We will then forward the articles to our friends in case they missed them, contributing to the temporary meme-like status of the stories in question. We might also cc copies to our own in-boxes, should we want to reconsult them in the future. All this can lead to unexpected sameness in what we are focused on and in what we read and talk about—a paradox and a real surprise, given the endless world of information available online, and the Internet's limitless potential to expand our interests and diversify our discourse.

Because we can e-mail ourselves the information that interests us or download it directly onto our computers, we also no longer see as much of a reason to memorize things. When information is at your fingertips all the time, why commit neurons to storing it in your brain? This is another big change in our approach to knowledge, and one that has real implications, especially for kids who are growing up wondering why it is that they need to retain facts and remember details. British psychologist Susan Blackmore warns that the heavy reliance on the Internet in school curricula is drastically reshaping the educational paradigm, with potentially scary consequences that are as yet unknown. "Traditionally, what has primarily been an issue for education has been putting knowledge into kids' heads," she says. "But now it will be about showing them how to navigate in [the online] world." E-learning, she concludes, because it does not need to emphasize memorizing, could produce children with brains that are wired very differently from adults'. Her concerns are valid, despite science still being far from proving the neurobiological changes that she fears might be taking place.

We will be coming back to memory, but the other crucial component to our cognitive life and to remembering is *attention*. All learning starts with the ability to focus and heed a teacher's imploration to "pay attention." Yet our kids, like Nicholas Carr and like many of us, are showing an attention span in the classroom that is increasingly like their attention span on Facebook: Many have become more distractible and are unable to focus on Mrs. Wilson for longer than it would take them to write a status update. This problem is suggested by the tremendous increase in the number of Ritalin prescriptions written over the last decade. Our children (and we) are less attentive than ever, and studies are questioning what role the virtual lifestyle may be playing in this.

Attention deficit/hyperactivity disorder (ADHD) is the most commonly diagnosed behavioral disorder of childhood, estimated to affect 3 percent to 5 percent of children, although adults are not spared. Children with ADHD typically show impairment across multiple areas of functioning, including home, school, and peer relationships, and can have long-term problems with academic performance, professional success, and social development. The inattentive type of ADHD is defined, in the *Diagnostic and Statistical Manual–IV*, as the presence, for at least six months, of six or more of the following symptoms:

- fails to give attention to details or makes careless mistakes in schoolwork, work, or other activities;
- has difficulty sustaining attention in tasks or play activities;
- does not seem to listen when spoken to directly;
- does not follow through on instructions and fails to finish schoolwork, chores, or duties in the workplace;
- has difficulty organizing tasks and activities;
- avoids, dislikes, or is reluctant to engage in tasks that require sustained mental effort (such as homework);
- loses things necessary for tasks or activities (school assignments, pencils, toys);
- is easily distracted by extraneous stimuli;
- is forgetful in daily activities.

To date, several studies have shown a link between ADHD and excessive Internet use. The largest of the studies conducted in school-age children involved 752 elementary students in South Korea and found that 33 percent of those who suffered from ADHD were "addicted" to the Internet. (More on the clinical definition of Internet addiction later.) A study in an older age group—216 college students in Taiwan—compared the rate of ADHD in adults who met criteria for Internet addiction to the rate of ADHD in those who were "normal" users of the Internet. The results showed that 32 percent of Internet addicts had

ADHD, compared to only 8 percent of nonaddicts. While these studies do not prove causality, the correlations are certainly striking and form a legitimate basis for questioning whether the Internet may be making us attention-deficient.

And in this age of compressed attention spans and library allergies, what would learning be without Wikipedia, the popular user-compiled online encyclopedia that has formed the backbone of countless term papers and graduation theses? Most of us visit the site on a regular basis, filling in the holes in our knowledge, whether the subject is history, current events, or pop culture. As an unregulated and dynamic repository of a certain kind of knowledge, Wikipedia is infinitely expandable and modifiable, without meaningful peer review or editorial scrutiny. So if the biography of your favorite historical figure wounds your sensibility, all you have to do is log on and edit the entry, in essence changing the course of history to your liking. Stephen Colbert famously poked fun at the site by encouraging his audience to edit the entry for "elephant" to reflect the "fact" that Africa's elephant population had tripled in the previous six months. "Together we can create a reality we can all agree on—the reality we just agreed on," as Colbert deftly put it.

Similarly, Yale prankster John Behan decided to define on Wikipedia a new condition of his creation. He called it "emysphilia" and described it as "a rare sexual fetish in which the practitioner experiences sexual arousal from visual and tactile stimuli relating to turtles and tortoises." Keeping with medical tradition, he coined the term based on the Greek roots for turtle and love. The fetish, according to his Wikipedia entry, was discovered by a "Dr. Daniel Schechner" in 1959, based on his patient, a "Mr. Gor." Two works by Dr. Schechner on the subject are referenced to lend legitimacy to the article, and the author acknowledges that the American Psychiatric Association has yet to recognize the fetish as a true disorder. Although Wikipedia eventually removed the article, and Behan pulled the plug on the joke, telling the student newspaper that emysphilia is "totally absolutely fake," and that Dan Schechner and

Ankit Gor are actually his roommates, the term apparently survived on Answers.com and other user-based Web sites. A new disease was born. (While no patient has ever come to me complaining of emysphilia symptoms, I have seen several with self-diagnosed "Morgellons," a total Web invention of a condition, with significant Wikipedia presence and over a million Google hits, where patients are convinced of a skin infestation and complain of stinging, crawling, and biting sensations.)

Such inventions can be seen as an exercise in "democracy," but what democracy truly requires is a process to reliably produce an informed citizenry. The few seconds we spend visiting each Web site do not add up to deep knowledge or meaningful retention. Can we learn things on Wikipedia? The answer is absolutely yes. But should we mistake the superficial knowledge we often pick up on the Internet for genuine mastery of a subject? I would say that the answer is no and, further, that the quick online information fix, dispersed over innumerable subjects, means that many of us are learning less and less about more and more—a process that, taken to the extreme, will leave us knowing nothing about everything.

John Gehl and Suzanne Douglas express their fear that the Internet is devolving into mindlessness, " . . . creating a citizenry that can't think or read, is unfit for jury duty, and can be entertained . . . but not enlightened." Yes, the great equalizing effect of the Internet wipes out differences in experience, stature, and roles by erasing discrepancies in our access to information. But instead of seeing our democracy truly enhanced by this, we risk moving toward demagoguery, where everybody is indeed equal—equally misinformed. Given how the Internet has shortened our attention spans when it comes to reading and meaningful analysis, and given the *psychological* 140-keystroke limit we now set for ourselves before declaring "information overload," it can become easier for demagogues to spread their rhetorical bullets and one-liner propaganda slogans. So that they are not believed, their veiled half-truths require vertical probing, dissection, and debate, but one is too distracted for that. One just got tweeted. Researching this book was made much easier by Google Books, which has given us free access to millions of books that are difficult to find or out of print. But, ironically, the net effect of Google may be that fewer and fewer of us are interested in reading them.

CHAPTER 9

INTERNET ADDICTION

WHETHER WE GO online to learn, find love, shop, play virtual games, diagnose ourselves, connect with friends and loved ones, or read our favorite blogs, the Internet sucks up a shockingly large amount of time— over forty-five days per year in some urban centers, according to some estimates. The consequences of spending too much time in the virtual world are sometimes no less serious than those associated with a mental illness or substance abuse problem. This has given rise in the media, and among some mental health professionals, to a new concept—"Internet addiction." The debate over whether it is an independent disease that deserves to be included in the *DSM* or simply a new manifestation of old conditions, such as pathological gambling and compulsive shopping, has created a split of sorts in the mental health community, eliciting some uncharacteristically strong reactions from psychiatrists, a normally placid bunch. Add to the problem of classifying Internet addiction the uncertainty about how to treat it, and you get a controversy that rivals the one surrounding multiple personality disorder, and echoes of the "hysterical response to hysteria" we talked about.

There is no shortage of opportunities to waste time online. Many of us have had the experience of going in search of a specific piece of information only to fall down the rabbit hole and find ourselves, an hour later, reading something entirely unrelated to our original search. Our browsing trajectory is, almost by definition, tangential, even when we approach Google knowing exactly what we want. So intent are we sometimes on *not* wasting time, on finding something specific, that we take advantage of a Google "advanced search" feature. By bracketing our search phrase with quotation marks, we can make sure we retrieve only exact instances of that phrase. Entering *"2010 Oscar nominees,"* for example, as opposed to the quoteless *2010 Oscar nominees*, should, technically, avoid related results like *Oscar betting games*, *best Oscar acceptance speeches*, and *Netflix*. In reality, however, this specificity-enhancing feature hardly narrows things down enough, as pictures of worst-ever Oscar fashions from years past and self-assured predictions of this year's winners still manage to pop up, diverting us from the task at hand. Despite our best intentions, eye-catching finds along the way always derail us online, so that a well-circumscribed search bifurcates and trifurcates in a manner that is guaranteed to yield much more, or much less, than our original aim. "Advanced" search option or not, a simple Internet search is never that simple, and before we know it, we have spent too much time browsing. Perform a dozen such searches a night and your spouse might start calling you an Internet addict, and some experts might agree.

Much conspires online to make any attempt at focusing almost futile. Resisting reading or answering personal e-mails at work is a challenge that most of us fail. How often does our in-box carry in it alerts that an out-of-stock item that we had expressed interest in is available again on Amazon, or that new status updates by our friends have been posted on Facebook since we last checked an hour before, or that new matches are waiting for us on Match as soon as we log in? Not to mention newsletters and blog feeds we subscribe to, and the waves of spam e-mail that most of us automatically delete—even that can be time-consuming—but that on occasion might steal our attention. All this adds up to real time, and, potentially, to a real waste of time, and we didn't even need to initiate a Google search to be thus diverted.

Embedded links, or "hyperlinks," are another reason for our Brownian motion in cyberspace and for the many days a year we spend moving that way. On the surface of it, hyperlinks are perfectly convenient pointers that guide us to resources with more specific information on our topic of interest. In reality, however, they can be loaded missiles that send us on a wayward journey away from the Web page at hand, and toward greener pastures where the links lead. And where the links lead, of course, has more links embedded, and following those takes additional time and introduces further degrees of separation between us and our original goal. A hyperlink, like the non-urgent e-mail we feel compelled to answer and the unsolicited search result that distracts us, is a mini-tangent we go on, one that is easy to initiate but can be very difficult to return from. These mini-tangents, along with virtual games, blogs, pornography, and other online pursuits, can translate into a mega time drain—one that, when destructive and consuming enough, may justifiably be called "Internet addiction."

Many people find it difficult to resist the enticing pull of a medium that contains endless content, whether it is news, blogs, message boards, or online retailers, yet not everyone can be said to have a pathological relationship with the Internet. What constitutes a legitimate pathology when it comes to the Internet? How much is "too much," and what are the real-life consequences of too much? These are some of the questions that researchers, therapists, and policymakers are grappling with. The previous chapters have been about the personality traits that the virtual world unleashes and some specific offline consequences, including romantic confusion and compromised knowledge. Internet addiction, on the other hand, is a blunt-edge label that does not always take into consideration what the individual finds so irresistible about the virtual experience, what aspects of his or her personality emerge online, or what the specific consequences to the person are. Rather, and despite some relatively limited variability, the Internet addiction diagnosis as most experts have defined it is concerned with two main features: (a) too much time is wasted online (regardless of what it is wasted on), and (b) the time taken from other activities and other relationships results in a major loss to the individual, such as divorce or significant difficulties at school or work. For the most part, the personality changes are lost under the label, and the more moderately affected individuals—those whose relationships and school and job performances have suffered but perhaps not enough to meet the diagnostic criteria—are missed. While measuring the prevalence of Internet addiction as it has been defined is important in justifying public health interventions and research funds, one should not lose sight of the more subtle transformations and consequences occurring in all of us as a result of virtual life, even if we are not spending forty-five days yearly tethered to our computers, or suffering greatly as a result. In other words, even if we do not meet the definitions for "Internet addiction" and because of that are not captured in the statistics, our psychology is still affected by the Internet, and how it is affected deserves to be investigated and understood.

Depending on the definition used, the population studied, and the quality of the research, Internet addiction rates have varied widely—from 0.3 percent in a U.S. population survey to nearly 38 percent in a study of Hong Kong teenagers and young adults. When we started seeing, in our clinic, individuals who were fired from their jobs for spending too much time browsing the Internet on company time, or who would wait for their spouses to fall asleep in order to check e-mail one last time, we wondered whether this was a function of being in Silicon Valley; whether the area most credited with birthing the Internet might be more likely to show pathological signs of inappropriate Internet use. In part to see whether this problem was somehow overrepresented in our territory, our group conducted a large nationwide survey of Internet use. We interviewed by phone 2,513 adults taken from all 50 states, in a manner proportional to the population in each state. Given the lack of an established *DSM* diagnosis, we developed the survey questions by borrowing from diagnostic criteria for well-accepted psychiatric conditions that share features with Internet addiction, including OCD, pathological gambling, and substance addiction.

The sample was obtained by random-digit telephone calls, and all listed and unlisted residential telephone numbers within each state had an equal chance of being called. Cell phone numbers were not included— to avoid the cost to the respondent. To help ensure that busy individuals were represented, telephone numbers were called fifteen times before being abandoned.

Over 50 percent of people contacted agreed to participate in the survey—a rather good rate for a phone-based health-related survey. The interview was conducted with the first person to answer the phone who was eighteen or older. The average age of respondents was forty-eight, and most (51 percent) fell in the middle-class socioeconomic stratum, reporting an annual household income between $50,000 and $150,000. Their responses to our survey questions, which we published in 2006, were surprising. They suggested that 4 percent to 14 percent of the general population showed evidence of problematic Internet use. More specifically,

- 4 percent said they were preoccupied with the Internet when they were offline;
- 6 percent said their personal relationships suffered as a consequence of their Internet use;
- 6 percent regularly went online to escape negative moods;
- 9 percent felt they had to hide their Internet use;
- 11 percent regularly stayed online for longer than they intended; and,
- 14 percent had a hard time staying offline for days in a row.

Two comments should be made about the results: Our figures would have been higher if we had included cellular phone numbers, because a significant proportion of heavy Internet users may no longer use landlines. Also, the fact that many red flags were found in a study where the average age of participants was forty-eight (as opposed to eighteen or twenty-eight) suggested how widespread problematic Internet use might be in the general population. Twentysomething "Sili Valley" techies may have sparked the Internet revolution, but our study indicated that people of all ages and in all geographic locales seem to be experiencing some negative consequence of virtual life.

Not everyone was equally struck by our data. When we submitted the study to a leading psychiatric journal for publication, we felt relatively optimistic that the survey—the largest at the time to assess the effects of the Internet on people's lives—would get a positive response from the editorial board. That was hardly the case. The anonymous peer reviewer, interpreting our work as advocacy for a new psychiatric diagnosis that he or she clearly did not believe in, saw little value in disseminating our work. "What next? Microwave abuse and ChapStick addiction?" the reviewer snipped, in a written rejection. "Do Not Publish" was the journal's non-negotiable decision. Fortunately, the anonymous reviewers and editorial board of *CNS Spectrums*, another widely read psychiatric journal to which we submitted our manuscript next, seemed rather taken by the study, since they proceeded to quickly accept and publish it, with few revisions.

These difficult to reconcile responses reflect the controversy surrounding Internet addiction as a clinical concept today and the strong feelings it generates. Opponents of the inclusion of Internet addiction in the next edition of the *DSM* (*DSM-V*) often make the point that it is not the Internet itself that is addictive, but the experiences that it makes available to a previously unimaginable degree. Dr. Michael Craig Miller of the *Harvard Mental Health Letter* summarized this position eloquently in a 2007 editorial. "The Internet is the equivalent of an electronic needle," he wrote, "a potent and efficient delivery system that provides ready access to a wide range of rewards and pleasures. Shopping, gambling and pornography can be infused directly and in high doses from the Internet, anywhere and any time." One does not get addicted to the sensation of being pricked by a needle, the argument goes, but to IV heroin. Target the underlying addiction, then, not the route of administration.

But even if the behavior itself is ancient—and few things can claim to be more ancient than sex or even gambling and buying—the Internet confers on it new qualities like anonymity, virtual connectedness, omnipotence, and the possibility of personal reinvention. Together, these can transform a well-worn activity into a novel one. As we have seen, many people are not simply "shopping" online; they are channeling William Randolph Hearst or Princess Diana. Gambling, they may feel the confidence of Minnesota Fats. Sex, negotiated online, is for some a more thrilling experience than its offline counterpart. This can help explain how someone might get hooked only on online gambling and shopping (as my patients Richard and Liz from chapter 1 did) but not be particularly moved by a real-life casino or the sight of a sale sign in a store window. Saying that the Internet is simply a needle that is passively delivering a dose of something else underestimates it. For many people, the Internet *is* the dose.

The fact that, to date, research has not found a biological cause for Internet addiction strengthens the position of those who question the validity of an Internet addiction diagnosis. For example, imaging studies that consistently show abnormal activity in part of the Internet addict's brain, or genetic studies that show the problem clustering among blood relatives, are lacking. Such data, if available, might convince many skeptics, fast-tracking problematic Internet use into the *DSM*. But the data are not available. (The brain imaging information presented earlier focused on virtual games, not Facebookers or other, more "classic," Internet addicts. Although this information points to altered brain activity among players and suggests that similar changes may be present in other types of virtual world abuse, it is not incontrovertible proof of pathology.)

Also, studies, ours included, that tried to assess the prevalence of

Internet addiction did not rule out other conditions that might better explain online habits. Is someone who is recklessly spending money online, like Liz was, doing so because she has bipolar disorder (sometimes called manic depressive illness), one of the cardinal symptoms of mania being prodigious buying? That was not the case for her, but Alex and Jill did drop out of real life and "become" someone very different in large part because of debilitating social anxiety. That is why it would be a mistake to simply call such people Internet addicts. Yet studies (and media stories) often make the mistake of labeling "Internet addiction" something that is clearly the downstream effect of something else.

Besides separating Internet addiction from established diagnoses like social anxiety disorder and bipolar disorder, we have the challenge of separating it from other electronic addictions—yes, this is as much about Xbox, Wii, and BlackBerry addicts as it is about superbloggers. Are these novel "addictions" different from one another in whom they strike, how costly they are to the individual, and how treatable they may be, or are they part of one big digital addiction overtaking our culture? And is it possible to dissect the various components anymore, when the iPhone has become an all-encompassing magic wand, incorporating within its sleek contours our browser, personal digital assistant, music source, and game console? The result of all this is a confusing diagnostic picture, where it is hard to understand where one putative new pathology begins and another one ends. (Some researchers have wisely stopped using "Internet addiction" or other Internet-specific designations altogether, opting for labels like "pathological use of electronic media" instead.) The diffuse nature of the problem might prove too much for *DSM* committee members who are entrusted with categorizing human psychopathology in discrete, relatively closed boxes.

Finally, part of the resistance to a formal Internet addiction diagnosis is psychiatry's sometimes problematic history of pathologizing human behaviors simply because they are different. Homosexuality, for instance, was until 1973 a *DSM*-certified psychiatric illness, likely *causing* clinical depression and other genuine *DSM* disorders in a generation of gay individuals by so thoroughly invalidating them. It is a good lesson to have learned, then, not to coin a new diagnosis if in doubt. When it comes to the *DSM*, an error of omission is better than an error of commission.

Together, these factors make a "no" vote by the *DSM-V* committee on adding Internet addiction to its list of sanctioned diagnoses quite conceivable. But for mental health professionals who take the opposite view, Internet addiction clearly satisfies the *DSM*'s overarching definition of a mental disorder as a "clinically significant behavioral or psychological syndrome . . . that is associated with present distress . . . or with a significantly increased risk of suffering death, pain, disability, or an important loss of freedom." In arguing that Internet addiction is such a syndrome, they draw parallels with well-accepted DSM disorders, especially OCD, substance addiction, and impulse control disorders. They say that Internet addicts, like OCD patients, have intrusive, recurrent urges to use the Internet—the obsession equivalent. Once in cyberspace, they often behave in ritualized ways, repetitively cycling among their Gmail account, MySpace Web page, and favorite blogs, often in preset patterns—the compulsion equivalent. (According to the online measurement service Hitwise, most surfers head to Google immediately after they leave Twitter, with Facebook the second most popular destination. This indicates some degree of patterned, ritualized movement in cyberspace.)

Like OCD, substance addiction has a place in the *DSM*, although the *DSM* avoids the term *addiction*, preferring *abuse* and *dependence* instead. Comparisons between Internet and substance addiction are based on two states—tolerance and withdrawal—familiar to individuals addicted to alcohol and drugs, and seen in some Internet users as well. Tolerance refers to needing more and more of the fix, be it Oxycontin or YouTube, to achieve the same level of "high." In discussing his own tolerance to the Internet, and how purposeless Web surfing was eating up an ever larger chunk of his day, a patient recently shared with me the story of a thirty-year-old man who died in the Chinese city of Guangzhou, apparently from a continuous three-day Internet binge at a cybercafé. "I guess you can say the guy overdosed on the Internet," my patient said, only half-jokingly. He could relate, to some degree. He knew how difficult it can be to sever one's Internet connection. When he tried to do it, or when his server would fail without forewarning, he experienced significant "withdrawal," a state of heightened anxiety and physical restlessness familiar to heavy smokers who try to quit cold turkey. Just as one can be addicted to a substance, the argument goes, one can be addicted to a behavior, even if the behavior is Web surfing, and just as alcohol dependence is, and deserves to be, in the *DSM*, so, too, should being dependent on the Internet.

A third comparison that supporters of an Internet addiction diagnosis make is with impulse control disorders. As we saw in chapter 1 and in the discussion of compulsive shopping and pathological gambling in the last chapter, these conditions have in common a difficult-to-resist urge to perform a behavior that is highly rewarding in the moment but that leads to long-term guilt and distress. My patient Liz felt helplessly drawn to a fun online experience that rewarded her with an immediate thrill every time she clicked the "add to my cart" button. Richard, who developed an online gambling habit, felt similarly thrilled in the short term, and equally devastated over the long term. Although neither had an impulse control problem before going online, the series of short-lived online thrills that were followed by relationship difficulties, depression, and bankruptcy is a sad scenario they share with individuals who have real-life impulse control disorders.

Based on the similarities with impulse control disorders, substance addiction, and OCD, researchers have developed screening questionnaires for Internet addiction using criteria for these conditions borrowed from the *DSM*. The most commonly used screening tool was developed by University of Pittsburgh psychologist Kimberly Young. In 1996,

Young was the first to publish a case of "addictive use of the Internet." The patient to launch this chapter in psychiatry, Young's "Sybil," was a "nontechnologically oriented" forty-three-year-old homemaker with a "content home life and no prior addiction or psychiatric history," who later became "addicted to using the Internet" in a way that "resulted in significant impairment to her family life." Based on this and other cases she saw, Young developed the Internet Addiction Test to screen for what she was convinced was a new clinical disorder. The test, available online and adapted, with scoring instructions, in the appendix, is composed of twenty "how-often" questions. Each question is rated on a scale of 1 to 5, and a total score of 80 or above is consistent with what Young has no qualms calling Internet addiction.

There is little doubt that Young's twenty questions can be helpful in screening for Internet-related trouble. Still, a high score on the Internet Addiction Test does not seal the diagnosis. As mentioned earlier, someone can have a high score as a result of another clinical problem, such as severe depression that is keeping the person at home, with no energy, motivation, or desire to do anything but mindlessly surf the Net. Diagnosing this person with Internet addiction could divert attention from a more serious, and treatable, condition. That is why much more work remains to be done to validate these scales statistically—that is, test their accuracy in a large group against the gold standard of a face-to-face interview where other diagnoses can be ruled out. Only then can we be sure that these scales measure what they tell us they are measuring—Internet addiction—and not something else, such as major depression or social anxiety. Unfortunately, the largest study to try to do that was rather unrepresentative: It tested the Chinese Internet Addiction Inventory, a scale similar to Young's, in 1,029 Beijing undergraduates. Its results, therefore, cannot be assumed to apply to Liz, my middle-aged Caucasian homemaker logging on from the suburban United States. (Dr. Ran Tao, the principle author of the study, lists his affiliation as the Medical Center for Internet Addiction, General Hospital of Beijing Military Command; more on militaristic and other approaches to treating Internet addiction later.) The validity of Young's scale was tested in an even more limited sample—86 volunteers.

Because of the controversy surrounding Internet addiction, and because of the limited studies conducted to date, there is still much debate over where patients like Liz and Richard might fit in the *DSM*, which, at 943 pages in its fourth revision, still has no category for prob lematic human-machine interactions, including problematic Internet use. In an e-mail exchange, Dr. William E. Narrow, of the *DSM-V* Task Force, told me that Internet addiction "will be considered" for inclusion, given the rising "public concern in the U.S. and other countries." It is far from certain, however, that consideration will lead to formal acceptance into the next DSM, scheduled to appear in 2012.

But even for mental health professionals who believe, as I do, that the virtual world can lead to psychopathology in otherwise healthy individuals, some cases we see or read about can challenge that belief. These cases remind us of the far-reaching consequences of medicalizing Internet-related problems and make us want the *DSM-V* gatekeepers to take all the time they need before allowing Internet addition in. Aaron, a thirty-two-year-old software engineer I saw in my clinic, did not ask for my help logging off Second Life, although he found himself lingering on the site at the office for hours at a time until he got fired. Instead, Aaron wanted me to appear in court on his behalf as he contested his termination on medical grounds. Aaron's argument was that he had a psychiatric illness that required treatment and should be covered by his insurance plan as a legitimate disability. Aaron's basis for his provocative argument? Our study!

Aaron is not alone. The media and research focus on Internet addiction has contributed to a new crop of legal cases in which "patients" are suing to reverse the negative consequences, especially termination from work, that are brought about by their "symptoms." In perhaps the most storied case, James Pacenza, 59, a man from Montgomery, New York, was fired by IBM in 2003 for continuing to visit adult chat rooms at work despite having been reprimanded about the behavior. In response, Pacenza sued IBM for $5 million, claiming he was an Internet addict whose diagnosis was protected by the Americans with Disabilities Act. Pacenza attributed his Internet condition to seeing his best friend die in Vietnam in 1969—a tragedy that left him with severe post-traumatic stress disorder (PTSD), from which, apparently, only pornographic online chat rooms could provide relief. "I felt I needed the interactive engagement of chat talk to divert my attention from my thoughts of Vietnam and death," he told the Associated Press. IBM should have offered him sympathy and treatment, he contended, not fire him. After all, his lawyer said, IBM workers who have a drug or alcohol problem are routinely referred to specialized programs for help and rehabilitation, and a decorated Vietnam veteran in the throes of a double-attack of PTSD and Internet addiction deserved at least as much. The case is ongoing, and a judgment could affect how employers regulate non-work-related Internet use.

As the jurors would have undoubtedly realized if the case had gone to trial, it is sometimes a fine line between being legitimately ill and illegitimately abusing a difficult to prove and controversial illness for personal gain. While Internet addiction might become an officially recognized condition, cases like these underscore the desperate need for much more research (and public research dollars) to study this problem. Real consequences—disability protection, insurance coverage, research fund allocation, among others—are attached to elevating a psychological problem to the ranks of a *DSM* diagnosis. But as our profession and society at large continue to debate the merits of such elevation, the Internet and other electronic media are increasingly being blamed for derailing people's professional and personal lives, and Aaron's and Mr. Pacenza's line of thinking is increasingly being voiced in courtrooms across the country.

If Aaron did indeed suffer from Internet addiction, and if a judge ruled that IBM should offer Mr. Pacenza help, what treatment options would be available for them? Few, unfortunately, that have been scientifically shown to work. But in view of the similarities with other conditions, doctors and therapists often adapt treatments used to address OCD, substance addiction, and impulse control disorders. These include Prozac-like drugs that enhance serotonin levels in the brain and that have been proven to work in OCD; twelve step programs like Alcoholics Anonymous (AA); and new applications of cognitive-behavioral therapy. Such relatively old tools, however, can feel painfully rudimentary when used with a patient who is barely present in your office because of various preoccupations with the virtual misadventures of his virtual persona, or who is asking permission to check his MySpace account on your office computer, as a college freshman I recently evaluated wanted to do. "It's like using the old concept of the four humors to treat physical illness today," a colleague recently told me. He runs a busy practice located in Silicon Valley, somewhere on the axis between Facebook's old and new headquarters, and sees a large number of individuals who are overwired and suffering from it. "Health was seen as a balance of the four 'humors'—black bile, yellow bile, phlegm, and blood," he explained. "Too much blood, and you have a headache. No one, today, is advocating bloodletting as a treatment for migraines, but they want us to give Prozac to treat Second Lifers!"

Old tools would be acceptable if they worked, but studies have yet to show that they do. The first well-designed medication trial in problematic Internet use failed to show clear superiority for Lexapro, a serotonin-enhancing drug in the Prozac family, over placebo. The study was conducted by Dr. Eric Hollander's research group, and published in 2008 in the *Journal of Clinical Psychiatry*. Nineteen volunteers (seven women and twelve men) with problematic Internet use were enrolled. Their average age was thirty-eight, and, at the beginning of the study, they spent an average of 36.8 hours per week online. Their excessive online activities spanned different categories of Internet use, including e-mail, online dating, information searching, pornography, and gambling. They were diagnosed with problematic Internet use because they saw their online habit as "time-consuming," "uncontrollable," and "distressing," as well as a source of social, professional, and financial difficulties. Based on a comprehensive interview with the study doctors, no other psychiatric condition could be blamed for the subjects' symptoms.

The study began with an "open-label" phase in which all nineteen participants received Lexapro. After ten weeks of taking the medication, subjects had a significant drop in the amount of time they spent online—down to an average of 16.5 hours per week, from 36.8 at the beginning of the study. Study subjects were then blindly randomized to either continue their treatment with Lexapro for another nine weeks or be switched to placebo. Beyond that point, neither doctor nor subject knew who was taking what. Following the nine-week double-blind phase, the study was unblinded, revealing interesting results: The group that had been switched to placebo did just as well as the group that was kept on Lexapro (16.1 online hours per week, compared to 15.9). In other words, there was no advantage for drug over placebo in maintaining the response seen in the first phase. For the study authors to be able to make a stronger argument in favor of using a Prozac-like medication in patients with problematic Internet use, they would have had to see significantly higher relapse rates in subjects who were switched to placebo, compared to those who were continued on the active drug, but that was not the case.

It might be that because of all the deeper issues highlighted so far in the book, Internet addiction is more complex than OCD, a condition that several double-blind studies have shown to respond rather well to serotonin-enhancing drugs. More than an empty or automatic ritual, which is what doctors might see in a patient with OCD, Internet addiction is also about an interaction with a machine that engages us by acting directly on the various parts that make us who we are—our dreams and frustrations, and our need for information, entertainment, titillation, and an alternative scenario of being. The Internet stirs these components up in a parallel, unreal universe, adds a couple of as yet unknown ingredients, then ejects a new, somewhat independent personality that might be less accessible to Prozac than the excessive hand washing of someone with "plain" OCD.

Rigorous studies have also yet to prove the efficacy of AA-style programs. Still, twelve-step interventions are sometimes used, with one important modification. Unlike the complete abstinence vow often required of AA members, moderated and "dosed" use may be the more appropriate expectation when it comes to treating Internet addiction. Computers have become an indispensable part of normal, everyday life, and it would be unreasonable for us to expect people to sever the umbilical cord. (With the godlike attributes some people take on in cyberspace, the surrender to a higher power advocated in traditional AA models might present its own interesting challenges.)

A third treatment strategy, and one that has received much media coverage, is the boot camp–style rehab option gaining popularity, especially in Asian countries. South Korea boasts of being the most wired nation on the planet, with at-home high-speed access approaching 90 percent of households. As the *New York Times*'s Martin Fackler described it, in a 2007 article, "online gaming is a professional sport, and social life for the young revolves around the 'PC Bang,' dim Internet parlors that sit on practically every street corner." Given the culture's focus on discipline, education, and achievement, when young people started skipping school in large numbers to stay online, with some dropping dead out of sheer exhaustion from marathon sessions of virtual games, the situation was viewed as a national threat akin to Kim Jong-il up north. The government's response was swift and aggressive: It opened an extensive network of Internet addiction outpatient clinics, hospital-based programs, and, for the more treatment-refractory, intensive boot camps with names like Jump Up Internet Rescue School. One addict profiled in the *Times* piece could easily have been taken from my practice:

Lee Chang-hoon, 15, began using the computer to pass the time while his parents were working and he was home alone. He said he quickly came to prefer the virtual world, where he seemed to enjoy more success and popularity than in the real one.

He spent 17 hours a day online, mostly looking at Japanese comics and playing a combat role-playing game called Sudden Attack. He played all night, and skipped school two or three times a week to catch up on sleep.

When his parents told him he had to go to school, he reacted violently. Desperate, his mother, Kim Soon-yeol, sent him to the camp.

"He didn't seem to be able to control himself," said Mrs. Kim, a hairdresser. "He used to be so passionate about his favorite subjects" at school. "Now, he gives up easily and gets even more absorbed in his games."

Her son was reluctant at first to give up his pastime.

"I don't have a problem," Chang-hoon said in an interview three days after starting the camp. "Seventeen hours a day online is fine."

Located in a forested area an hour south of Seoul, Jump Up's curriculum consists of drill instructors driving young men through military-style obstacle courses, horseback riding, and group activities aimed at strengthening the bonds with the real world and weakening those with the virtual one. Participants are denied any digital access, except for one hour of cell phone calls daily. Knowing that Chang-hoon was spending at least seventeen hours a day online, one can only imagine how uncomfortable his withdrawal symptoms must have been.

The efficacy of these grueling, baptism-by-fire types of interventions has not been independently assessed in well-designed studies. One would need at least that level of scientific scrutiny to recommend them to patients and to begin justifying suspending a person's rights, since it is questionable whether patients in some of these programs are truly there voluntarily. One also needs such evidence to explain charging desperate parents $1,200 a month to cure their child, as some camps in China do. Instead, the advertised success rates of Internet boot camps are based largely on what the camp masters tell us they are. Dr. Ran Tao, the research psychologist who worked on the Chinese Internet Addiction Inventory, runs a camp on a military base outside Beijing—one of over three hundred in the country. He claims a remarkable 70 percent cure rate for his treatment. Part of the therapy he offers is a game with toy guns, aimed to wean youngsters off World of Warcraft by encouraging a real-life substitute. At least he seems to take a more gradual approach.

Most therapists I know who treat Internet addicts employ toyless cognitive-behavioral therapy. As discussed in the first chapter, CBT tries to correct faulty assumptions people make about situations, such as the common belief among Internet addicts that online friendships are a good substitute for real-life ones. As patients confront their thoughts, they are encouraged to replace problematic online behaviors such as prolonged unnecessary surfing with healthier pursuits, often with the help of relaxation tools. Cognitive-behavioral therapy is the only form of psychotherapy to have been scientifically examined in Internet addiction, although, once again, only in a rather limited number of studies. The largest was conducted by Dr. Kimberly Young and published in the journal *CyberPsychology and Behavior* in 2007. Subjects (sixty-six men and forty-eight women) who met the Internet Addiction Test criteria for the diagnosis were enrolled in a CBT program. The average age was thirty-eight for men and forty-six for women. Overall, 96 percent reported significant time management problems because of excessive Internet use; 85 percent cited negative relationship repercussions; and 75 percent reported sexual problems—specifically, favoring online pornography or sex-based chat rooms over sexual relationships with their offline partners.

The weekly CBT sessions consisted of asking subjects to keep a detailed log of their cyberspace whereabouts in order to help them better understand the nature and scope of their Internet problem. Researchers taught them more efficient time management and coping skills, and confronted the rationalizations they used to justify their time online, such as "Just a few more minutes won't hurt." Using this intervention, Young reported that most subjects achieved effective control of their symptoms by the eighth session, and that their gains were sustained over at least a six-month follow-up period. While far from definitive, this study suggests that CBT can be a helpful tool in managing Internet addiction. It also provides an opportunity to discuss an interesting paradox that a self-diagnosed Internet addict faces when he or she types "Internet addiction treatment" in the Google box, and sifts through the search results looking for a cure.

Sooner or later, an embedded link will lead the person to a treatment for Internet addiction, conducted virtually, online. Like most things, the traditional practice of CBT is being challenged by a movement to outsource it—where else—to cyberspace. The long-held belief that improvement in psychotherapy requires a supportive relationship with a therapist is being challenged as CBT is replaced by CCBT (computerized CBT). Writing in the *British Journal of Psychiatry* in 2007, Dr. Isaac Marks, of London's King's College, defines CCBT as "any computing system that aids cognitive behavioral therapy by using patient input to make at least some computations and treatment decisions." He cites ninety-seven English-language computer-aided psychotherapy programs, whose delivery methods include the Internet, "virtual reality devices," DVDs, and personal digital assistants.

The advantages that Dr. Marks and other CCBT enthusiasts see in computerizing psychotherapy include wider access to treatment in geographic locations usually underserved by therapists; 24/7 availability, including at times when therapists prefer not to work; reduction in the cost of therapy; and the notion that computers are more likely to deliver reproducible, consistent treatment, and are less likely than human therapists to err away from a standardized intervention that has been shown to work. Their argument received a big boost in 2007, when the

British National Institute for Clinical Excellence recommended that the National Health System offer two CCBT programs: Beating the Blues, for depression; and FearFighter, for panic disorder and anxiety.

Fearing that their profession will go the way of travel agents, and concerned about the kind of support a computer is capable of delivering, traditional therapists are mounting a spirited defense of nondigital, face-to-face, human-to-human therapy. But the economic and access pressures are such that time may well be on Dr. Marks's and the computer's side. Writing for *Impulse Control Disorders*, the book that I coedited with Dr. Lorrin Koran, Dr. John Greist, a University of Wisconsin psychiatrist who has developed several CCBT programs, evokes Max Planck's maxim when predicting the future landscape of therapy: "A new scientific truth does not triumph by convincing its opponents and making them see the light, but rather because its opponents eventually die and a new generation grows up that is familiar with it." In his view, then, the next generation of fully wired mental health professionals and mentally ill patients might think it most natural for someone with OCD to log on for a cure.

There would be nothing inherently wrong about that. In my experience, some patients do benefit from Beating the Blues and FearFighter, and from CBT-inspired Web programs like those available at stopping overshopping.com, stoppicking.com (helps compulsive skin pickers for "a dollar a day"), and, in all seriousness, ucanpooptoo.com (treats children with encopresis, or fecal soiling). A patient I see swears by Flying without Fear, an app for iPhone and iPod available to download from Virgin Atlantic. One push of the "fear attack" button, and you have breathing exercises, relaxation tips, and soothing mantras at your fingertips. It is much more doubtful, however, that the Internet addiction treatments now proliferating online work as well. Programs that invite the Internet addict to linger longer in cyberspace remain inherently flawed—there is something fundamentally wrong in telling someone to "Click here if you are addicted to the Internet." The ancients, at least, knew to give you a purgative if they suspected a harmful surplus of phlegm. We, on the other hand, will sometimes treat excess with excess.

The virtual world is making us prone to a new addiction. Like many other addictions before it, this one's definition is controversial, and accepting it implies having to assume social consequences that are uncomfortable, provocative, and expensive. Also, like many other addictions, its cure has proven to be elusive so far.

Still, the focus on defining and treating Internet addiction should not take attention from the more subtle ways in which the Internet affects the psychology of the nonaddicts among us. We will likely not meet Young's or anyone's criteria for Internet addiction if we spend only two hours a day online and have not failed in school, been reprimanded at work, or gotten a divorce because of it. But this does not mean that aspects of our psychology have not been affected by the Internet and that the fractures we have talked about are irrelevant to us. What people have called Internet addiction represents an extreme on a spectrum. It is worthy of vigorous debate, media attention, and much more research investigation, but not at the expense of the rest of the spectrum, and not if the rest of us end up feeling deceptively immune.

_CHAPTER 10

THE END OF PRIVACY

"I'M RELIEVED you don't look anything like a mouse," my new patient said on first meeting me. After an awkward exchange in which I tried to clarify why he would assume such a thing about his new doctor—was he being disrespectful or was he being psychotic?—it became clear that Tim had Googled my "image," a feature of the search engine I had been previously (and blissfully) unaware of. Unfortunately, the only picture that came up for him was that of a mouse—a computer mouse. It took some investigating, but I later came to understand that because of the media attention our Internet study had received, my name had become linked to pictures that accompanied the various articles that mentioned it. Since most of those articles were written by people who did not interview—let alone photograph—me, the accompanying illustrations were pictures of keyboards, laptops, and, apparently, a computer mouse.

This encounter drove me to perform my first online search of myself. The results included quoted statements I made in languages I do not speak, my office and home phone numbers, the address and satellite pictures of my newly purchased house, my medical license number, reviews of my bedside manner by unidentified supposed patients, and still and video images of me, along with the mouse picture. The effect of this seemingly simple search can best be described as denuding. The search highlighted, more dramatically for me than ever before, a critical side effect of the Internet revolution: the impossibility of privacy in the online age, and the psychological consequences of living in a post-privacy world. While most of us have Googled someone's name prior to meeting them, either to reduce the anxiety of interacting with a stranger or out of simple curiosity, the fact that much of our private information can now be found online can have repercussions for our psychological well-being. Put simply, I believe that for the sake of our mental health, we all need a small inviolate zone around our person and that such a zone has become virtually impossible.

From Margaret Mahler to Erik Erikson to Carl Jung, all the great thinkers in the field of human development have highlighted the importance of *individuation*, a process by which a person reaches psychological maturity and forges an independent identity through achieving a healthy separateness and distinction from others. It represents the individual outgrowing a state of dependency and need, and gradually gaining mastery over his internal and external worlds. For famed child psychoanalyst Margaret Mahler, because the limits between self and caregiver have not been established yet, the infant in the earliest phases of development perceives the mother as part of his self-experience (most developmentalists concerned themselves primarily with the male infant and generalized their theories from there). The baby and the mother are merged in one symbiotic whole, and distinct boundaries between "self" and "other" are lacking. The infant is confused by his dependence on an entity that is both an outsider and a part of him, and anxious about losing the mother. As he becomes more aware and more physically capable, his no-mean-feat task is to succeed at the "separation/individuation" test— a goal that, if reached, will result in the child's having a portable image of Mom that he can carry within him and that can continue to soothe and comfort him even as he moves further and further in the direction of physical and psychological autonomy. A developmental milestone, then, individuation implies the ability to feel comfortable in one's own skin without the constant presence and support of nurturers. In the case of the growing child, it means the ability to tolerate the anxiety born out of the mother's (or the caregiver's) temporary absence.

Although we are first faced with this challenge at the dawn of life, being able to individuate and feel contentedly independent is a lifelong quest. In the context of an adult couple, for example, it means being a less clingy, "codependent" spouse. Developmental psychologist Erik Erikson places individuation firmly ahead of social or romantic success as a barometer of health. To some degree, he deemphasizes social interactions and relationships in general, saying that mature involvement with another person can happen only if one has attained self-identity—if one is comfortably autonomous and happy in his relationship with himself. One can be a "good" child, parent, or spouse only to the extent that one can tolerate being alone, and not feel too anxious or disoriented by the experience. "True engagement with the other is the result and test of firm self-delineation," he writes.

Writing before Mahler and Erikson, Carl Jung, the great Swiss psychoanalyst and one-time Freud competitor, seemed to be saying something similar. He saw individuation as the person's fortress against the sometimes crushing weight of group mentality and group demands. For him, it is at least as important to be oneself—that is, to be separate—as it is to belong:

> Individuation is, in general, the process by which individual beings are formed and differentiated; in particular, it is the development of the psychological individual as a being distinct from the general, collective psychology. . . . [It] is a natural necessity inasmuch as its prevention by leveling down to collective standards is injurious to the vital activity of the individual.

According to various schools of development, then, that "vital activity of the individual," and the one from which other important functions stem, is to become an individual. This crucial goal assumes certain safe-guards that protect one's privacy. You are a psychologically autonomous individual if you have the option to keep your personhood to yourself and dole out the pieces as you see fit, enjoying the process of sharing them with people you think are worthy and with whom you want to form a special bond.

And you don't have to be a developmentalist to agree. "Privacy is partly a form of self-possession," writes novelist and technology writer Lew McCreary, in the *Harvard Business Review*. You don't truly possess your "self" if you don't have "custody of the facts of [your] life, from strings of digits to tastes and preferences." However, with so much of our "facts" now readily available online for anyone to consult, con-trol over our personal business has become a chimeric goal. This can threaten our self-possession and make true autonomy a moribund con-cept from a bygone era. (McCreary provocatively titled his essay "What *Was* Privacy?" Emphasis mine.) Today, parents regularly invade their children's MySpace accounts (often for good reason); children often read their parents' e-mail (my eight-year-old niece easily figured out that her nickname is her mother's Hotmail password); our genealogy is public knowledge—just bring up your family tree on Ancestry.com; blind dates are no longer blind, because they involve the requisite pre-date Google search; and your boss has access to, and could be read-ing, everything that goes through your server at work. From school to work to extended family, everybody is, or everybody can easily be, in everybody else's business. It is like development in reverse. We live in an increasingly incestuous—I use the word elastically—world, when psy-choanalysts warned us for decades about the apocalyptic consequences of incestuous tangles. This should give us serious pause, even if we think of psychoanalysis itself as moribund.

Consider the ever loosening Facebook definition of "friend." Just between December 2008 and March 2009, the average number of friends per Facebook member grew from 100 to 120. Has humanity suddenly grown more congenial? No, but it might have grown more incestuous. It is common on Facebook for a person to be "friending" his or her boss, mother, current love interest, an ex or two, a real-life best friend, several acquaintances, and several acquaintances' acquaintances. In 2009, Silicon Valley author Randall Stross wrote an article titled "When Everyone's a Friend, Is Anything Private?" Stross had this to say about people's promiscuous friending patterns on the site:

> Among members, a Law of Amiable Inclusiveness seems to be revealing itself: over time, many are deciding that the easiest path is to routinely accept "friend requests," completing a sequence begun when one member seeks to designate another as a Facebook friend. In other words, they are defining "friend" simply as any Facebook member who communicates a wish to be one. . . . When the distinction blurs between one's few close friends and the many who are not, it seems pointless to distinguish between public and private.

The phenomenon is so widespread and unregulated that the *New York Times* felt the need to publish some ground rules on "How to Friend Mom, Dad, and the Boss on Facebook . . . Safely." Here is how Sarah Perez opened the piece: "Oh no! Your mom joined Facebook and what's even worse, she wants to be your friend." The problem Perez and Stross seem concerned about is the "benefits" that a Facebook friendship comes with, not the least of which is unfettered access to much of the friend's life.

People often bare it all on Facebook, across family generations, professional hierarchies, and social circles. While the site does offer a feature called Friend Lists, which allows you to segregate friends as a function of the kind of access you want to give them, very few people take advantage of it. It is possible, for example, to interact in a no-holds-barred way with only a certain category of friend, like your current or former fraternity or sorority siblings, and with more self-consciousness and restraint when it comes to other friends, like your boss and office colleagues. Facebook does allow multiple online identities, if you will, per member per account, but this feature remains highly underutilized, maybe because the process is rather daunting-looking, at least to this novice Facebooker. Still, it behooves us to customize access permissions by serial-clicking through the multiple drop-down menus: "It may seem like quite a bit of work to set up, but you'll thank yourself for doing this later . . . like every Monday morning when you go back to work after a *great* weekend . . . or the next time you need to borrow money from mom and dad," Perez writes. "You get the idea. Better safe than sorry."

Another "benefit" to friendship that Stross warns about is a benefit to Facebook itself and to its third-party businesses partners. "An application installed by a friend can vacuum up and store many categories of a member's personal information." In other words, software used by one of my Facebook friends can be storing my information, to be used by the software company down the road. In fact, the default setting that Facebook assigns to fifteen of nineteen information categories in people's profiles is "Share." Shared categories include "activities," "interests," "pictures," and "relationship status"—all of which can be pulled from Facebook accounts and stored on servers outside its control. This encourages the polymorphous spread of personal information among members but also outsiders. Again, as with the Friend Lists, heightened privacy options exist for members to try to limit the sharing, but few people go through the trouble of adjusting the all-important default settings. How few? Only about 20 percent of members, according to Facebook's Chief Privacy Officer. (The title itself is a by-product of the Internet age, first used in 1999 by AllAdvantage, the start-up that coined the phrase "Get paid to surf the Web," then died a violent death in the 2001 crash.) The remaining 80 percent are not aware of the privacy-enhancing features that Facebook offers, find them too cumbersome, or, worse yet, do not mind being an open e-book, browsable by friend, "friend," and foe alike.

Or maybe they agree with Sun Microsystems cofounder Scott McNealy, who, as early as 1999, was quoted in *Wired* saying, "You have zero privacy anyway. Get over it." Sadly, his insensitive remark now seems prescient. We are inching closer to an Orwellian vision of the world, where our tastes, relationships, and pinpoint GPS locations are public knowledge to whomever is manning the server. As someone once jokingly told me, it's Facebook's world; we just update our status in it.

This overexposed state of being became more apparent in February 2009, when Facebook moved to assert its ownership of its members' information. It updated its terms of use—its governing document—hiding behind obtuse legalese to essentially delete a provision that had said that users could remove their personal content at any time. The change was interpreted to mean: "Anything you upload to Facebook can be used by Facebook in any way the company deems fit, forever, no matter what you do later," and "Facebook owns you." The move to control members' data, with its marketing gold mine of name, sex, age, marital status, and favorite brands of beer and lipstick, sparked an uproar that eventually led Facebook to reverse its decision. Their pattern, however, suggests that they might try again: Already in 2007, a tracking tool called Beacon caught members off-guard by broadcasting to their Facebook friends information about their shopping and other activities on other Web sites—something like "Your friend so and so just saved two recipes on Epicurious; come find out what you've been missing" (not an actual example). After a torrent of complaints, Facebook offered an opt-out option.

They seem to want to own us, and it's hardly an equal fight. Still, we cannot afford to "just get over it" as McNealy suggested, for nothing short of our self-custody seems to be at stake. This is about much more than a passing curiosity about a recipe. At its heart, this is about our psychological autonomy and the maintenance of some semblance of control over the various little details that make us.

But if being stunted in our lifelong challenge to individuate by profit-driven corporations is too abstract a concept, much more practical reasons exist for why it is generally a good strategy to say less than more online:

- According to a 2006 survey of 100 executive recruiters by the search firm ExecuNet, 77 percent routinely run Web searches to screen applicants, and 35 percent have eliminated a candidate based on information uncovered online (one firm said it disqualified an otherwise highly competent candidate because her sex somewhere online was listed as "yes, please").
- According to a 2008 survey of 453 admissions departments by the University of Massachusetts, 26 percent use search engines to research potential students, and 21 percent use social networking sites like Facebook and MySpace.
- According to 2006 data from the Pew Internet and American Life Project, 53 percent of American adults use search engines on a "social" basis to find information about each other.

A majority of us act as though we are not very concerned about the neighbor, admissions committee, or boss learning what we do for fun. We tweet our whereabouts, post our family pictures, blog our politics, and discuss in considerable detail our favorite and least favorite things. "TMI"—for "Stop! Too Much Information already"—is an acronym that is increasingly popular in our everyday vernacular but does not seem to apply in the virtual world. The problem is that people may judge us based largely on the information we make public on the Web. They may assume that, in the real world, we are the same as the "yes, please" persona of our online profile and, because of this misconception, may decide not to befriend us offline, give us a job, or welcome us into the incoming class. Yet given the gap that often exists between e-personality and what people are "really" like, those decisions can be unjustified.

The two domains of Web life where many of us verbalize more caution are personal finances and health care. Yet our behaviors do not always match the anxiety we express. Almost all respondents to the 2008 Digital Future Project reported concerns about financial identity theft and credit card information being stolen during an online transaction. However, as we have seen, this is hardly a meaningful obstacle when the online impulse to buy or bid overtakes a person. People also say they worry about the health coverage implications of having a public online life. In fall 2007, Microsoft unveiled HealthVault.com, a "free Web-based platform that enables patients to collect, store, and share health information with hospitals and physicians—using enhanced security and privacy measures—in ways that can help healthcare providers increase efficiency, reduce errors, and improve care." Note the Web site's name and language, designed to preempt obvious concerns about sensitive medical data remaining private. In fact, according to a 2005 nationwide study of 2,100 adults from the California Healthcare Foundation, 13 percent of consumers practice what some researchers call "privacy-protective health behaviors," including: declining diagnostic tests for fear of other people learning the results; asking a doctor not to record a diagnosis or to record a less serious or embarrassing one; and paying out of pocket rather than submitting a claim for a test, procedure, or counseling. Still, the immense popularity of such processes as the RealAge test makes one think we are not privacy-protective nearly enough.

RealAge claims to promote healthier living through nonmedical solutions. So far, nearly thirty million people have taken the online quiz, which consists of about 140 questions that dissect in great detail one's habits, medical history, and family and relationship background. Slightly modified sample questions include: What is your resting heart rate? Do you take vitamin supplements? How many servings of red meat do you eat per week? Have you ever had a sunburn that caused blistering? and How many close friends and relatives do you have, including your spouse and children? At the end of the exhaustive interrogation, one is assigned a "biological age," dictated not by years on the planet but by lifestyle.

The optimistic, Benjamin Button–like message RealAge sells is that, with the help of the "personalized" recommendations that the site makes based on your honest test answers, you can, indeed, grow younger.

Because test takers are very invested in knowing their "RealAge" and in unlocking the secrets of aging in reverse as customized for their own lifestyle, they are motivated to be as truthful as possible in answering the questions. The scandal to focus on here is not the claim that someone may have found the elixir of youth—that is hardly news. Rather, it is that the very specific, highly accurate information that test takers are freely providing is being sold to drug companies (Pfizer, Novartis, and Glaxo-SmithKline, makers of Lipitor, Maalox, and Paxil, respectively, have been listed as customers). The drug companies can then use it to find the perfect audience to whom to market their potions. That takes place in the form of an e-mail that comes from RealAge, usually sponsored by a pharmaceutical company, about a condition that the person might have based on his or her test answers, and that the company happens to sell a product for. Although RealAge does not give personally identifiable information to the drug industry, "leaks," as we will see, can happen. Having our entire health history, medical risk factors, and genetic load in the hands of a profit-driven entity with close ties to Big Pharma might be an invitation for trouble. And that's a realm of online life where we say we're very cautious about what we publish and share.

So how might the privacy-protective, "self"-preserving, 20 percent or so among us be feeling? Even if we diligently close down our old profiles, keep our boss and mother in mind with everything we upload, and never post our pictures, much of our private information is still easily findable. Anyone can locate your address, date of birth, and phone number free of charge on ZabaSearch. For $39.95, the person can get a full "background check" on you, which includes a statewide criminal check, bankruptcies and liens attached to your name, small claims and judgments made against you, your home value, your aliases, your neighbors' and relatives' names, and, if this is not enough bang for his buck already, "much more." Despite our best efforts, there is a surfeit of personal data that anyone can retrieve, and this fact is enough to make some of us suspicious, even paranoid. *Slate*'s Michael Agger describes this state quite well, although his ire is focused on Google, when our paranoia is, or should be, more diffuse and generalized:

> Once you start thinking of Google's potential reach, it's easy to become paranoid. I am presently a happy user of Gmail, Google Calendar, Google Reader, Google Earth, Google Maps, Google Docs, Google Chat, Google Groups, Google Video, and Google Notebook (which I use to clip interesting things online). I also love Google Desktop, which has indexed the contents of my computer. What has Google made of all this information? If they wanted, they could know my friends, my family, my weakness for homemade YouTube soccer highlights. They could know what car I drive, where I drive it to, and where I shop. They definitely know what blogs I read and how often I read them. They took a picture of the building where I live. They just started a 411 service that will give them my voice. They're making me a mobile phone. The attention they've lavished on me would be flattering, if it weren't so vaguely menacing. I'm not alone in this feeling.

With every favorite link we bookmark on our browser or search item we enter into the search engine box, we say something about our preferences, values, and interests. "By Googling, we are supplying the company data with which to parse and analyze us," Agger writes. The culled information can be used to fill in the details of a profile that gradually develops for us. This profile, coupled with our Internet Protocol (IP) address, which locates us geographically, offers unparalleled opportunity to marketers and makes search engines and sites we subscribe to willing to fight to hold on to every last byte of our private data for as long as possible, Terms of Use agreement or not.

The online trail we leave behind follows us offline. Agger reminds us of the supposedly anonymous search logs of 650,000 users, each given a random number, which a well-intentioned AOL released in 2006 as an "academic resource." They included a sad soul, No. 672368, whose searches evolved over several weeks from "you're pregnant he doesn't want the baby" to "foods to eat when pregnant" to "abortion clinics charlotte nc" to "can christians be forgiven for abortion." It is plausible that someone could have identified user No. 672368, just as several other AOL members were identified based on their search logs. A "dog that urinates on everything," for example, turned out to be the unfortunate problem of Thelma Arnold, a sixty-two-year-old widow of Lilburn, Georgia. "My goodness, it's my whole personal life," she exclaimed as the reporters who tracked her down showed her three months' worth of her AOL searches. "I had no idea somebody was looking over my shoulder."

She would be justified in feeling a bit paranoid. One can imagine her being subjected to "target ads" from local veterinarians, online pet pharmacies, or dating services for mature women (her AOL log included a search for "60 single men"). It also included queries about "hand tremors," "nicotine effects on the body," and "bipolar." Should Ms. Arnold want to apply for a private medical insurance plan, and should the plan have access to her online profile, she would probably be automatically ruled out based on three quick assumptions: "She has Parkinson's, a slowly progressing illness that will cost us for years;" "she's going to get heart disease and/or lung cancer—very expensive illnesses;" and "she's psychiatric." In reality, they would be very wrong, because Ms. Arnold suffered from none of these ailments. As she told interviewers, she was simply a curious woman trying to educate herself to better comfort some sick friends. But an insurer considering her application and facing the odds of having to treat her potential maladies would never take her word for it. Another reason to save Medicare and support extending medical health coverage to the uninsured.

However, as we have seen, it is hardly just insurers, Google, or Big

Brother that we have to fear, but simply "the other," because so much of our personal information is readily available to any casual Web surfer. Yahoo! Inc. may plant a sophisticated "cookie" on our computer to better track our comings and goings on the Web, but anyone who uses the yahoo.com search box can still find out too much about us for our own comfort. Realizing the extent of what is out there, and how it can haunt us offline, is enough to suffuse some people's lives with paranoia that extends well beyond the corporations behind the search engines to include anyone who can look us up—that is, everyone. Rob, a patient I saw in my clinic, would routinely spend hours Googling himself. But he was not narcissurfing. He was not looking for the satisfaction some people feel from leaving a big mark on the Web. To the contrary, he really wished his virtual footprint would disappear altogether.

Rob was a reserved forty-five-year-old single father and a county hospital emergency room nurse. The chronic nursing shortage many of the country's hospitals suffer from, combined with Rob's willingness to work overtime whenever asked, tripled his baseline salary, effectively making him one of the highest-paid county employees. One day, a popular online newspaper decided to publish his salary, along with that of other "overpaid" state employees, in an "exposé" that seemed to imply that these individuals were somehow taking advantage of the taxpayer rather than working extra time to fill a very important need. Hate e-mail soon followed, flooding Rob's in-box. Cancelling his e-mail account only shifted the abuse into real life—people had found his home address and phone number online and were now phoning in and snail-mailing their misplaced hatred and jealousy. Worse yet, Rob's teenage daughter started dreading going to school because of harassment from her classmates. The paper's issuing of a belated clarification did not help, as the article had now taken on a life of its own, cut and pasted into countless blogs, and cc'd and bcc'd to innumerable in-boxes. Rob had been publicly humiliated, and he was helpless and without recourse when he tried to defend himself. His paranoia made sense, and I could understand why he asked to see me under a pseudonym, refused to show ID to the clinic clerk, and paid out-of-pocket for my services to suppress any evidence of his treatment. He knew what the consequences of having an electronic record of his private life were and could not trust that his confidential medical record would not somehow also be searchable by Google.

A 2009 story from NPR's *On the Media* offers a tragicomic solution to the problem of living life "on the record." A young man invited his friends and family, and a reporter, to a funeral he hosted for his former name. The deceased, who was referred to as Peter, greeted his guests at the door. Three years earlier, then a college senior, Peter had written a piece for his school newspaper about his experience using Craigslist to look for sex with closeted Harvard men. "It was a big hit. It's my number one Google result, of course," he said of the reception the article got. "But now, you know, three years later, I find that I'd really like to be an elementary schoolteacher. So I'm really wary of the possibility that, you know, a ten-year-old kid coming across this, because, you know, if I were like, in fourth grade I'd be Googling my teachers all the time. It's really nothing I want coming back to haunt me."

So Peter requested that the *Harvard Crimson* pull the story. Unsuccessful, he looked for ways to outrun his Google hits. He registered a domain name, did some other writing, and kept hoping that the piece would at least recede to the second page of search results. But that did not happen. Desperate to move past the risqué article and to become an elementary schoolteacher, he decided to bury his former identity altogether and to officially change his name. "In this world . . . you just can't compartmentalize your life," his mother said at the funeral. Your online indiscretions will always haunt you, she seemed to be warning. The only answer, if you want to avoid her son's untimely "death," is to have a very quiet, totally Google-unworthy, existence. "May he lead a timid, uneventful life—marked by no accomplishments that anyone would ever care to document online," a friend of Peter's said in his eulogy.

It is telling that the person responsible for the biggest Web leaks finds it necessary to lead a very secretive existence himself. "Information on the self-appointed king of transparency is scant," writes columnist Richard Tomkins of Julian Assange, founder of WikiLeaks. The Web site is devoted to posting highly classified documents and has been responsible for many prominent scoops, including the publication of the contents of Sarah Palin's private Yahoo! e-mail account. More recently, WikiLeaks released a secret military video taken in 2007 showing a U.S. helicopter attack in Iraq that killed at least eighteen people, including two Reuters journalists. The video was posted during a meticulously guarded operation conducted out of a small house in Reykjavik, Iceland, that became known as the Bunker. Raffi Khatchadourian, who wrote about the operation for the *New Yorker*, describes how Assange, despite having ostensibly rented the house to cover the country's volcanic eruption, pulled the drapes over the windows and made sure they remained closed for the duration of his team's work. "A low-grade fever of paranoia runs through the WikiLeaks community," Khatchadourian says of the engineers, hackers, and activists who run the Web site. The transparency they espouse in accessing the closely guarded information of governments, corporations, and public figures does not seem to apply to them. "[Assange's] phone numbers and e-mail address are ever-changing," Khatchadourian writes, "and he can drive the people around him crazy with his elusiveness and his propensity to mask details about his life." The man who knows more than anyone about the no-secrets world we live in operates as though the only way to survive anymore is to be a paranoid itinerant, traveling the world with nothing but a backpack and computer and refusing to confirm his age or give a fixed address.

Assange may, of course, be living in partial hiding because of worries about his safety—no less an organization than the Pentagon is extremely angry with him. Safety concerns, however, do not explain Apple's paranoia. The company (and man) that brought us the iPhone, with all its wondrous capabilities but also its confidentiality-busting potential, is obsessed with secrecy. According to the *New York Times*, "Secrecy at Apple is not just the prevailing communications strategy; it is baked into the corporate culture." Employees assigned to top-secret projects "must pass through a maze of security doors, swiping their badges again and again and finally entering a numeric code to reach their offices." Engineers in critical product-testing areas "must cover up devices with black cloaks when they are working on them, and turn on a red warning light when devices are unmasked." Unlike the approach taken by other companies that embrace blogging and tweeting, Apple severely limits communication with news media, shareholders, and the general public. This is evident in how it vehemently denied that it was developing a cheaper iPod with no screen until it released just that: the iPod Shuffle. It is also evident in how the company handled its chief executive's health problems in 2009, initially announcing that Steve Jobs suffered from a hormonal imbalance, only for him to resurface on the Apple campus a couple of months later having undergone a liver transplant. If anyone can be said to fully understand the virtual media landscape, it must be Mr. Jobs. And maybe that is why he chooses to navigate it with sealed lips.

While we do not all experience the level of exposure—and paranoia—that Rob and Peter did, the Internet is making some of us more wary of sharing pieces of ourselves with others offline. Some of us feel naked enough as it is, like the "world knows enough about me already," and also fear that the information will somehow end up online. Our reluctance to have our personal information broadcast to the world can lead to unhealthy paranoia and excessive withholding in personal relationships. As in Rob's case, it can also lead to attempts at camouflage and disguise in real life, as we desperately try to stop the loss of more of our life's details. Will Julian Assange's and Steve Jobs's extreme self-guardedness become our way of life as we continue to appreciate the dangers of the search engine?

In civil society and in intimate matters such as health, parenthood, and sexuality, we are supposed to be able to make selective disclosures of personal information. Possessing personal information is a source of power. When we lose the right to withhold information, we are weakened compared to the person, large organization, government, or other entity that, against our wishes, now possesses it. One can make a long list of the ways in which the virtual revolution has served to make us feel empowered. At the top of that list is probably the ability to quickly access information about anything or anyone. However, when we pause between searches involving others to think about how we no longer control our own personal information, we can end up feeling distinctly *dis*empowered. In the end, this may prove more weakening to us than having so much information at our fingertips is strengthening.

Rob's overtime pay figures, Peter's account of his college-day adventures, and Thelma Arnold's medical searches can never be reclaimed. People are starting to appreciate the difficulty of "taking back" something private once it has leaked. They are thinking more about, and wanting to avoid, that predicament. But this is only part of their challenge, one of two main contributors to their disempowerment and paranoia.

Just as concerning as the leak of accurate details of our lives (paycheck value, writings, home address, Google searches we conducted, etc.) is the inability to confront outright lies involving us once they have been posted. Even if we have never published or searched anything remotely incriminating, we may still have reason to be suspicious. For, in trying to protect our online reputation, we are utterly defenseless, with no effective way to dust off digital dirt that people attach to our names, regardless of how unwarranted it may be. As a review of the review site Yelp shows, it is very easy to sully one's reputation, and all but impossible to unsully it (until very recently, Yelp would not allow defamed individuals to publicly respond on the site to critiques, no matter how outrageous). Just as we cannot unpost our phone number, we cannot challenge a slur or a baseless accusation. Either way, what is on the Web is probably there to stay.

In two 2009 articles about Yelp that she wrote for the *San Francisco Chronicle*, journalist Deborah Gage wonders whether the Internet, which "sought to put power in the hands of the people by tapping the so-called wisdom of the crowds to change the world," may have "turned into mob rule." We talked about the fine line between Internet democracy and mob mentality. Gage's specific focus is the democratic online rumor mill and how quickly word of mouth spreads in cyberspace, with potentially heart-wrenching effects when the stories being circulated are motivated more by the poster's vindictiveness than his democratic ideals.

Yvonne Wong is a pediatric dentist practicing near San Francisco who was shocked to read a one-star Yelp review by a couple who claimed she used "laughing gas" on their son and fillings containing mercury. No such thing happened, insisted Dr. Wong, and the couple had signed a consent form disclosing the use of mercury. Seeing how the claim was scaring away new patients, but unable to make it disappear or to respond to it adequately on the site, she decided to take legal action against the parents. "I'm not looking for money," she told the newspaper. "I don't want these lies to be posted on the Web site about me." Feeling considerable heat from the press, Yelp eventually pulled the review (keeping the one-star rating), but a simple Google search still yields the story of Dr. Wong intoxicating a little boy with laughing gas, a scarlet letter that will likely always be linked to her license number.

Likewise, Steven Biegel, a San Francisco chiropractor, saw no other recourse but to sue a reviewer who had accused him of dishonesty in his billing practices, "charging people whatever [he] feel[s] like hoping they'll pay without a fuss." Despite settling the lawsuit out of court to his satisfaction and receiving a written apology from the reviewer, Biegel's Yelp page was barraged with negative commentary about his chiropractic technique—some coming from people he had never treated—and about his decision to sue a fellow "yelper." He may well have won, legally speaking, but Biegel surely still looked like a loser in the end. "It's called flaming," he told the *Chronicle*. (I can relate to Dr. Wong and Mr. Biegel's experiences: A thirty-something patient recently threatened to write a "scathing" review of me on Yelp if I refused to write her a prescription for Xanax, a highly addictive drug she did not really need.)

And flaming is hardly limited to clinicians or small business owners. In chat rooms and on blogs, it is very easy to call someone, anyone, a racist, an idiot, a wife beater or a faggot, for no reason other than the author's whim. There is a good chance the epithet will then stick to the person. The feedback wars that would regularly erupt on eBay were a good manifestation of that: A negative score from a less than thrilled buyer would trigger retaliation from the seller in the form of even worse feedback for the buyer, bringing the all-important average feedback scores for both of them down. The process devolved to such levels, and eBay got so tired of breaking up feedback fights, that, in 2008, it took away altogether sellers' ability to leave negative reviews. Only positive feedback or no feedback at all is permitted now. Once again, an Internet characteristic that seems so empowering (being able to publicly diss a chiropractor or dentist you feel wronged you) stops being so when you realize that anyone can invent and post worse things about you.

Sites like eBay and Yelp are themselves largely absolved from responsibility for what their members post by the Communications Decency Act (CDA) of 1996. In particular, Section 230 states that "No provider or user of an interactive computer service shall be treated as the publisher or speaker of any information provided by another information content provider." This effectively immunizes Internet service providers (ISPs) and online forums from torts committed by users over their systems, and leaves people like Wong and Biegel with lawsuits directed against *individuals* as their most realistic legal option. Yet although the number of such lawsuits has risen sharply (up 68 percent in 2007 from 2006 levels, according to statistics from Harvard's Berkman Center for Internet and Society), they are ineffectual if the goal is to make a defamatory remark disappear—before the verdict is in, the online comment has already metastasized in cyberspace, and one is already "flamed." On our own, we are no more likely to succeed in making hurtful lies about our business practices disappear than in taking back our honest answers to the RealAge quiz. This has opened the door wide for the latest booming Internet business: the online reputation concierge who prowls the Web for published dirt on your behalf, a large virtual dustpan in hand.

That is more or less the service that ReputationDefender, among other Web sites, offers, and for a lot of money. "It's quite simple,"

ReputationDefender writes about its reasons for existing and why we should all sign up. "We constantly search the Internet for information about each other and use that information to make judgments. . . . Everyone has an online reputation, whether they realize it or not. You cannot afford to leave yours unattended for another day!" Founded in 2006, the self-described "world's first comprehensive online reputation management and privacy company" charges $14.95 a month to locate negative content involving you, such as an unflattering picture from a Christmas party two jobs ago, politically incorrect blog entries, and risky outpourings on social networking sites that appear to have happened under the influence. Then, for $29.95 per "Destroy assistance," it tries to delete the offending item. For another $14.95 a month, it will also enroll you in MyChild—there is no mention of a family plan—because "knowing what's [written online about your offspring] is part of parenting in the 21st Century." But if you *really* want to have an edge in the online defamation wars, you should opt for their MyEdge service. For a reported $10,000, ReputationDefender will hide unwanted Web dirt about you behind a barrage of unrelentingly positive, Google-friendly content, either created by the company or found elsewhere on the Web, and optimized to appear at the top of search-engine results. The idea is to scrub your reputation clean essentially by gaming Google. This is today's version of the old PR offensive, only now the battle is waged against an anonymous, unrestrainable enemy. The good news is that you may finally have a chance at destroying that revealing piece of information or that downright lie. The bad news is twofold: You have to pay to gain your autonomy back, and $10,000 can buy anyone a sparkling reputation. Discretion and playing by the rules are no longer reasonable guarantors of an individuated existence or a decent reputation.

"What Was Privacy?" Lew McCreary asked in the title to his essay. One thing privacy was, author Ayn Rand might say, was proof of civilization. She would have a point. "Civilization is the progress toward a society of privacy," she wrote in *The Fountainhead* several decades ago, when "to yelp" meant something different. "The savage's whole existence is public, ruled by the laws of his tribe. Civilization is the process of setting man free from men." Just as Freud saw the id as a threat to civilized existence, so, Rand thought, is an overly open life. Yet men are in other men's business like never before as today's life is lived publicly and with no boundaries that delineate one person from another.

These issues came to the fore recently with the news of an eighteen-year-old Rutgers freshman, Tyler Clementi, who jumped to his death from the George Washington Bridge after his roommate streamed a video of him having sex with another man. By all accounts, Clementi followed appropriate, in retrospect perhaps old-fashioned, dorm etiquette. To avoid surprises, the shy music major would ask to have the room to himself for specified blocks of time when he planned an intimate meeting. But etiquette is overrated in our digital culture, and a promise of privacy holds no water when you live in a post-privacy world. "Roommate asked for the room till midnight," Dharun Ravi, Clementi's roommate, apparently tweeted before streaming the first video live. "I went into Molly's room and turned on my webcam," he added, referring to the dorm neighbor whose computer Ravi used to remotely activate his webcam. "I saw him making out with a dude. Yay." Two days later, Ravi's 148 Twitter followers received another message: "Anyone with iChat, I dare you to video chat me between the hours of 9:30 and 12. Yes it's happening again."

The exposed young violinist was driven to suicide by a critical by-product of our time: the small zone of privacy that we all need and that is crucial to our psychological equilibrium is now nowhere to be found. It is a natural necessity to be able to assume that a sexual moment one worked hard to keep private will not be that easy to record and, if it is recorded, will not be that easy to broadcast. But those basic confidentiality (and mental health) safeguards no longer exist. Clementi paid the ultimate price, but we all have something to mourn. We are not being rendered suicidal, but the detailed and indelible online record of our lives that is being produced is a threat to our psychological autonomy, to our control over our reputation and legacy, and, it would seem, to civilization itself. As we contemplate and realize the answer to the "What Was Privacy?" question, we are feeling weakened and are hitting a paranoid moment in our history.

_CHAPTER 11

MARKING TIME, MAKING MEMORIES

MY EIGHT-YEAR-OLD NIECE who guessed that her nickname was what my sister used for her Hotmail password could have also accessed her mother's online bank and credit card statements, as well as her Amazon, Travelocity, and Flickr accounts. Like most of us, my sister's memory can hold only a limited number of relatively straightforward passwords that she recycles across several Internet registration needs. In fact, according to a 2007 study of over 500,000 users conducted by Microsoft researchers, the average Internet user has twenty-five password-protected Internet accounts, but only six passwords, which means that, on average, each individual password is used for roughly four different sites. This simplifies the problem from one of remembering twenty-five distinct passwords to remembering which of only four passwords the person uses is associated with what account.

What also helps is that many of us choose simple passwords, like a loved one's nickname. While, for the most part, we recognize the risks inherent in this, memory limitations often trump privacy concerns, and out go unfamiliar characters, alphanumeric hybrids, and upper-case/lower-case combinations, unless we are forced to use them by a Web site that will not let us in otherwise.

Still, even when we juggle a relatively limited number of easy-to-remember passwords, we rely on sticky notes and trial and error—typing each of our usual passwords in sequence until one works. And when everything fails—hardly an infrequent occurrence—password resets are invoked. As our struggle with this most ubiquitous feature of virtual life indicates, memory is a delicate thing, and the Internet, by fortifying certain memories and helping others more readily slip away, is changing the nature and content of what we remember in very interesting ways.

My Google self-search of the last chapter revealed more information yet. It brought back memories of a contentious lawsuit I had taken part in years earlier. I thought I had processed and shelved away all its unpleasantness, and I was not keen on resurrecting any of it. But there it was, archived for the benefit of I don't know whom, with total disregard for the desire of the lawsuit participants to never revisit that minefield again. Yes, the simple experience/mistake/excuse of forgetting—a process as human as DNA—has become more difficult, because so much of our lives can now be documented online before our, and the world's, eyes.

There is something very healthy and fundamentally human about being able to forget, about being able to selectively recall those experiences that are worth remembering and to stuff into the deep recesses of our brain those that are less fair or flattering to our concepts of who we are. "I can forgive, but I can't forget," goes the popular adage, perhaps privileging forgiveness over amnesia in our recovery from painful experiences and in our ability to move on. But there is nothing wrong with forgetting, which in itself can be wonderfully therapeutic—nothing wipes the slate equally clean, and nothing is a harbinger of a fresher start. Indeed, to truly forgive, we have to make the traumatizing details less present, even a little bit fuzzy in our minds. They have to be more difficult to access and less quick to spring to the fore at the first mention of the person who wronged us, or the ugly situation that made us victims. Time is needed to soften the negative charge. If we say we have forgiven when the memory of an injustice is still crisp or when only a couple of days have elapsed, we are either being slightly disingenuous or showing sainthood potential. Better let time and amnesia work their magic.

In sometimes acting as a reminder of things that we are better off forgetting, the Internet can interfere in that process, making it difficult to truly file disturbing memories away. This can challenge the notions of ourselves that we hold most dear, and in some cases can even compromise our well-being, both online and offline.

Post-traumatic stress disorder is a serious psychiatric illness that can follow severe trauma. One way to conceptualize it is as a disorder of intense remembering of a terrible event. For patients with PTSD, every memory of the trauma can perpetuate the pain and cause them to relive the tragedy. Part of how they cope is by avoiding all cues associated with it. I treated Tina, a twenty-one-year-old college student, for PTSD. Tina's symptoms began shortly after she was sexually assaulted by a male college friend following a party at their dorm. Although Tina had indeed been raped, it took her a while to be able to verbalize it—she wondered what role alcohol or her dress might have played, and whether she somehow had led her friend on. With that realization came terrible anxiety, as well as flashbacks and nightmares of that night. To avoid reliving the awful experience with every sighting and every reminder of her attacker, Tina destroyed their pictures together, deleted his phone number from her cell phone, stopped eating in the student cafeteria, and even moved out of the dorm they had shared. The depression that set in after the attack made her withdraw from her larger circle of friends, too.

Months later, however, when Tina slowly began to recover and regain interest in connecting with old friends, she decided, naturally, to reactivate her Facebook account, for to be a social twentysomething today means to have an active Facebook life. And there he was, listed as "friend" on several of her close friends' profiles, often with a quoted joke and always sporting an innocent smile in his photographs. And there was Tina herself, seemingly always sitting next to him in all the group photos, making a funny face at him in one, and forcing a goofy hat over his head in another. Tina wished she could tear those pictures, too, but that, alas, was not an option. For her, the real-life work of forgetting and moving on, which was well under way offline, was being hindered by a deep cache of online memories that she could not escape or run away from, possibly ever. Tina's offline recovery was being dealt a setback because of the permanence of her relationship history online.

While it is important not to be always confronted with terrible memories from our past like Tina was, it is also important to be able to delete neutral and insignificant memories. Just as it can be helpful to forget the traumatic, it is also helpful to forget the mundane. This, neuroscience research is beginning to show, is crucial to our ability to lay down new, more important memories. Indeed, the brain is programmed to forget certain events as it tries to remember others.

Consider the daily commute. Much catches our eye on the way to work: a fuel gauge nearing empty, traffic lights, kids hopping on a school bus, a police officer issuing a speeding ticket, and so on. The fact that none of these non-events is stored in our long-term memory helps make it possible for us to remember the important meeting that took place once we got to work. Likewise, if we remembered the last five passwords we used for our online banking account, it would be significantly more difficult to summon up the latest one we picked. An all-inclusive, "photographic," memory, as manifested in so-called savant syndrome and dramatized in the movie *Rain Man*, is not necessarily a happiness-inducing quality to have. Sure, it might help us recall the cards dealt from all six decks in a blackjack game, but can you imagine the "weight" of having to store all the irrelevant numbers you come across over the course of a typical day? In contrast, there is lightness and freedom in being able to forget some things, in being able to develop a hierarchy of memories, whereby certain events are designated for long-term preservation in our cortex, while others are discarded without second thought, never to be heard from again.

In a study published in 2007 in the journal *Nature Neuroscience*, Stanford neuroscientist Anthony Wagner and his research group used functional MRI to prove that memory centers in the brain can strengthen important memories only if they weaken or suppress irrelevant ones. As described in the article and in the *Stanford Report*, twenty students, ages eighteen to thirty-two, took part in the three-hour study. Each participant was shown forty capitalized words (for example, ATTIC) and, for each capitalized word, six attached associate words (for example, ATTIC-dust and ATTIC-junk). In total, there were 240 word pairs. Each word pair flashed for four seconds on a screen inside the MRI scanner. For each capitalized word, there were six memories being formed—based on the six associate words. Participants practiced remembering the word pairs and were given clues, such as ATTIC-j for ATTIC-junk, to improve their ability to remember one pair over the others. They practiced the prompted word pair (ATTIC-junk) three times as the scanner recorded their brain activity. The first time they practiced remembering it, the prefrontal cortex area of their frontal lobes "lit up," suggesting that the brain was working hard to form the new memory as it competed with the other word pairs. However, when they practiced remembering it for a second and third time, their frontal lobes showed significantly less activity.

After twenty minutes, study participants were tested on all the word pairs. As expected, they best remembered the pairs they had practiced and tended to forget the competing ones. More importantly, there was a direct relationship between the level of decrease in brain activity seen on the scans and how likely it was that participants would later forget the competing pairs. In other words, the participants who forgot the competing words the most were the ones who showed the greatest decrease in prefrontal cortex activity—that is, it was easier for them to learn new information. For the first time, a study had demonstrated the advantages of forgetting.

"As irrelevant memories are forgotten, the neural systems that help us remember do not need to work as hard," Wagner said about his results. The economy of our memory is such that new things can be encrypted only if others can be lost. Our brains have finite storage capacities, and it is crucial to forget in order to remember. "Any act of remembering reweights memories, tweaking them to try to be more adaptive for the next time you try to remember something," Wagner says. "The brain is plastic—adaptive—and one feature of that is not just strengthening some memories but also suppressing or weakening others. . . . It's an important property of our memory system that the memories change in both directions—they get both stronger and weaker—and that this confers benefits." While forgetting can certainly be frustrating, it represents real benefits for our ability to remember.

If our brains are cluttered with insignificant memories, making and accessing new ones naturally—make that *neurally*—becomes more challenging. "Remembering the past is fraught with competition," Wagner and his colleagues write. The "competition" is in the form of the numerous less important, superfluous memories that can clog the system. I would argue that because of the Internet, competing memories have become harder to forget. They are archived somewhere in cyberspace where they linger, seemingly in perpetuity, waiting to be Googled.

Just like a Facebook account, that bottomless storage unit of all sorts of average memories, online memories can be quite sticky. "How Sticky Is Membership on Facebook? Just Try Breaking Free." That is the title of a 2008 *Times* article in which one "trapped" member described the site as a "Hotel California:" "You can check out anytime you like but you can never leave." To truly leave, members have to painstakingly delete, line by line, Wall post by Wall post, and group affiliation by group affiliation, all the profile information that they created over the course of their Facebook life. (A cottage industry of unofficial Web pages has sprung up to help people escape the social network; a popular one is tellingly named "2,504 Steps to Closing Your Facebook Account.") But even after the labor-intensive process, the account cannot be considered permanently removed, since footprints, in the form of archived user content, can persist in backp copies on the company's servers.

The technical reasons for the survival of data online even after we delete it are complicated and have to do in part with the way information is stored online. Here is how Yahoo! technology blogger Christopher Null explains it:

> While your personal computer only keeps one copy of a file, large-scale services like Facebook rely on what are called "content delivery networks" [CDNs] to manage data and distribution. It's a complex system wherein data is copied to multiple intermediate devices, usually to speed up access to files when millions of people are trying to access the service simultaneously. . . . But because changes aren't reflected across the content delivery networks immediately, ghost copies of files tend to linger.

This was scientifically demonstrated in 2009, in a Cambridge University study, where a group of computer scientists found that nearly half of sixteen social networking sites they tested, including Facebook, did not immediately remove pictures when a user requested they be deleted. To perform their experiment, they uploaded photos to each of the sites, then deleted them, noting the direct URL addresses to the pictures from the sites' content delivery networks. When they checked thirty days later, these links continued to work for seven of the sites, even though the typical user would safely assume the photos had disappeared. (And if the picture or other content has somehow escaped the confines of the social networking site, then all bets are off, and the likelihood of success deleting it diminishes reverse-exponentially.)

While the nature of CDNs may be one reason online data can survive long after we thought it was deleted, some services are intentionally working to make sure Web content is never lost. The mission of the Wayback project, for example, is to copy entire sites for posterity, archiving Web pages, images, and texts forever. Others, such as the Digital Library Project, the Online Computer Library Center, and Alexa, are starting to offer access to archived versions of pages after those pages have been removed from the Web. This means that the life span of data online is, if anything, increasing, and the "404—Page Not Found" message we are used to getting when we click on a defunct link will gradually stop being part of our World Wide Web experience.

There is much good in building a digital Library of Alexandria and saving every Web page ever uploaded—nothing would more comprehensively capture this moment in our history. Similarly, there might be something to celebrate in the decision by the Library of Congress in April 2010 to keep a digital archive of every public tweet that has ever been broadcast on Twitter. But there can also be a psychological downside. We saw in the last chapter the consequences to our privacy and reputation of "sticky" online content and discussed the disempowering and paranoid-making effects of others finding out too much about us. Here, we are seeing how memory, too, can be affected; how the Internet can remind us of things that we should not burden our hippocampus with. "Too much information" cuts both ways: Others can know too much about our business and so, in a sense, can we.

Forty percent of Twitter tweets can be categorized as "pointless babble," according to a 2009 study by the marketing research firm Pear Analytics. (The second biggest category is conversational tweets.) They, like the inane Facebook Wall posts that are difficult to delete and the nominal "friends" we accumulate, can act like the ATTIC-dust word pair that is distracting us from remembering ATTIC-junk in the MRI machine. Countless long-lost best friends have reconnected through social media sites, and many formidable new friendships have formed, but for the most part, there is a reason we had forgotten all about our seventh-grade lab partner until our paths crossed again in cyberspace. For better or worse, forgetting him or her is in part what has allowed us to vividly remember other relationships with perhaps more compatible souls. But, like it or not, that lab partner is now in our life again, in the form of a superficial memory and a superficial friendship that have floated back to the surface and that might dislodge other, perhaps more promising, associations that we might want to concentrate on and remember.

The attention-deficient, distracted Web surfer we talked about, who is spread across several browser tabs, texting platforms, and e-mail accounts, is also increasingly forgetful and in need of ATTIC-j–like clues to refocus and remember. The next must-have digital accessory better be a mnemonic-producing device.

According to Moore's Law, for the same price, digital computing power and the closely linked computer memory capacity increase exponentially over time. It is the prediction of Gordon E. Moore, cofounder of Intel, a world leader in silicon technology. Moore first articulated his law in a 1965 paper for *Electronics* magazine, titled "Cramming More Components onto Integrated Circuits":

> The complexity for minimum component costs has increased at a rate of roughly a factor of two per year. . . . Certainly over the short term this rate can be expected to continue, if not to increase. Over the longer term, the rate of increase is a bit more uncertain, although there is no reason to believe it will not remain nearly constant for at least 10 years. That means by 1975, the number of components per integrated circuit for minimum cost will be 65,000.

In 1975, Moore revised his prediction, saying that the doubling was now occurring every two years. This formulation remains accepted by many information technology experts today. They believe that as electronic miniaturization continues to improve, up to 15 billion components will be "crammable" on a chip by 2015, and that, by 2020, molecular-scale production, or nanotechnology—where each individual atom can be precisely positioned—will dominate. In his original paper, Moore foresaw that "integrated circuits will lead to such wonders as home computers . . . automatic controls for automobiles, and personal portable communications equipment," adding that "the electronic wristwatch needs only a display to be feasible today." Digital watches, personal computers (PCs), personal digital assistants (PDAs), and automated car functions are, of course, the norm today, but so, and for the same reasons, is vast hard drive capacity and vast virtual storage. In fact, as much as a terabyte in virtual stores per person now seems within reach. (One terabyte equals $1,024^2$ megabytes; as a reference point, the typical free Hotmail account comes with about a gigabyte, or 1,024 megabytes, in storage capacity.)

One direct effect of this trend is that people are able to hold on to an ever-increasing amount of electronic information about the world and about themselves, with little need to be selective or discriminating in what gets digitally saved and what gets deleted. E-mails, Word documents, PDF files, images, and audio and video recordings of varying quality and importance—all are more likely to get preserved, simply because there is no longer an imperative to shed or downsize. In my Gmail in-box are some eight hundred e-mails that I keep, not always because of the crucial information they contain or because of a sentimental attachment to the sender. Rather, I have become an electronic hoarder of bytes and pixels and of important and not-so-important content, when hoarding was never really a problem for me before. Why do I do this? Probably, because I can. I have 7,320 megabytes allotted to me by Google, and a visit to the "Settings" section of my account reveals that I have used only 1 percent of it so far. So why not keep a distant relative's Christmas e-card from three years ago and the predictable e-mail exchange that preceded a not particularly memorable business meeting last quarter?

Nondigital, real-life hoarding is defined as the acquisition of, and difficulty getting rid of, worthless items. It is considered a subset of OCD, and treatments similar to those used for more classic presentations of the disorder, such as contamination-based OCD, are often tried. Traditionally, hoarders have collected old magazines, newspapers, receipts, junk mail, clothing, and furniture. The negative effects on the hoarder's life can be devastating and include frequent loss of important items in disorganized homes, falls, fires, and, among the elderly, malnutrition and the inability to comply with medication regimens because of difficulty navigating the kitchen or locating the pills. Fortunately, only a relatively small percentage of people are afflicted with clinical hoarding (OCD strikes about 2 percent of the population; roughly 20 percent of them are hoarders). However, I believe electronic hoarding is starting to affect many of us. Our virtual desktop is infinitely larger in surface area than our real desk ever was and can hold infinitely more clutter. And while this does not constitute a fire hazard like a real-life hoarder's collections might, it does make it easy for us to save information that is of questionable quality and importance and that might pose other kinds of hazards. Coming across items in my virtual files that I would have discarded and forgotten about in real life consolidates memories I would normally not work hard to store in my brain, perhaps at the expense of something more meaningful that I should be retaining. We saw, in chapter 8, the effects on knowledge of swimming in a sea of so-so information. It turns out the deluge of electronic material can play tricks on another crucial aspect of cognition—remembering.

The impossibility of forgetting (because everything is preserved and ready to jog our memories) may also translate into difficulty remembering. The democratizing and leveling effects of the Web apply to our memories as well—it's one memory, one vote—and it can be hard for any single special detail to stand out amid all the irrelevance. It's thousands of digital pictures on Picasa, Flickr, and various jump drives, instead of a truly cherished one that we carry around in our wallet or display on the mantelpiece. So far as I can tell, I have not started misplacing my keys or forgetting phone numbers as a result of my e-clutter, but I do wonder whether taxing my neurons with insignificant detail might compromise something in my ability to recall important things down the road. Metaphorically speaking, as our virtual memory expands into terabyte territory, our real memory for important things stays within the kilobyte range, and may even be shrinking. Our brain, unlike our laptop's brain, does not obey Moore's Law.

Forgetting may have become a lost art, but at least we have nanotech in our future, right? Mr. Moore himself is not so sanguine. I don't think he had in mind the possible consequences to our cognitive lives of his law, but I love what he told an interviewer in 2005 about the ultimate end result of ever-increasing hard drive capacity and computing power: "It can't continue forever," he said. "The nature of exponentials is that you push them out and eventually disaster happens."

Memory matters because it is the currency that makes it possible for us to hold on to time. "God gave us memory so we might have roses in December," James M. Barrie, the author of *Peter Pan, or, The Boy Who Would Not Grow Up*, once said. And just as our concept of memory is changing, so is the way we experience and relate to time. Some understanding of time has always factored into our ideas of religion, philosophy, mythology, and mortality. Throughout our history, we have been haunted by time. We have lived in fear of its ravages as we saw them in the environment and on our faces. We struggled to understand its cycles, and developed elaborate rituals and entire religions around them. As much as possible, we have tried to master time. To give ourselves the illusion of subjugating this monster, we broke it down into more manageable components—years, months, hours, minutes, and seconds— and categorized it into weekdays, weekends, vacations, and holidays that commemorate time. In organizing it and forcing it into some form of grid or calendar, we were organizing our lives and allaying our anxieties. Much of that seems to be changing.

We often refer to virtual life as being "there," whereas real life is what happens "here." "Where did you meet?" "We met online," goes the common exchange, reflecting the notion that cyberspace is, well, a space. In our collective thinking, it is an extension of geography, a second home, or a home away from home. The popularity of terms such as My "Space," chat "room," Web "site," and "home" page speaks to this. Overall, virtual life is the response to a "where" question. But virtual life is also a *time*; a time that is dislocated from time, and that marches to its own rhythm and nonstandard metronome. "Online" is just as valid a response to a "when" question. We talked about how Internet addicts lose their sense of time, and by the time they "catch" themselves idling on a Web site, it is too late, and they have wasted another afternoon. They cannot comprehend how time just "flew" by. We also talked about how we compress time in our online decision making, e-mails, and texts, as we sacrifice time-intensive reflection and deliberation in favor of expediency and impulsive, knee-jerk actions. Unlike our new, expansive concept of space, which seems to have extended our geography into novel territory, our new concept of time is abbreviated, shrunken, and preoccupied with the present moment. And a very busy present moment it is, for it is given to multitasking. This phenomenon often involves putting both our online and offline selves to work simultaneously in order to squeeze two or more activities out of the same timeslot (responding to a work e-mail while talking to our spouse on the phone, or tracking an eBay auction while helping our child with homework). As a result, our new time is really a point in time; one that blends work, play, and everything in between.

One facet of the Internet and of the digital age in general is the explosive growth in work productivity, with the unquestionable economic benefits that have accrued as a direct result. Another is that we are now constantly on call for work. The lines that demarcated weekends from weekdays, "eight to five" from the rest of the twenty-four-hour cycle, and workdays from holidays and vacation—these distinctions now feel very "early nineties," like relics of an age so foreign and removed from our experience that it might as well be Victorian. Simply put, in our hyperconnected, always "on" culture, true time off does not exist in any practical sense anymore.

Our e-personality cannot tolerate down time. There is always a discovery or connection to be made; always some fun to be had. Yet idle time, when the browser is shut down, the smart phone is out of charge, and the other electronic gadgetry is silenced, is necessary to our ability to reflect on the world around us and our ability to *self*-reflect. Lose that productive idleness and we lose the opportunity to assess ourselves and our place in the world, as well as consider the downsides of the new technologies that are keeping us constantly busy. And without that ability to cogitate, ponder, and deliberate what is at stake, we will automatically upgrade to the newer and faster model, which, seemingly inevitably, will only add more pressure on our time. And so the cycle goes. Like many people, I routinely respond to work e-mails after-hours and on weekends, and am apt to start feeling ignored if a work-related missive I send Friday evening is not returned by Sunday morning. I also love to telecommute and look at my nonclinic workdays as an opportunity to catch up on paperwork, charting, and scheduling issues, all from my favorite couch in the sunroom of my house. What is not to like about this arrangement? It liberates me from my commute, saves me time, is environmentally friendly, and allows me to tend to my garden as I work. I would be mad not to feel gratitude toward my employer for allowing me that opportunity. Yet the fact that I don't question it is a symptom of our culture's new sense of time and of the blurring that is happening between our professional and personal lives, between being on- and off-duty. As our work responsibilities and preoccupations encroach deeper into our other time, a new identity is emerging: one that may be defined more by what we do than any other consideration. Reacting to a 2008 survey by the Elon University/Pew Internet Project site, here is what one commentator had to say on the subject of too much after-hours online connectivity with work:

> [People's] very existence will be dictated by their belonging to that company or corporation, such that they may as well be labeled as "slaves." . . . In this scenario, employees will have very little choice as to where and when they devote their time to the profit-making of the company. Of course I may see this as a negative thing, but perhaps the generation of today are already being trained to recognize that being a company employee first means they can be recognized as an identity/a person only as a function of that.

We should have an advantage over the generation of millennials the writer is referring to. We *remember* what it was like to work for four consecutive months, then take a break or get sick or go on maternity or paternity leave. Yet we embrace our longer hours and work harder than ever before, either because we are metaphorically enslaved or because this is the new norm. Increased economic productivity may be defined simply as the ability to produce more work in the same amount of time. One would expect the digital revolution, which has remarkably enhanced productivity, to be leading to more generous vacation leaves and more personal time. Instead, many of us find ourselves working more hours, even as we continue to express outrage at child labor in the Far East and other obvious workplace injustices. Maybe the e-personality traits that come out in cyberspace make it more palatable, so the workload ends up feeling less like work and more like being online with all the omnipotence, freedom, and play opportunities that brings. Or maybe, just maybe, we are not really working that much harder after all—it only looks that way.

Just as we spend too much time at home working for the boss, we also spend too much time at work being social on Facebook, looking up items on Amazon, or playing our favorite virtual game. Several studies point to how pervasive this new phenomenon with a new name—cyberloafing—is:

- A 2008 report by a New Zealand network security firm estimated personal Internet use at work to be as high as 25 percent of total online time;
- According to a 2005 America Online/Salary.com study, 45 percent of the over 10,000 workers surveyed listed Internet use as the number one distraction at work (the insurance profession apparently leads other industries in time wasted);
- A 2005 Harris Interactive/Websense study put the cost to U.S. employers of cyberloafing at $178 billion annually.

A cynic would say that it is only fair that the "abuse" should be mutual.

We seem to be losing the ability to enjoy things or immerse ourselves fully in them, one at a time and for a prolonged period of time. We work, play, consume, and live on the run and in the moment—this very moment—like there is no tomorrow. Our memory of things past potentially compromised, we do not seem to be looking to the future, either. We are doing three tasks simultaneously, while also looking at an RSS feed and conducting an IM exchange, and it is hard to pause, look ahead, and question what this pace may portend for the future. This deeply concerns computer scientist W. Daniel Hillis, who has proposed an impressive monument that can help us think beyond the frenzied moment. Its critical role is to remind us that it can be salutary for our mental health and overall good for us to be able to take a deep breath from time to time, grab a number, and wait.

Hillis speaks from experience and authority. His background is distinctly technological. He comes from a generation of scientists devoted to helping us get the most out of every moment we spend in front of our computers. In the 1980s, as a graduate student at MIT, Hillis rethought the architecture of the modern computer. Instead of its "brain" consisting of a single processor, he imagined a supercomputer that would contain thousands of processors all working together at the same time. "I want to build a computer that would be proud of me," he once said. The then revolutionary idea of parallel processing became the subject of his doctoral thesis, and, while still in graduate school, he started Thinking Machines, a company that would put his theories to practical use. His firm succeeded in building Connection Machines, or computing behemoths with up to 65,536 processors. However, finding success and fortune through ultraspeedy computers must have still left him empty, for instead of leveraging his background and experience to branch into nanotechnology—perhaps the next logical career move—the "mad scientist" decided to pursue a drastic change of pace. He started devoting his time to building a monument that would force us to slow down, relieve the current moment of its to-do list, and ponder the seasons and what lies ahead:

> When I was a child, people used to talk about what would happen by the year 2000. For the next thirty years they kept talking about what would happen by the year 2000, and now no one mentions a future date at all. . . . I think it is time for us to start a long-term project that gets people thinking past the mental barrier of an ever-shortening future. I would like to propose a large (think Stonehenge) mechanical clock powered by seasonal temperature changes. It ticks once a year, bongs once a century, and the cuckoo comes out every millennium.

Today, the year 2000 is a blur perhaps best remembered for Y2K, the drama that never was. The millennium bug that would bring the Internet to a screeching stop and arrest its development was hardly millennial in significance. Still, the year 2000 and Y2K were milestones of sorts: They oriented us toward a point in the future. Worms, viruses, and "Trojan horses" have followed in steady succession since, including such global annoyances as ILOVEYOU (2000), Sobig (2003), Mydoom (2004), Storm (2007), and Conficker (2008). But none of them filled us with Y2K-like dread or anticipation. We paid attention to their threat for only as long as it took us to download the latest security patch, then went on merrily multitasking. Expecting a future event with the intensity that we did the new millennium or even Y2K might be refreshing at this point, but nothing on the horizon has nearly that hold on the collective consciousness.

That is why the Long Now Foundation set out to realize Hillis's dream of building a monument in honor of the future tense. (Hillis also co-chairs the board.) According to company literature, the foundation was formed in the year "01996"; the extra zero, we are told, is to solve the deca-millennium bug which will come into effect in the year 10000 (this should give you an idea). The group's hope is to give us a future landmark, in the form of a 10,000-year clock that would stretch time out again.

> Civilization is revving itself into a pathologically short attention span. The trend might be coming from the acceleration of technology, the short-horizon perspective of market-driven economics, the next-election perspective of democracies, or the distractions of personal multi-tasking. All are on the increase. Some sort of balancing corrective to the short-sightedness is needed—some mechanism or myth which encourages the long view and the taking of long-term responsibility, where "long-term" is measured at least in centuries.

The clock is meant to supply that mechanism and myth. It is an attempt to offer a counterpoint to today's in-the-moment mindset and to promote slower (and better) thinking and living. Hillis's first prototype of the monument is on display at the Science Museum in London, and he is working on the second version. According to the team of engineers who have already patented several of its elements, the proposed clock is so accurate, its precision will equal one day in 20,000 years. It will self-correct by phase-locking to the noon sun.

Beyond the revolutionary science involved in building it, formidable obstacles to the clock's survival remain, and Hillis and his team are trying to find ways to increase their enterprise's likelihood of success. "The only way to survive over the long run is to be made of materials large and worthless, like Stonehenge and the Pyramids, or to become lost," Hillis says. With that in mind, his group is researching samples and sizes and considering ways to hide, camouflage, or even lose the clock. How long might it take them to resolve these challenges and erect the monument? If we ask, we are probably missing the point. True to their mission, Hillis and his associates are giving themselves all the time in the world. "There is no projected completion date," they tell us. (A visitor to their headquarters in San Francisco's Presidio National Park is greeted by a sign that reads: "You can virtually never be late to our opening.") Hillis will not be here to see the cukoo come out the first time on his clock (that is scheduled to take place in the year 03000). Still, whether or not his clock starts ticking, and whether or not it survives the deca-millennium bug, the parallel-processing whiz, Connection Machine inventor, and one-time living embodiment of Moore's Law has already accomplished much simply by remembering to pause and think about time, and imploring us to do the same:

> I know I am a part of a story that starts long before I can remember and continues long beyond when anyone will remember me. I sense that I am alive at a time of important change, and I feel a responsibility to make sure that the change comes out well. I plant my acorns knowing that I will never live to harvest the oaks. I have hope for the future.

I want to have hope, too.

CHAPTER 12

VIRTUALISM, OR THE ART OF BEING MORE REAL THAN REAL

WHILE STILL IN TRAINING, desperate for additional income to supplement my meager resident salary, I spent many weekends moonlighting in a small clinic in California's Central Valley. The clinic was run by someone I will call Dr. Susan Taylor. To the young, newly licensed physician I was, Dr. Taylor provided opportunity, mentorship, and the promise of greener pastures on the other side of a demanding residency. To her adoring patients, she was the caring doctor from a bygone period who still made house calls, remembered small details about her patients' personal lives, and forgave them the occasional bill if she felt that paying it would constitute a hardship. Her kindness was reciprocated with kindness as they heaped praise and prayers on her, along with beautiful baskets of whatever they picked from their gardens that morning. While Dr. Taylor deservedly kept praise and prayers, she generously shared heirloom tomatoes, figs, and persimmons with her city-dwelling underling and staff. "You just can't find produce like this anywhere else," she would say, to my gastronomic delight, as I ended each shift and packed my trunk with Central Valley bounties in preparation for the long drive back home.

The wonderfully healthy tableau I had painted in my mind of Dr.

Taylor's practice was seriously disrupted one Saturday when I agreed to cover for her after her elderly out-of-state mother fell ill and Dr. Taylor had to leave town on short notice. I found myself in the middle of the shift needing to access a pain specialist's report on one of her patients, who was insisting it had been e-mailed directly to Dr. Taylor. Unable to reach the specialist on the weekend, I decided to call Dr. Taylor, starting my conversation by apologizing for bothering her while she was preoccupied with a family emergency. "I'm not sure what I can do from here," she said hesitantly. "Mother doesn't have Internet access," she added after a long pause. "Her one neighbor doesn't, either, and I don't know of any Internet cafés around here."

This was well before the age of smart phones, and it was becoming obvious that I would have to access Dr. Taylor's personal e-mail account myself if I wanted to read the report—an awkward resolution to the issue that I perhaps should have anticipated. Not wanting to deprive her patient of information that could potentially change the course of treatment and help her pain, she asked me if I was ready to write down her log-in information. Little did I know, but I answered affirmatively.

"My e-mail address is 'DoctorSusan,' and my password is 'Doctor Bitch.'"

I was not ready for *that*. "Doctor what?" I started to ask, but quickly ended the conversation, after muttering a few words about how sorry I was for intruding on her weekend and how something in the clinic required my attention.

But I couldn't get past the fascinating choice of password. Why not "Susan123" or "Doctorwithoutborders," a reference to the international medical humanitarian organization, I wondered? If she wanted something a little bit on the dark side, why not "shadylady," a Central Valley tomato varietal that she was particularly fond of? All would have been more in line with the personality everyone had come to know and love, but it had to be DoctorBitch. I found it hard to shake off the feeling that this revelation was giving me a glimpse into a parallel existence that was somehow significantly less content and rosy. Feeling embarrassed for her and more than a little guilty, I headed home a bit early, my trunk empty this time. Shortly thereafter, I stopped moonlighting altogether. Supermarket tomatoes, I decided, weren't so bad after all.

Over time, I dreamed up wild scenarios involving Dr. Taylor. Whenever I would read about a medical professional running afoul of the medical board's rules, I would somehow expect her name to pop up at the bottom of the article. As I prepared, more than ten years later, to write about e-personality, I sought an update on Dr. Taylor, maybe expecting a juicy tidbit that would fit into my "Ordinary Everyday Viciousness" chapter. So I did what we all do when we are curious what became of someone—I Googled her. My search, however, did not reveal any booking mug shots or public reprimands by the board. I learned, instead, that Dr. Taylor has expanded her low-income clinic to meet the growing needs of the community she was serving. Other search results linked her to other noble causes: the fight against childhood obesity, the rights of immigrant farmers, even a connection to the slow food movement. From everything I could glean reading the many pages my search retrieved, I could not have been more wrong to jump to sordid conclusions about the good doctor, and I should consider myself lucky to have been associated with her so early in my career. She would be an ideal person to try to friend on Facebook—if she will accept my invitation . . .

Indeed, not everyone is less disciplined in real life because of the Internet or is on shakier moral, relationship, or cognitive grounds. Not everyone is in danger of developing depression-, paranoid-, PTSD-, addiction-, and ADHD-like states from spending too much time online. Not everyone is more impulsive or spatially lost or temporally disoriented. Sometimes a password is just a password.

There are people who are remarkably adept at compartmentalizing. They may have an online life that is very different from their offline life but still manage to keep the two rather separate. For these individuals, it may be as simple as having a group of friends with whom they do certain things and another group of friends that they are equally comfortable with but with whom they socialize around completely different activities. In their case, the two spheres of existing—online and off-, virtual and real—remain neatly separate, like the proverbial oil and water. For the rest of us, however, this separation is no longer feasible, and we are living in something that resembles a cloudy emulsion, the existential equivalent of a well-shaken vinaigrette. Hard as we may try, there are significant obstacles to our ability to maintain the dichotomy—to how much we can keep our virtual life neatly encapsulated. I am referring here not only to potentially compromising Google searches we may have conducted or to other Internet activities that we may want kept behind password-protected accounts, but also to the distracting banalities that target us from all digital directions: Facebook status updates that don't tell us anything significant but still pull us back to the screen, tweets of the "pointless babble" variety, "K" text messages we feel compelled to send, and so on. All these seemingly inescapable interruptions impinge on our reality and our offline life and make it so we feel constantly tethered to, and enmeshed with, our virtual lives.

Few things sound as far removed and freeing as "cloud computing," which allows data and applications to be accessed over the Internet from remote services without the need to invest in bulky infrastructure or expensive software. But its effects are close to home, not in the upper atmosphere. For us, unlike in Vegas, what happens online does not stay online. For even if we manage to close the browser at the end of a long day, a window remains open in our psyche, and through it continue to percolate tastes and traits that were born out of the virtual experience but that demand to be incorporated offline. Saying that it takes one click of the mouse to close a browser significantly underestimates the browser's hold on our psyche. It may well take a click or two to log on, but logging off is a more difficult challenge and a whole different story.

Saying we have successfully logged off, then, is an expression of seriously wishful thinking: Most of us are never truly offline anymore. With every text, e-mail, or emoticon we launch into cyberspace, an imperceptibly small something is lost or at least altered in our offline life, and remains that way even after we turn our computers and other electronic gadgetry off. These losses and alterations, infinitesimal in and of themselves, add up to a life that is different from the one we led only a decade ago, and to "a whole new you," as countless products that have nothing to do with technology often promise but almost never deliver. This product—the Internet and other purveyors of the virtual experience—does deliver, and the signs are all around us, as I have argued.

More and more, we straddle the digital divide within us and increasingly fuse and confuse e-personality with personality, virtual life with life, cloud computing with a more grounded way of interacting and transacting. This is what I call "virtualism," and it is our new reality.

And it will only become more problematic as the tide of technology decidedly moves, and moves us with it, in the direction of more blending of our different worlds, more multitasking, and more lack of privacy guarantees for how we conduct ourselves in cyberspace. But it is bad enough right now. The consequences of virtual life's taking over real life are no longer theoretical, and one can already see manifestations of that around us. In the town hall meetings that convened to discuss health care reform in the summer of 2009, for instance, we saw people across the country carrying swastikas and wearing "Proud Member of the Mob" t-shirts. We heard them getting into shouting matches with one another, making a mockery of intelligent debate, and bringing the level of discourse to rarely seen lows. We felt the pain of the baffled, drowned-out speakers, to whom no one really went to listen anyway—everyone's own voice was louder and more interesting, and everyone felt more entitled to the audience and the spotlight. And all this was taking place in the time-tested, couldn't-be-more-democratic format of the town hall meeting. The scenes that were generated looked at once familiar and bizarre, like something we have witnessed before but not necessarily offline. Were we engaged in a serious public discussion of a most serious issue, or were we watching nutty people on YouTube? One could not immediately tell.

Our statements, actions, and reactions are tending toward the extreme, because we have started thinking of them as worthless if they cannot be turned into YouTube moments or Internet memes; if they do not meet the criteria for irrationality and exuberance; if they cannot distract a multitasker from his multiple tasks; and if they do not carry within them that online mix of demagogue-ish pronouncements, facile entertainment, and provocation. More and more, offline, too, we see ourselves in pixels and hear ourselves in voxels, which is giving rise to a sobering realization: When life, like the democratic town hall, becomes a chat room, the outcome, seemingly inescapably, is an assault on civilization and society, and a town *brawl*.

Which raises the following big question: What if the virtual world, rather than *making us* more bellicose, immature, and impulsive, is simply allowing our true instincts to return? Could the new you be, in a sense, more real than the real thing? Is e-personality more true to our core? Is virtualism, by turning the clock on civilization and the social contract, simply taking us back to something that might be called our "state of nature"? That is the phrase used by the seventeenth-century English philosopher Thomas Hobbes to refer to the human condition left to its own devices.

According to Hobbes, in the state of nature, each person is driven exclusively by self-interest, and each person has a right to all things. He makes a threefold argument/prediction that suggests it is extremely unlikely that human beings will live in peaceful cooperation if left to their natural instincts: (1) We will ruthlessly compete with one another to secure our needs and make material gains; (2) we will challenge one another and fight out of fear; (3) we will seek reputation (or "glory"), both for its own sake and for its deterrent effects—so others think twice before challenging us. In this environment of universal insecurity, human cooperation is all but impossible, and all have reason to be afraid and mutually suspicious. In the mayhem that ensues, "nothing can be unjust," and "the notions of right and wrong, justice and injustice have . . . no place." Further,

> . . . there is . . . no culture . . . no knowledge of the face of the earth; no account of time; no arts; no letters; no society; and, which is worst of all, continual fear and danger of violent death; and the life of man, solitary, poor, nasty, brutish, and short.

Such was the case at the "beginning of time" and in "primitive societies," but the state of nature can occur anytime, such as in Hobbes's seventeenth-century England should the king's authority be successfully undermined, or even today. The only way to avert this doomsday scenario is for men to agree to a social contract that establishes a civil society where all individuals cede some of their natural rights to a powerful ruler or political system in exchange for stability and protection. For Hobbes, the alternative to strong and authoritarian rule is a situation no one could reasonably wish for. In his conception of the human condition, peace and harmony in the absence of an authority that contains us are chimeric notions impossible in the real world. The best we can hope for is peaceful coexistence under some form of external control.

One could draw a parallel between the state of nature that pushed Hobbes to his pessimism and the state of the World Wide Web today. The worst possible outcomes he feared have echoes in a medium he could not have imagined. Seeing the security risks that loom on the cyberspace horizon, Stanford Internet engineer Nick McKeown, for example, warns: "Unless we're willing to rethink today's Internet, we're just waiting for a series of public catastrophes." Rick Wesson, the chief executive of the computer consulting firm Support Intelligence, voices the same fear: "If you're looking for a digital Pearl Harbor, we now have the Japanese ships streaming toward us on the horizon." And, according to journalist John Markoff, who interviewed them, "there is a growing belief among engineers and security experts that Internet security and privacy have become so maddeningly elusive that the only way to fix the problem is to start over."

And starting over, Markoff writes, involves building a gated online community, "where users would give up their anonymity and certain freedoms in return for safety"—something that, when you think about it, sounds like a Hobbesian solution to a Hobbesian crisis. As more of us become worried about online safety and convinced of the need for a new Internet model, Markoff predicts more of us will be willing to accept the freedom-in-exchange-for-security bargain. And as more of us retreat into relatively closed-off communities that are organized to look more like real life, "the current Internet might end up as the bad neighborhood of cyberspace. You would enter at your own risk and keep an eye over your shoulder while you were there."

Markoff and the cybersecurity experts he quoted, however, are primarily concerned with ways to bolster the Web's defenses against cybercrime. Their Armageddon comes in the form of a more virulent Conficker strain. These are the same fears that led President Obama to create a cyberczar position in his administration and led some senators to go further, proposing a solution that was likened to an "Internet kill switch." Radical as they may be, however, none of these measures begin to address the other fronts on which we need to bolster our defenses and the other forms of mass disruption that have been the subject of this book. Additional controls are needed to help defend against those, because more is at stake than painful but comparatively straightforward security breaches.

Such additional controls can sometimes come from outside. To the extent that the recession of 2008–2010 may have been exacerbated by a new relationship with money that was born or practiced online, reining in our financial impulsivity would seem to make sense. Remarks made in early 2010 by Ben Bernanke, the Federal Reserve chairman, pointing out that it was lack of regulation and oversight, not low interest rates, that caused the housing bubble and subsequent economic meltdown, speak to that. The more muscular approach to financial regulation that followed ostensibly aims to correct the problem. As overzealous borrowers, we might benefit from a system that can help better protect us against ourselves (and, at least as importantly, against unscrupulous lenders). This is not that different from the kind of watchful benevolence that Google is capable of through initiatives like the Goggles program. But not all controls can be legislated or imposed or can come from outside. Nor should they. Ultimately, they have to come from within the wakeful and aware self; from a genuine conviction that our offline standards and other things we value should continue to carry weight as our lives become more digitalized, for they are the result of a long civilizing process and should not be gambled or experimented with, even as we gamble and experiment with so much else online.

One principal way to try to achieve this self-discipline is through a well-rounded, balanced education about the good and the bad that have come with the virtual revolution. Courses abound, at every level, in every language, and for every audience, on how to master new software, build a catchy Web site, or take a business idea online. Extremely little is available, however, for the individual interested in learning more about how virtual technology has reshaped our inner universe and may be remapping our brains. As centers of learning, public libraries, schools, and universities may be disproportionately responsible for this deficiency. They outdo one another in digitalizing their holdings and speeding up their Internet connections, and rightfully see those upgrades as essential to compete for students, scholars, and patrons. In exchange, however, and with few exceptions, they teach little about the unintended, less obvious, and more personal consequences of the World Wide Web. The irony is, at least in some libraries' case, that their very survival seems threatened by a shift that they do not seem fully engaged in trying to understand, much less educate their audiences about.

Like teachers and schools, parents can do more to mold a better virtual citizen. In general, parents are well aware of the risks posed by MySpace predators and do a good job warning their kids about those. Many have learned to use blocking software and keyloggers-type monitoring of online activity to curtail their kids' access to pornographic and other extreme content. But more can be done to inculcate good World Wide Web morals and habits in children. This can happen only through a more nuanced understanding of what kids do and become online; one that goes beyond knowing how much pornography they are being exposed to and whether they have befriended adults masquerading as children. Parents need to be more curious, for example, about whether their kids are more quick to cyber-harass a classmate online than in the playground or are more readily bullied themselves. How often do they cut-and-paste answers to their homework, and do they see anything wrong with that? Is their attention span suffering as a result of quick-paced, superficial online interacting, and how is that affecting their ability to focus, learn, and be patient with the world? Are they valuing real-life friendships less because of a surfeit of Facebook friends? Are they mindful of how their online reputation is shaping up? And so on. The truth is, however, many parents do not ask these questions of themselves, making it less likely that they will ask them of their offspring. (Reading text message exchanges between teenagers and their parents for a different project I was involved in, it was hard sometimes to tell which party ignored writing rules more.)

Parents might also be feeling intimidated by a new technology that they know their kids are more facile with. Parents often rely on their children for tips on maintaining a Facebook page, editing a digital photograph, or downloading an iPhone app. This might make them feel unqualified when it comes to advising their children on the possible negatives associated with a technology that they do not fully master—"What do *I* know about Facebook?" To the extent that their technophobia may be causing them to doubt their instincts and whether they know what is best for their kids, they should reverse the reverse parenting going on.

Much more research needs to be done to understand the biological changes that happen in our brains as we interact with the virtual world. What is it that mediates, at the level of brain pathways, neurons and neurotransmitters, the disinhibition that seems to come naturally online, and the other personality traits I have tried to highlight? Because of the potential for conflict of interest, designing and conducting such studies is probably not the role of a pharmaceutical company or the R&D arm of an online powerhouse. Rather, this objective might be best met through a well-funded collaboration between a government-supported entity like the National Institute of Mental Health and academic institutions with a proven track record in conducting research. The East is well ahead of the West in that regard, although the focus, as we have seen, has been on "Internet addiction." The more subtle changes that have been the subject of this book and that occur in people who cannot be called "addicts"—that is, most of us—also deserve rigorous study. Strong scientific proof, should we find it, of Web-mediated changes at the level of our brain cells would serve as a wake-up call and could go a long way toward convincing us that our virtual lifestyle is indeed changing our internal chemistry. We might then start logging on a little bit more self-consciously.

It would be easy to counter this call to action, or for that matter this book, by saying that those who raise concerns about virtual life, and ask for publicly funded research into it or measures to try to contain it, are simply rehashing old fears that surface with every new technology. But this would be missing the point. It is true that every wave of new media technology has brought with it its loud detractors: People agonized over the effects of films in the early 1900s, radio in the 1920s, television in the 1940s, the personal computer in the 1970s, and primitive video games in early 1990s. However, the Internet's much deeper penetration into every aspect of our lives today makes it more insidious, and potentially more dangerous, than these historical scares. Its immersive and interactive qualities, how it can talk back to us, engulf us, break us down and then reconstitute us into something different—all distinguish it from other waves of technology that have caused panic over the decades, and all make it so that there might be more at stake today.

I have tried to make the case for the existence of the online self as a relatively independent creature that does not necessarily answer to us. I have drawn on clinical work and personal experience, as well as research in the fields of linguistics, neuroscience, sociology, psychoanalysis, and philosophy, to identify what I see as the most common, and often negative, psychological characteristics that tend to define it. I outlined a series of potentially dangerous impulses that are unleashed by the Internet and showed how they can turn the user's psychology on its head. Although for clarity's sake I have separated them into distinct forces—tendencies toward immoderation, self-aggrandizement, dark thoughts, impulsivity, and infantile regression—we are all capable of exhibiting all of these qualities simultaneously or in succession. The part of our psyche that usually reins in these instincts—what psychoanalysts have traditionally called the superego—finds a worthy competitor in the Internet-assisted id, with its infantile self-centeredness and its dark dreams that demand to be satisfied. The new disequilibrium, brought about by virtual life, between the brake system that keeps us in check and the stubborn (Hobbesian) urges that lie underneath the surface, helps unleash an online self that can be quite foreign to the person sitting behind the computer.

Leaving it at that, however, would have captured neither the dynamic flow across the digital divide nor the full breadth of the problem. In reality, there is a constant back-and-forth between our online and offline lives—and the border between the two is quite porous. The rudeness we are capable of in our e-mails and the lack of judgment we show in our online purchases and sexual hookups do not stay "there." These behaviors bleed into our real lives, leading to the propagation, offline, of personality traits such as impatience, immoderation, and impoliteness. Although these qualities may be useful or even advantageous in cyberspace, they can negatively affect our well-being when imported into the real world. For example, how does easy access to Internet pornography affect our sex and love lives? Does the Internet enrich us with its surfeit of information ipso facto, or could it provide a false base of knowledge upon which we try to diagnose ourselves and fix whatever ails us? Does the immediate gratification promised by the Internet lead us to become Web junkies, incapable of stepping away from the screen, regardless of how our online habit is affecting our relationships with friends and loved ones? And what of the permanence of the Internet, the fact that our personal information and, for some of us, critical events in our lives are memorialized in perpetuity on the Web? Does this affect the way we behave in our dealings with others or have an effect on our general well-being and mental health? How are our day-to-day reality and sense of ourselves changing as a function of our online browsing?

The whole new you that is the end result of this process is larger than life, convinced of its specialness, alternately dark and infantile, both compulsive and impulsive, and feeling its way through relationships, knowledge, space, and time. Yet foreign as it may seem, it is still you, virtually speaking, and you still own it and own its consequences—that our virtual half has a mind of its own is hardly a good enough defense when it gets us in trouble. That is why it is imperative that we carefully dissect and contemplate our new psychology, even as the virtual world, a contemplation-averse medium, may be slowly compromising the mental skills we need to fully assess its impact on our lives. Whether we use the Internet for e-mail and the occasional eBay purchase or conduct much of our lives in cyberspace, we can no longer afford to ignore the psychological dimension to going online. Beside the established economic, educational, entertainment, and civic realities that are urging us to log on—indeed, before all of these—there exists a psychological being busy meeting his social and emotional needs even as he unknowingly creates new ones. There is someone, for example, who goes online out of loneliness or boredom, only to start devaluing offline relationships because of the comparative difficulty of forming them, something that in the long run can lead him to feel lonelier and more bored. Or someone who feels stuck in an unhappy marriage and finds in the virtual world a welcome breath of fresh air, only for that seemingly innocent and free outlet to make him put off working on his marriage or deciding to leave if that is what needs to be done. Our understanding of the psychological needs of the person logging on, and of how they are being met and unmet in cyberspace, is essential to our ability to maintain our equilibrium, anchoring, and important associations.

This book is not intended as a manifesto for renouncing the virtual world. It would be both naïve and futile to preach that—no one can imagine life without Google, and, even if it were possible, few people I know would be interested in living it. One senses a sad inexorability to all this, and we are all "hooked," if not clinically, then functionally and practically. A few years ago, I took a six-day trip to a country officially listed by Reporters without Borders as one of thirteen "enemies of the Internet" because of severe oppression of online freedom of speech. As I struggled to access my university e-mail account and to log on to Pubmed, the government-sponsored database of scientific publications, and as I found search engines much less useful because of irrational restrictions on search results, I felt something that I can only describe as a mini-withdrawal: a malaise that steadily grew over the course of my six days there, and that only getting back on U.S. soil and in front of my laptop with the 20-megabyte/second DSL connection could cure. The list of thirteen includes other places I have always wanted to visit, but knowing that they are Google-unfriendly and that they might read what I type gives me serious pause, a little bit like knowing it was malaria season in my vacation destination would.

My goal, then, is less painful and more modest than to suggest that we log off. I have tried, instead, to offer a note of caution, an exhortation to think before we click, to proceed in the virtual world with increased caution, knowledge, and, above all, self-knowledge. Just as a teenager becomes one naturally, without planning it or necessarily working toward it, we all have, whether we approve it or not, already come of age as virtual beings. We cannot, any more than a teenager can, reverse the clock or unrelease those hormones. The question before us is what to do with ourselves now, not how to capture some romanticized pre-virtual innocence. The answer, unfortunately, is far from clear, but will have to pass through an appreciation for what is at stake and for how ungrounded and unreal so much of our world and our identity have become. Understanding this unreality, and calling for awareness of and research into it, and for new parenting and educational paradigms, are the requisite first steps toward doing something about it even if this book is not a self-help or how-to manual—I may be a psychiatrist who has lived in Silicon Valley and researched and treated problematic Internet use, but I claim no secret recipe for how to extricate us from the virtual thicket. What I do have, and what I have tried to convey here, is a big belief in "know thyself," and I hope that my book will serve as an invitation to look through the laptop screen and into the mirror.

Virtualism, as enabled especially by the Internet, is a major signpost in our journey through history. There can be no doubting that it has opened windows and brought opportunity—for social connection and outreach, for liberation from anxiety and doubt, for financial and personal success, and for self-realization and fulfillment. Similarly, there can be no doubting any longer the big experiment we are conducting with our psyches. To offer a psychological read of the virtual age is to offer a candid assessment of an encounter between humankind and a new type of machine—one that is not entirely inanimate; that can be alluring, deceptive, and addictive at the same time; and that can efficiently prey on our basic instincts and impulses, our need for amusement and information, and our never-ending search for belonging and self-betterment. Yet for all the problems and "for the worse" changes this machine might have introduced into our lives, we are not any lesser for it; only much more complicated. And just as we survived the steam engine, that other watershed machine, and are now able to assess, relatively objectively, both the progress and the deprivation brought about by the Industrial Revolution, I hope that we will someday be able to measure the World Wide Web's legacy beyond gross domestic product indexes, efficiency gains, and the number of smiling emoticons flying through the ether. Only then can we honestly rejoice in the Internet's many real bounties. Only then can we claim it as proof that, despite what philosophers have been telling us for centuries, history is not over yet, and the human race is not living in an irrelevant era of stagnation and zero achievement—the "Sunday of life" that follows history's long labor, according to Hegel. Only then can we genuinely feel that we, our time, our contributions, still matter and can still mark, even make, history.

_ACKNOWLEDGMENTS

Above all, I wish to thank my patients, some of whose stories I adapted for the book. They are my best teachers and an endless source of inspiration.

I am deeply grateful to my agent, Rachel Sussman. Her vision helped me think up the book, and her support along the way helped make it a reality. My gratitude also goes to Rachel's colleagues at Zachary Shuster Harmsworth, especially Todd Shuster.

I owe much to my editor, the indomitable Maria Guarnaschelli. Maria believed what I had to say and helped me say it the best way I could. A unique mix of experience, instinct, and opera, she was a pleasure to work with. Other members of the W. W. Norton family, including Melanie Tortoroli and Janet Byrne, also gave generously of their time and talent toward the publication of this book.

Finally, for their valuable advice on different aspects of the book and for their sustained, and sustaining, enthusiasm, I wish to thank Dr. Robin Apple, Nona Gamel, Dr. Khalil Ghanem, Dr. Lorrin "Larry" Koran, and Dr. Debby Rovine.

_APPENDIX
YOUNG'S INTERNET ADDICTION TEST*

Answer each of the following 20 questions on a scale of 1 to 5, where
1 = rarely; 2 = occasionally; 3 = frequently; 4 = often; 5 = always.

1. How often do you stay online longer than you intended?
2. How often do you neglect household chores in order to spend more
   time online?
3. How often do you prefer the excitement of the Internet over intimacy with your partner?
4. How often do you form new relationships with fellow online users?
5. How often do others complain about the amount of time you spend
   online?
6. How often do your grades or schoolwork suffer because of the
   amount of time you spend online?
7. How often do you check e-mail before something else that you need
   to do?
8. How often does your job performance or productivity suffer
   because of the Internet?
9. How often do you become defensive when someone asks you what
   you do online?
10. How often do you block out disturbing thoughts about your life
    with soothing thoughts of the Internet?
11. How often do you find yourself anticipating when you will go
    online again?

*Adapted from K. S. Young, *Caught in the Net: How to Recognize the Signs of Internet
Addiction—and a Winning Strategy for Recovery* (New York: Wiley, 1998).

12. How often do you fear that life without the Internet would be boring, empty, and joyless?
13. How often do you snap, yell, or become annoyed if someone bothers you while you are online?
14. How often do you lose sleep due to late-night Internet use?
15. How often do you feel preoccupied with the Internet when offline, or fantasize about being online?
16. How often do you find yourself saying "just a few more minutes" when online?
17. How often do you try to cut back on your online time but fail?
18. How often do you try to hide how long you've been online?
19. How often do you choose to spend more time online over socializing?
20. How often do you feel depressed, moody, or nervous when you are offline, [a feeling] which goes away once you are back online?

A total score of 49 or less suggests typical Internet use by a nonaddict; 50 to 79 correlates with possible Internet-related problems; and 80 or above is consistent with Internet addiction.

_NOTES

PREFACE

9 **The news story introduced me**: Alejandro Martinez-Cabrera,"Web Sites Deal with Digital Assets after We Die," January 31, 2010, http://articles.sfgate .com/2010-02-01/business/17841840_1_digital-passwords-online (accessed February 8, 2010).

1: E-PERSONALITY

16 **ten million Americans whose information**: Identity Theft Assistance Center, *Javelin 2009 Identity Fraud Survey Report Reveals Fraud Is Up 22%, Impacting Nearly 10 Million Americans*, http://www.identitytheftassistance.org/pageview.php?cateid=47 (accessed December 6, 2009).

16 **all one billion or so**: Erick Schonfeld, "ComScore: Internet Population Passes One Billion," January 23, 2009, http://www.techcrunch.com/2009/01/23/ comscore-internet-population-passes-one-billion-top-15-countries/ (accessed October 1, 2009).

19 **According to the Digital Future Project**: Center for the Digital Future, *Annual Internet Survey by the Center for the Digital Future Finds Shifting Trends Among Adults About the Benefits and Consequences of Children Going Online*, 2008, http://www .digitalcenter.org/pdf/2008-Digital-Future-Report-Final-Release.pdf (accessed October 1, 2009).

20 **takes cyber-disobedience from Facebook**: *Washington Times*, "Iran's Twitter Revolution," June 16, 2009, http://www.washingtontimes.com/news/2009/ jun/16/irans-twitter-revolution (accessed December 6, 2009).

20 **On the eve of renewed student protests**: Ali Akbar Dareini, "Iran Chokes Off Internet on Eve of Student Rallies," December 6, 2007, http://www.chron .com/disp/story.mpl/ap/world/6756087.html (accessed December 7, 2009).

22 **over sixteen million virtual "residents"**: Tomi Ahonen, "Second Life at 16 Million Users, Says CNN Today," http://communities-dominate.blogs.com/ brands/2009/02/second-life-at-16-million-users-says-cnn-today.html (accessed October 1, 2009).

22 **over 100 million active accounts**: Patricia Sellers, "MySpace Cowboys," 2006, http://money.cnn.com/magazines/fortune/fortune_archive/2006/09/ 04/8384727/index.htm (accessed October 1, 2009).

22 **over 500 million users**: Jenna Wortham, "Facebook Tops 500 Million

Users," *New York Times*, July 21, 2010, http://www.nytimes.com/2010/07/22/technology/22facebook.html (accessed July 26, 2010).

26 **Celexa in compulsive shopping**: L. M. Koran, H. W. Chuong, K. D. Bullock, and S. C. Smith, "Citalopram for Compulsive Shopping Disorder: An Open-Label Study Followed by Double-Blind Discontinuation," *Journal of Clinical Psychiatry* 64, no. 7 (2003): 793–98.

26 **Paxil in pathological gambling**: S. W. Kim, J. E. Grant, D. E. Adson, Y. C. Shin, and R. Zaninelli, "A Double-Blind Placebo-Controlled Study of the Efficacy and Safety of Paroxetine in the Treatment of Pathological Gambling," *Journal of Clinical Psychiatry* 63, no. 6 (2002): 501–7.

26 **cognitive-behavioral therapy, or CBT**: J. Beck, *Cognitive Behavioral Therapy: Basics and Beyond* (New York: Guilford Press, 1995).

33 **160 million regular Internet users**: Erick Schonfeld, "ComScore: Internet Population Passes One Billion."

33 **The "patient zero"**: Mark Miller and Barbara Kantrowitz, "Unmasking Sybil: A Re-Examination of the Most Famous Psychiatric Patient in History," *Newsweek*, January 25, 1999, http://www.newsweek.com/id/87075 (accessed October 1, 2009).

34 **Dr. Cornelia Wilbur**: Ibid.

34 **fewer than a hundred cases**: J. P. Sutcliffe and J. Jones, "Personal Identity, Multiple Personality, and Hypnosis," *International Journal of Clinical and Experimental Hypnosis* 10 (1962): 231–69.

34 **Chris Costner Sizemore**: C. C. Sizemore, *A Mind of My Own: The Woman Who Was Known as "Eve" Tells the Story of Her Triumph over Multiple Personality Disorder* (New York: William Morrow & Co., 1989).

34 **a veritable avalanche of MPD case reports**: J. F. Kihlstrom, "Dissociative Disorders," *Annual Review of Clinical Psychology* 1 (2005): 227–53.

34 **best-selling book**: Miller and Kantrowitz, "Unmasking Sybil."

34 **a 1976 made-for-TV movie**: Ibid.

34 **overeager clinicians, determined to find it**: A. Piper, "A Skeptical Look at Multiple Personality Disorder," in *Dissociative Identity Disorder: Theoretical and Treatment Controversies*, ed. L. M. Cohen, J. N. Berzoff, and M. R. Elin (New York: Jason Aronson, 1995), 135–73.

34 **1 to 2 percent of the U.S. population**: Kihlstrom, "Dissociative Disorders."

34 **number of personalities *within* each case**: Ibid.

34 **Even Eve, not to be outdone**: Ibid.

35 **"profoundly ignorant of the whole hypnosis phenomenon"**: Mikkel Borch-Jacobsen, "Sybil—The Making of a Disease: An Interview with Dr. Herbert Spiegel," http://www.nybooks.com/articles/article-preview?article_id=1199 (accessed October 1, 2009).

35 **compare the size of the hippocampus and amygdala**: E. Vermetten, C. Schmahl, S. Lindner, R. J. Loewenstein and J. D. Bremner, "Hippocampal and Amygdalar Volumes in Dissociative Identity Disorder," *American Journal of Psychiatry* 163, no. 4 (2006): 630–36.

35 **measurable biological changes taking place**: G. E. Tsai, D. Condie, M. T. Wu, and I. W. Chang, "Functional Magnetic Resonance Imaging of Personality Switches in a Woman with Dissociative Identity Disorder," *Harvard Review of Psychiatry* 7, no. 2 (1999): 119–22.

35 **"Now we can watch multiple personalities emerge in the brain"**: Robert Adler, "Crowded Minds," *New Scientist*, December 18, 1999, http://www.newscientist.com/article/mg16422174.800-crowded-minds.html (accessed October 1, 2009).

36 ***Diagnostic and Statistical Manual of Mental Disorders***: American Psychiatric Association, *Diagnostic and Statistical Manual of Mental Disorders–IV*, text revision (Washington, D.C.: American Psychiatric Association, 2000); hereinafter *DSM-IV*, text revision.

36 **"dissociative identity disorder"**: Ibid.

36 **disruption of the normal integration**: E. M. Bernstein and F. W. Putnam, "Development, Reliability, and Validity of a Dissociation Scale," *Journal of Nervous and Mental Disorders* 174, no. 12 (1986): 727–35.

36 **the way the *DSM* defines it**: *DSM-IV*, text revision, 529.

36 **iatrogenic**: R. M. Wachter, L. Goldman and H. Hollander, eds., *Hospital Medicine*, 2nd ed. (New York: Lippincott, Williams & Wilkins, 2005), 147.

37 **Dissociative Experiences Scale**: E. M. Bernstein and F. W. Putnam, "Development, Reliability, and Validity of a Dissociation Scale."

38 **1998 study published in the journal *Nature***: M. J. Koepp et al., "Evidence for Striatal Dopamine Release during a Video Game," *Nature* 393 (1998): 266–68.

38 **Dopamine is a major player in the "pleasure system"**: K. C. Berridge and M. L. Kringelbach, "Affective Neuroscience of Pleasure: Reward in Humans and Animals," *Psychopharmacology* 199, no. 3 (2008): 457–80.

38 **It is also implicated in cognitive functions**: I. Wickelgren, "Getting the Brain's Attention," *Science* 278 (1997): 35–37.

38 **euphoria that is sometimes induced by cocaine use**: Ibid.

39 **2007 study led by Harvard psychiatrist**: D. H. Han et al., "Dopamine Genes and Reward Dependence in Adolescents with Excessive Internet Video Game Play," *Journal of Addiction Medicine* 1, no. 3 (2007): 133–38.

39 **Another study, published in 1992**: R. J. Haier et al., "Regional Glucose Metabolic Changes after Learning a Complex Visuospatial/Motor Task: A Positron Emission Tomographic Study," *Brain Research* 570, nos. 1–2 (1992): 134–43.

40 **"online disinhibition effect"**: J. Suler, "The Online Disinhibition Effect," *Cyberpsychology and Behavior* 7, no. 3 (2004): 321–26.

45 **fifty-six innocent seconds**: Nielsen Company, "Nielsen Online Provides Topline U.S. Data for March 2009," http://www.nielsen-online.com/pr/pr_090414 .pdf.

2: DELUSIONS OF GRANDEUR

46 **639 skeletal muscles**: Brian Samuel Beckett, *Biology*, 2nd ed. (London: Oxford University Press, 1983), 8.

48 **like those of Larry Page and Sergey Brin**: *Forbes*, "The 400 Richest Americans," September 17, 2008, http://www.forbes.com/lists/2008/54/400list08_The-400-Richest-Americans_Rank.html (accessed October 2, 2009).

48 **Pierre Omidyar, the forty-three-year-old founder of eBay**: Ibid.

48 **Mark Zuckerberg, the twenty-six-year-old founder**: Dell Jones, "*Forbes*: Facebook CEO Is Youngest Self-Made Billionaire," *USA Today*, http://www .usatoday.com/money/2008-03-05-forbes-billionaires_N.htm (accessed October 2, 2009).

49 **According to official Google history**: Google, *Google Milestones*, http://www .google.com/corporate/history.html (accessed October 2, 2009).

49 **The googol represents the numeral one**: Russ Rowlett, *How Many? A Dictionary of Units of Measurement*, 2001, http://www.unc.edu/~rowlett/units/dictG.html (accessed October 2, 2009).

49 **Google Books**: Jeffrey Toobin, "Google's Moon Shot," *The New Yorker*, February 5, 2007, http://www.newyorker.com/reporting/2007/02/05/070205fa_fact_ toobin (accessed October 2, 2009).

49 **Google Earth, which photographically maps**: Google, *Google Earth High Resolution Imagery Coverage (USA)*, 2005, http://earth.google.com/coverage/google_ earth_coverage_list_2005-05-07.pdf (accessed October 2, 2009).

50 **to the tune of over five billion hits a month**: Danny Sullivan, "Nielsen: Google Hits New Search Share High," 2008, http://searchengineland.com/ nielsen-google-hits-new-search-share-high-14038.php (accessed October 2009).

50 **two old company jokes**: Google, *Google Milestones*.

50 **"*googol*plex," a number even larger**: Rowlett, *How Many?*

50 **10 duotrigintillion in the American system**: Russ Rowlett, *Names for Large Numbers*, http://www.unc.edu/~rowlett/units/large.html (accessed October 2, 2009).

50 **Sixty billion is grandiose enough**: eBay Inc., *2008 Annual Survey*, 2009, http:// www.shareholder.com/visitors/dynamicdoc/document.cfm?documentid=2493& companyid=ebay&page=1&pin=400276241&language=EN&resizethree=yes& scale=100 (accessed January 2, 2010).

50 **by its 80 million or so**: eBay Media Center, *eBay Inc.: A Short History*, 2009, http://news.ebay.com/about.cfm (accessed October 2, 2009).

50 **figure grew from $14.83**: eBay Media Center, *Our History*, http://news.ebay
.com/history.cfm (accessed October 2, 2009).

50 **According to company lore**: eBay Media Center, *eBay Inc.: A Short History*.

50 **human kidney was auctioned off**: Amy Mullen, "Learn How eBay Began as
a Small Business in Someone's Living Room and Grew into One of the Top Earning Websites on the Internet," http://www.happynews.com/living/online/history-
ebay.htm (accessed October 2, 2009).

51 **seats to view executions**: "A Brief History of eBay," *Industry Standard*, July 30,
2001, http://www.thestandard.com/article/0,1902,28323,00.html (accessed October 2, 2009).

51 **put his soul up for auction**: "EBay Blocks Man's Attempt to Sell Soul," *USA
Today*, February 9, 2001, http://www.usatoday.com/tech/news/2001-02-09-ebay-
soul.htm (accessed October 2, 2009).

51 **"Hacker. Dropout. CEO"**: Ellen McGirt, "Facebook's Zuckerberg: Hacker.
Dropout. CEO." May 1, 2007, http://www.fastcompany.com/magazine/115/
open_features-hacker-dropout-ceo.html (accessed October 2, 2009).

52 **chronicles the rise of Amazon**: Robert Spector, *Get Big Fast: Inside the Revolutionary Business Model That Changed the World* (New York: HarperCollins, 2000).

52 **the day of the Netscape IPO**: John Shinal, "Netscape: The IPO That
Launched an Era," August 5, 2005, http://www.marketwatch.com/story/netscape-
ipo-ignited-the-boom-taught-some-hard-lessons-2005851850 (accessed October
2, 2009).

53 **" . . . Clearly, sustained low inflation implies less uncertainty"**: Alan
Greenspan, "Remarks by Chairman Alan Greenspan," 1996, http://www.federal
reserve.gov/boarddocs/speeches/1996/19961205.htm (accessed October 2,
2009).

53 **a record high of 5132.52**: David. R. Francis, "How Stock Rout Hits
America Inc.," March 10, 2000, http://www.csmonitor.com/centennial/on-
this-day/2009/03/march-10-2000-the-nasdaq-composite-stock-market-index-
peaks-at-513252-the-beginning-of-the-slide-of-the-dot-com-technology-sec
tor-boom/ (accessed October 2, 2009).

53 **the NASDAQ ended 2009 at 2269.15**: New York Stock Exchange, *History of
the NASDAQ Composite Index*, http://www.nyse.tv/nasdaq-composite-history.htm
(accessed October 2, 2009).

53 **seven-trillion-dollar drop**: Shinal, "Netscape: The IPO That Launched an
Era."

53 **Two hundred thousand people in "Sili Valley"**: Adam Kress and Mike Sun-
nucks, "Financial Services among Job Sectors with Big September Losses," September 29, 2008, http://sanjose.bizjournals.com/sanjose/stories/2008/09/29/
daily98.html (accessed October 2, 2009).

54 **The roughest of all the dot-com landings**: Melanie Farmer and Greg San-doval, "Webvan Delivers Its Last Word: Bankruptcy," http://news.cnet.com/2100-1017-269594.html (accessed October 2, 2009).

54 **accuse Webvan of "historical innocence"**: Nicholas Hodson and Tim Las-seter, "Sweeping Webvan into the Dustbin of History," 2001, http://www.strategy-business.com/press/enewsarticle/22494 (accessed October 2, 2009).

55 **was among the first to make it**: Andrew P. Morriss, "The Wild West Meets Cyberspace," http://www.fee.org/Publications/the-Freeman/article.asp?aid=3446 (accessed October 2, 2009).

56 **John Ashcroft, then a U.S. senator**: John Ashcroft, "Keep Big Brother's Hands Off the Internet," 1997, http://www.swans.com/library/art8/zig080.html (accessed October 2, 2009).

57 **"cybersecurity czar"**: "Cybersecurity Revamp, New 'Czar,' " May 29, 2009, http://www.cbsnews.com/blogs/2009/05/29/politics/politicalhotsheet/entry5048128.shtml (accessed October 2, 2009).

58 **2003 UCLA Internet Report**: The Center for the Digital Future, *The UCLA Internet Report Surveying the Digital Future*, 2003, http://www.digitalcenter.org/pdf/InternetReportYearThree.pdf (accessed October 2, 2009).

58 **10 percent of the so-called millennial**: J. Roberts, "Compulsive Spending in Younger Generations," *Futurist* 38, no. 2 (2004): 2.

58 **44 percent of adolescents**: Helga Dittmar, "Compulsive Buying—A Grow-ing Concern? An Examination of Gender, Age, and Endorsement of Materialistic Values as Predictors," *British Journal of Psychology* 96, no. 4 (2005): 467–91.

58 **consumer debt reached $2.52 trillion**: Gregg Robb, "U.S. January Consumer Credit Up $6.9 Billion or 3.3%," March 7, 2008, http://www.marketwatch.com/story/us-jan-consumer-credit-up-69-bln-or-33-rate (accessed October 2, 2009).

58 **credit file is responsible for $16,635**: Kimberly Palmer, "The End of Credit Card Consumerism," August 8, 2008, http://www.usnews.com/articles/business/economy/2008/08/08/the-end-of-credit-card-consumerism.html (accessed Octo-ber 2, 2009).

58 **hovered close to 0 percent**: Ibid.

58 **four of the top-ten online advertisers**: Peter Kafka, "Will Mortgage Woes Spread to Online Ads?" August 16, 2007, http://www.businessinsider.com/2007/8/will-mortgage-w (accessed October 2, 2009).

61 **gossip blogger Perez Hilton**: Andrea Chang, "How I Made It: Perez Hil-ton," *Los Angeles Times*, June 13, 2008, http://articles.latimes.com/2008/jun/13/business/fi-howimadeit13 (accessed October 2, 2009).

61 **YouTube superstars Obama Girl**: Jake Tapper, "Music Video Has a 'Crush on Obama,'" June 13, 2007, http://abcnews.go.com/Politics/story?id=3275802 (accessed October 2, 2009).

61 **lonelygirl15**: Jonathan Richards, "Worldwide Fame for a Lonely Girl," London *Times*, August 19, 2006, http://www.timesonline.co.uk/tol/news/uk/article613683 .ece (accessed October 2, 2009).

61 **Christian Lander of the wildly successful satirical blog**: Gregory Rodriguez, "White Like Us," *Los Angeles Times*, February 25, 2008, http://www.latimes .com/news/opinion/la-oe-rodriguez25feb25,0,1952462.column (last accessed October 2, 2009).

62 **over six billion videos posted on YouTube**: ComScore, "YouTube Surpasses 100 Million U.S. Viewers for the First Time," http://www.comscore.com/Press_ Events/Press_Releases/2009/3/YouTube_Surpasses_100_Million_US_Viewers (accessed October 2, 2009).

62 **the next Tila Tequila**: MTV.com, "A Shot at Love," 2008, http://www.mtv .com/ontv/dyn/tila_tequila/series.jhtml (accessed October 2, 2009).

62 **Justin Bieber, the sixteen-year-old**: Marco R. della Cava, "Tween Heartthrob Justin Bieber Pops into the Fame Machine," *USA Today*, June 21, 2010, http://www .usatoday.com/life/music/news/2010-06-21-justinbieber17_CV_N.htm (accessed June 29, 2010).

62 **thousands of "citizen journalists"**: Reyhan Harmanci, "CNN Discovers Downside of 'Citizen Journalism,'" October 4, 2008, http://www.sfgate.com/ cgi-bin/article.cgi?f=/c/a/2008/10/04/MNIV13B9E4.DTL (accessed October 2, 2009).

62 **Matt Harding is one of the millions**: Charles McGrath, "A Private Dance? Four Million Web Fans Say No," *New York Times*, July 8, 2008, http://www.nytimes .com/2008/07/08/arts/television/08dancer.html (accessed October 2, 2009).

63 **Mahir Cagri, a man from Izmir**: Oddee, "Ten Craziest Internet Memes," 2006, www.oddee.com/item_63440.aspx (accessed October 2, 2009).

63 **3-D digital rendition of a lifeless baby**: Ibid.

64 **the meme as a unit of cultural information**: Richard Dawkins, *The Selfish Gene* (Oxford: Oxford University Press, 1999), 192.

65 **"a premium on short, catchy memes"**: Gary Marshall, *The Internet and Memetics*, http://pespmc1.vub.ac.be/Conf/MemePap/Marshall.html (accessed October 2, 2009).

65 **"There is nothing, or next to nothing"**: René Girard, *Things Hidden Since the Foundation of the World*, trans. Stephen Bann and Michael Metteer (Stanford, CA: Stanford University Press, 1987), 7.

66 **"If the model, who is apparently already endowed"**: René Girard, *Violence and the Sacred*, trans. Patrick Gregory (Baltimore: Johns Hopkins University Press, 1977), 146.

3: NARCISSISM

68 **According to the DSM, people with narcissistic personality**: *DSM-IV*, text revision, 717.

69 **less than 1 percent of the population**: K. N. Levy, M. A. Chauhan, J. F. Clarkin, R. H. Wasserman, and J. S. Reynoso, "Narcissistic Pathology: Empirical Approaches," *Psychiatric Annals* 39, no. 4 (2009): 203–13.

69 **men are more likely to be afflicted**: Ibid.

69 **The popularity of "narcissurfing"**: Peter Hartlaub, "The Hip, Overused and Abused Business Buzzwords of 2007," December 21, 2007, http://www.msnbc.msn.com/id/22286283/ (accessed October 4, 2009).

69 **"Narcissurfing: Googling yourself to see"**: UrbanDictionary.com, http://www.urbandictionary.com/define.php?term=narcissurfing (accessed October 4, 2009).

69 **the iPad, whose name**: Clair Cain Miller, "The iPad's Name Makes Some Women Cringe," *New York Times*, January 27, 2010, http://bits.blogs.nytimes.com/2010/01/27/the-ipads-name-makes-some-women-cringe (accessed April 21, 2010)

70 **"It's Y!ou"**: Clay Dillow, "Yahoo!'s New Ad Blitz: It's All About 'Y!ou,'" September 22, 2009, http://www.fastcompany.com/blog/clay-dillow/culture-buffet/yahoo-launches-new-ad-blitz-its-all-about-you (accessed October 4, 2009).

70 **"EarthLink revolves around you"**: EarthLink Inc., *Earthlink Marks*, www.earthlink.net/about/policies/copyright.faces (accessed October 4, 2009).

70 **your own portable Wi-Fi bubble**: David Pogue, "Wi-Fi to Go, No Café Needed," *New York Times*, May 7, 2009, http://www.nytimes.com/2009/05/07/technology/personaltech/07pogue.html (accessed October 4, 2009).

70 **"Unlike real bubble wrap"**: Suzanne Choney, "iPhone's i-Centric Programs: It's about You 24/7," November 5, 2008, http://www.msnbc.msn.com/id/27524782 (accessed October 4, 2009).

70 **Zit Picker**: App Shopper, http://appshopper.com/entertainment/zit-picker-%E2%98%85 (accessed January 7, 2010).

70 **iCycle**: Choney, "iPhone's i-Centric Programs."

71 **"The Daily Me"**: Quoted in Robert Wachbroit, "Reliance and Reliability: The Problem of Information on the Internet," in *Ethics and the Internet*, ed. A. Vedder (Antwerp, Belgium: Intersentia, 2001), 139.

71 **has been called iSolation**: Sonja Haller, "iPod Era of Personal Media Choices May Be Turning Us into an iSolation Nation," September 12, 2005, http://www.azcentral.com/arizonarepublic/arizonaliving/articles/0912customize0912.html (accessed January 8, 2010).

71 **One VSL feed**: Very Short List, "I, Me, Mine," 2008, http://www.veryshortlist.com/science/daily.cfm/review/664/Other_print_publication/narcissism-and-social-networking-sites/?tp (accessed October 4, 2009).

72 **Dupré's MySpace page**: MySpace, http://www.myspace.com/ashleydupre (accessed October 4, 2009).

72 **Facebook found it necessary to lift its 5,000-friend limit**: Michael Arrington, "Facebook to Lift 5,000 Friends Limit," 2008, http://www.techcrunch.com/2008/05/09/facebook-to-lift-5000-friends-limit (accessed October 4, 2009).

72 **In Buffardi and Campbell's study**: L. E. Buffardi and W. K. Campbell, "Narcissism and Social Networking Web Sites," *Personality and Social Psychology Bulletin* 34, no. 10 (2008): 1303–14.

73 **"because narcissists have more"**: Very Short List, "I, Me, Mine," http://www.veryshortlist.com/science/daily.cfm/review/664/Other_print_publication/narcissism-and-social-networking-sites/?tp (accessed October 4, 2009).

74 **"self-presentational vehicle"**: Ki Mae Heussner, "Facebook: Where Narcissists Connect?" 2008, http://i.abcnews.com/print?id=5887520 (accessed October 4, 2009).

75 **Plato's theory of ideal forms**: Plato, *The Republic*, trans. Benjamin Jowett (New York: Plain Label Books, 1946), 171–83, 330.

76 **fusing the Form of the Good with God**: Vivian Boland, *Ideas in God According to Saint Thomas Aquinas* (Boston: Brill Academic Publishers, 1996), 314–20.

76 *The God Delusion*: Richard Dawkins, *The God Delusion* (Boston: Houghton Mifflin, 2006).

76 **act in a "God-like way"**: Google Videos, *Richard Dawkins Discusses Second Life*, 2007, http://video.google.co.uk/videoplay?docid=-7920532540725792452&hl=un (accessed October 4, 2009).

76 **"God mode," and comes with a "God menu"**: Second Life Wiki, "God Mode," 2009, http://wiki.secondlife.com/Wiki/God_Mode (accessed April 26, 2010).

77 **my book *Compulsive Acts***: Elias Aboujaoude, *Compulsive Acts: A Psychiatrist's Tales of Ritual and Obsession* (Berkeley: University of California Press, 2008), 137–61.

81 **"ordinary everyday psychosis"**: P. L. Gibbs, "Reality in Cyberspace: Analysands' Use of the Internet and Ordinary Everyday Psychosis," *Psychoanalytic Review* 94, no. 1 (2007): 11–38.

81 **"The Internet can also be seen as serving"**: Ibid.

81 **"Use of the Internet/computer, then, serve[s]"**: Ibid.

82 **For "all of us"**: Ibid.

82 **University of Southern California's 2008 Digital Future Project**: Center for the Digital Future, *Annual Internet Survey by the Center for the Digital Future Finds Shifting Trends Among Adults About the Benefits and Consequences of Children Going Online.*

84 **Craigslist, the hugely popular classifieds Web site serving**: Craigslist, Factsheet, http://www.craigslist.org/about/factsheet (last accessed October 4, 2009).

85 **God may be dead**: R. J. Hollingdale, *Nietzsche: The Man and His Philosophy* (Cambridge, UK: Cambridge University Press, 2001), 139.

86 **"The God of the Old Testament is arguably"**: Dawkins, *The God Delusion*, 31.

86 **"I have been in there myself as an avatar"**: Roger Highfield, "Virtual Worlds 'Could Replace Real Relationships,'" *Telegraph*, http://www.telegraph.co.uk/news/uknews/1554999/Virtual-worlds-%27could-replace-real-relationships%27.html (accessed October 4, 2009).

87 **Elysian Isle, a Second Life island**: RichardDawkins.net, "Richard Dawkins to Appear in Second Life," 2007, http://richarddawkins.net/print.php?id=1156 (accessed October 4, 2009).

87 **The inside of the auditorium looked suspiciously like a church**: Richard Dawkins.net, "Photos of the God Delusion Event in Second Life," 2007, http://richarddawkins.net/article,1215,Photos-of-The-God-Delusion-Event-in-Second-Life,SecondLifecom (accessed October 4, 2009).

4: ORDINARY EVERYDAY VICIOUSNESS

91 **Nearly ten million Americans**: Javelin Strategy and Research, 2009, "Latest Javelin Research Shows Identity Fraud Increased 22 Percent, Affecting Nearly Ten Million Americans: But Consumer Costs Fell Sharply by 31 Percent," http://www.javelinstrategy.com/2009/02/09/latest-javelin-research-shows-identity-fraud-increased-22-percent-affecting-nearly-ten-million-americans-but-consumer-costs-fell-sharply-by-31-percent/ (accessed October 6, 2009).

91 **at a worldwide cost of $1 trillion**: McAfee, http://resources.mcafee.com/content/NAUnsecuredEconomiesReport (accessed October 6, 2009).

91 **5,499 known breaches of American government**: CBS News, "Federal Sites Knocked Out by Cyber Attack," July 7, 2009, http://www.cbsnews.com/stories/2009/07/07/tech/main5142652.shtml (accessed January 15, 2010).

91 **attack against the White House network**: Demetri Sevastopulo, "Chinese Hack into White House Network," November 8, 2008, http://us.ft.com/ftgateway/superpage.ft?news_id=fto11062008193836072&page=2 (accessed January 15, 2010).

91 **Cramster supplies step-by-step**: Lisa W. Foderado, "Psst! Need the Answer to No. 7? Click Here," *New York Times*, http://www.nytimes.com/2009/05/18/education/18cram.html (accessed October 6, 2009).

91 **"download your workload"**: Theresa Gillis and Janeanne Rockwell-Kincanon, "From Download Your Work to the Evil House of Cheat: Cybercheating, Plagiarism and Intellectual Property Theft," 2000, http://www.wou.edu/provost/library/about/staff/kincanon/plagiarism/presentation_files/frame.htm (accessed October 6, 2009).

91 **$100 million was wagered**: John Walters, "Computer-Friendly Gambling Has Found a Growing Fan Base Online," *Sports Illustrated*, May 24, 2005, http://sports illustrated.cnn.com/2005/more/05/23/internet.poker/index.html (accessed October 6, 2009).

92 **Over 10 percent xof all Web pages**: Family Safe Media, "Pornography Statistics," 2006, http://www.familysafemedia.com/pornography_statistics.html (accessed October 6, 2009).

92 **one in five youths**: Office for Victims and Crime, *Youth Internet Safety Survey*, 2001, http://ovc.gov/publications/bulletins/internet_2_2001/internet_2_01_6 .html (accessed October 6, 2009).

92 **The number of such groups in the United State**s: Southern Poverty Law Center, "Hate Groups, Militias on Rise as Extremists Stage Comeback," 2004, http://www.splcenter.org/center/splcreport/article.jsp?aid=71 (accessed October 6, 2009).

92 **Al-Qaeda boasts a "media arm"**: Eben Kaplan, *Terrorists and the Internet*, January 8, 2009, http://www.cfr.org/publication/10005/ (accessed January 15, 2010).

92 **cybersecurity position**: David Sanger and John Markoff, "Obama Outlines Coordinated Cyber-Security Plan," *New York Times*, May 30, 2009, http://www .nytimes.com/2009/05/30/us/politics/30cyber.html (accessed October 6, 2009).

93 **Protecting Cyberspace as a National Asset Act**: Bianca Bosker, "Internet 'Kill Switch' Would Give President Power to Shut Down the Web," *Huffington Post*, June 17, 2010, http://www.huffingtonpost.com/2010/06/17/internet-kill-switch-woul_n_615923.html (accessed June 18, 2010).

93 **"the dark, inaccessible part of our personality"**: Sigmund Freud, *New Introductory Lectures on Psychoanalysis: The Standard Edition*, trans. James Strachey (New York: W. W. Norton, 1965), 91.

93 **"of a negative character"**: Ibid.

93 **"we call it a chaos"**: Ibid.

93 **"filled with energy reaching"**: Ibid.

94 **"represents what may be called reason"**: Sigmund Freud, *The Standard Edition of the Complete Psychological Works of Sigmund Freud*, vol. 19, trans. James Strachey (London: Hogarth Press, 1953), 25.

94 **superego is the voice of the authority figure**: Sigmund Freud, *Civilization and Its Discontents*, trans. James Strachey (New York: W. W. Norton, 1989), 89–92.

94 **Oedipus complex**: Jerome Neu, *The Cambridge Companion to Freud* (Cambridge, UK: Cambridge University Press, 1991), 161–65.

95 **"[T]he problem before us"**: Freud, *Civilization and Its Discontents*, 108.

95 **"polymorphous perversity"**: Neu, *Cambridge Companion to Freud*, 195.

97 **"Second Life communities"**: Cinderella Kesey, "Group Dynamics, Commu-

nities, and the Mob Mentality," December 27, 2007, http://cindykesey.wordpress
.com/2007/12/27/group-dynamics-communities-and-the-mob-mentality/
(accessed October 6, 2009).

98 **have posted nearly three billion images**: Chris Colin, "Nasty as They Wanna
Be? Policing Flickr.com," September 29, 2008, http://www.sfgate.com/cgi-bin/
article.cgi?f=/g/a/2008/09/29/onthejob.DTL (accessed October 6, 2009).

99 **"Behavior [on Flickr] must be moderated"**: Colin, "Nasty as They Wanna
Be?"

99 **the announcement came with a picture**: Flickr, "Heather Is the One with
the Muscles," May 25, 2005, http://blog.flickr.net/en/2005/05/25/heather-is-the-
one-with-the-muscles (accessed October 6, 2009).

100 **Megan Meier, a thirteen-year-old girl**: Lauren Collins, "Friend Game,"
The New Yorker, January 21, 2008, http://www.newyorker.com/reporting/
2008/01/21/080121fa_fact_collins (accessed October 6, 2009); Christopher Maag,
"A Hoax Turned Fatal Draws Anger but No Charges," *New York Times*, November
28, 2007, http://www.nytimes.com/2007/11/28/us/28hoax.html (accessed October 6, 2009).

101 **a federal judge threw out**: MSNBC, "Judge Finalizes Dismissal in MySpace
Hoax," August 31, 2009, http://www.msnbc.msn.com/id/32635205/ns/us_news-
crime_and_courts (accessed October 6, 2009).

102 *Cyber Bullying: Bullying in the Digital Age*: R. M. Kowalski, S. P. Limber,
and P. W. Agatston, *Cyber Bullying: Bullying in the Digital Age* (New York: Wiley-
Blackwell, 2008).

102 **"As tempting as it is to assume"**: R. M. Kowalski, "Cyber Bullying: Rec-
ognizing and Treating Victim and Aggressor," *Psychiatric Times* 25, no. 11 (2008):
45–47.

102 **more than 50 percent of children**: Ibid.

103 **"When people tease or bully"**: Ibid.

103 **90 percent of U.S. children**: National Institute on Media and the Family,
12th Annual MediaWise Video Game Report Card, 2007, http://www.mediafamily.org/
research/report_vgrc_2007.shtml (accessed October 6, 2009).

103 **over 90 percent of games classified**: D. A. Gentile, "The Rating Systems for
Media Products," *Blackwell Handbook of Child Development and the Media*, ed. S. L. Cal-
vert and B. J. Wilson (Oxford: Blackwell, 2008), 527–51.

104 **One recent "secret shopper"**: National Institute on Media and the Family,
12th Annual MediaWise Video Game Report Card, 2007.

104 **One of the largest studies to address**: C. A. Anderson et al., "Longitudinal
Effects of Violent Video Games on Aggression in Japan and the United States,"
Pediatrics 122, no. 5 (2008): 1067–72.

105 **"In the virtual world"**: Vladan Starcevic and Guy Porter, "Effects of Violent

Video Games: The Controversy Revisited," in *Impulse Control Disorders*, ed. Elias Aboujaoude and Lorrin M. Koran (New York: Cambridge University Press, 2010), 186.

107 **Dr. Jeanne B. Funk**: Jeanne B. Funk, "Children's Exposure to Violent Video Games and Desensitization to Violence," *Child and Adolescent Psychiatric Clinics of North America* 14, no. 3 (2005): 387–404.

108 **Some contend that the communication system**: A. Vedder, "The Internet: Moral Benefits, Drawbacks, and Innovations, in Vedder, *Ethics and the Internet*, 1.

109 **viral video from 2006**: Richard Spencer, "Just Who Is the Glamorous Kitten Killer of Hangzhou?" *Telegraph*, March 4, 2006, http://www.telegraph.co.uk/news/worldnews/asia/china/1512082/Just-who-is-the-glamorous-kitten-killer-of-Hangzhou.html (accessed October 6, 2009).

109 **According to the New York Daily News**: Beverly Ford, Erica Pearson, and Helen Kennedy, "Cops Have Philip Markoff, Suspected 'Craigslist Killer' of Model Julissa Brisman, in Custody," *New York Daily News*, April 20, 2009, http://www.nydailynews.com/news/ny_crime/2009/04/20/2009-04-20_massachussetts_police_arrest_suspect_in_craigslist_killer_case.html (accessed October 6, 2009).

109 **handed an eight-count indictment**: Beverly Ford and Oren Yaniv, "New Lurid Details in Case of Accused Craigslist killer Phillip Markoff," *New York Daily News*, June 22, 2009, http://www.nydailynews.com/news/ny_crime/2009/06/22/2009-06-22_new_lurid_details_in_case_of_accused_craigslist_killer_phillip_markoff.html (accessed October 6, 2009).

110 **attorneys general from forty states**: Megan Woolhouse, "Rhode Island AG Blasts Craigslist," *Boston Globe*, May 4, 2009, http://www.boston.com/news/local/breaking_news/2009/05/charges_expecte.html (accessed October 6, 2009).

110 **declared the National Enquirer**: *National Enquirer*, "Craigslist's Markoff May Be Psychosexual Serial Killer," April 30, 2009, http://www.nationalenquirer.com/celebrity/66605 (accessed October 6, 2009).

110 **Here is a sampling from one Web site**: Queerty.com, "Craigslist Killer Philip Markoff Went After Men & Transexuals, Too," http://www.queerty.com/craigslist-killer-philip-markoff-went-after-men-transexuals-too-20090427 (accessed October 6, 2009).

112 **As reported in the New York Times**: Brian Stelter, "Web Suicide Viewed Live and Reaction Spur a Debate," *New York Times*, November 25, 2008, http://www.nytimes.com/2008/11/25/us/25suicides.html (accessed October 6, 2009).

112 **on ABCnews.com**: Emily Friedman, November 21, 2008, http://abcnews.go.com/technology/mindmoodnews/story?id=6306126&page=1 (accessed October 6, 2009).

112 **on the Los Angeles Times blogs**: http://latimesblogs.latimes.com/technology/2008/11/strange-record.html (accessed October 6, 2009).

113 **Suicide Chat Room for Young People**: Mark Simkin, "Suicide Pacts

Arranged Over the Internet in Japan," January 10, 2005, http://www.abc.net.au/am/content/2005/s1279571.htm (accessed October 6, 2009).

113 **suicide plan involving thirty-two individuals**: CNN, "Others Sought in Alleged Mass Suicide Pact," February 11, 2005, http://www.cnn.com/2005/US/02/11/valentine.suicide/index.html (accessed October 6, 2009).

113 **"a mode of thinking"**: I. L. Janis, *Victims of Groupthink* (Boston: Houghton Mifflin, 1972), 9.

114 **"most of what's available via the Internet"**: Stelter, "Web Suicide Viewed Live and Reaction Spur a Debate."

114 **overall suicide rate in the United States**: G. Hu, H. C. Wilcox, L. Wissow, and S. P. Baker, "Mid-life Suicide: An Increasing Problem in U.S. Whites, 1999–2005," *American Journal of Preventive Medicine* 35, no. 6 (2008): 589–93.

114 **Many factors may have contributed**: Denise Gellene, "U.S. Suicide Rates Are Up," *Los Angeles Times*, October 21, 2008, http://articles.latimes.com/2008/oct/21/science/sci-suicide21 (accessed October 6, 2009).

115 **"These sites often describe"**: P. R. Recupero, S. E. Harms, J. M. Noble, "Googling Suicide: Surfing for Suicide Information on the Internet," *Journal of Clinical Psychiatry* 69, no. 6 (2008): 878–88.

115 **"As a human being, you don't"**: Stelter, "Web Suicide Viewed Live and Reaction Spur a Debate."

117 **an episode on National Public Radio's**: NPR, "Enforcers," 2008, http://www.thisamericanlife.org/Radio_Episode.aspx?episode=363 (accessed December 11, 2009).

5: IMPULSIVITY

119 **"Sometimes I send messages I shouldn't send"**: Jon Perlow, "New in Lab: Stop Sending Mail You Later Regret," October 6, 2008, http://gmailblog.blogspot.com/2008/10/new-in-labs-stop-sending-mail-you-later.html (accessed October 8, 2009).

120 **"Fuck off and cover something important you twats!"**: Tania Branigan and Jackie Ashley, "Campbell Suffers the Curse of the BlackBerry E-mailer," *Guardian*, February 9, 2005, http://www.guardian.co.uk/politics/2005/feb/09/uk.media (accessed October 8, 2009).

121 **"With the development of the Internet"**: Eric Hollander and Dan J. Stein, *Clinical Manual of Impulse Control Disorders* (Arlington, VA: American Psychiatric Publishing, 2006), 2.

121 **"the failure to resist an impulse"**: Ibid.

121 **"carelessness, an underestimated sense of harm"**: Ibid.

121 **"poorly conceived, premature, inappropriate"**: S. R. Chamberlain and B. J. Sahakian, "The Neuropsychiatry of Impulsivity," *Current Opinion in Psychiatry* 20, no. 3 (2007): 255–61.

122 **"The particular element is impulsiveness"**: Quoted in Donald Black, "Compulsive Buying: Clinical Aspects," in Aboujaoude and Koran, *Impulse Control Disorders*.

122 **"we all engage from time to time in impulsive acts"**: Chamberlain and Sahakian, "The Neuropsychiatry of Impulsivity."

124 **In a comprehensive review of compulsive shopping disorder**: Black, "Compulsive Buying: Clinical Aspects."

125 **"They went into my closets looking for skeletons"**: BBC, "Homage to Imelda's Shoes," February 16, 2001, http://news.bbc.co.uk/2/hi/asia-pacific/1173911.stm (accessed October 8, 2009).

126 **Compulsive Buying Scale**: R. J. Faber and T. C. O'Guinn, "A Clinical Screener for Compulsive Buying," *Journal of Consumer Research* 19 (1992): 459–69.

126 **surveys conducted over the last two decades**: Black, "Compulsive Buying: Clinical Aspects."

126 **rate of 44 percent seen in a study**: Helga Dittmar, "Compulsive Buying—A Growing Concern? An Examination of Gender, Age, and Endorsement of Materialistic Values as Predictors," *British Journal of Psychology* 96 (2005): 467–91.

126 **93 percent for twelve- to seventeen-year-olds in the United States and 89 percent**: PewInternet.org, *Generations Online in 2009*, http://www.pewinternet.org/Reports/2009/Generations-Online-in-2009/Generational-Differences-in-Online-Activities/2-Internet-use-and-email.aspx?r=1 (accessed October 8, 2009).

126 **Data from the UK**: Office of National Statistics, *Internet Access 2008*, http://www.statistics.gov.uk/pdfdir/iahi0808.pdf (accessed October 8, 2009).

127 **Another study, also conducted by Dittmar**: H. Dittmar, K. Long, and R. Bond, "When a Better Self Is Only a Button Click Away: Associations between Materialistic Values, Emotional and Identity-Related Buying Motives, and Compulsive Buying Tendency Online," *Journal of Social and Clinical Psychology* 26, no. 3 (2007): 334–61.

127 **In 2005, 2006, and 2007**: A. Benson, "Compulsive Buying: How Can We Stem the Tide of This Costly Epidemic?" in Aboujaoude and Koran, *Impulse Control Disorders*.

127 **In 2007, the average credit card debt per household**: Americans for Fairness in Lending, *Credit Cards*, 2009, http://www.affil.org/consumer_rsc/credit_cards2.php (accessed October 8, 2009).

127 **consumer debt reached an all-time high**: David Cho and Nancy Trejos, "Addicted to Debt," *Washington Post*, February 18, 2008, http://www.washingtonpost.com/wp-dyn/content/article/2008/02/17/AR2008021702487.html (accessed October 8, 2009).

128 **Helga Dittmar attempted to answer**: Dittmar, Long, and Bond, "When a Better Self Is Only a Button Click Away."

131 **"Research has shown a correlation"**: American Psychiatric Associa-

tion, *Advisory on Internet Gambling*, http://www.psych.org/Departments/QIPS/ Downloads/APAAdvisoryonInternetGambling.aspx (accessed October 8, 2009).

132 **A 2007 British survey of 9,003 individuals**: National Center for Social Research, *British Gambling Prevalence Survey 2007*, http://www.gamblingcommission .gov.uk/pdf/britsh%20gambling%20prevalence%20survey%2007%20-%20 sept%202007.pdf (accessed October 8, 2009).

132 **"medium of the Internet may be more likely"**: M. Griffiths et al., "Socio-demographic Correlates of Internet Gambling: Findings from the 2007 British Gambling Prevalence Survey," *Cyberpsychology and Behavior* 12, no. 2 (2009): 199–202.

132 **An American study published in 2002**: G. T. Ladd and N. M. Petry, "Disordered Gambling among University-Based Medical and Dental Patients: A Focus on Internet Gambling," *Psychology of Addictive Behaviors* 16, no. 1 (2002): 76–79.

133 **"We're not seeing a lot of recreational gambling"**: AddictionInfo.org, "Online Gambling May Be More Serious Addiction," http://www.addictioninfo .org/articles/642/1/Online-gambling-may-be-more-serious-addiction/Page1 .html (accessed October 8, 2009).

133 **signs of offline trouble as defined in the *DSM***: *DSM-IV*, text revision, 674.

133 **more than double between 2000 and 2008**: National Council on Problem Gambling, *Helpline Statistics 2000–2008* (Washington, D.C.: National Council on Problem Gambling, 2008).

134 **Unlawful Internet Gambling Enforcement Act**: Lawrence G. Walters, "On Second Thought . . . What Does the UIGEA Really Mean for Internet Gambling?" http://www.firstamendment.com/UIEGA.html#_ftnref2 (accessed October 8, 2009).

134 **distance themselves from disgraced gaming lobbyist**: Ibid.

134 **made oversight complicated**: I. Nelson Rose, *Gambling and the Law®: The Unlawful Internet Gambling Enforcement Act of 2006 Analyzed*, 2006, http://www .gamblingandthelaw.com/columns/2006_act.htm (accessed October 8, 2009).

134 **a self-declared "pretty good poker player"**: James McManus, "Aces," *The New Yorker*, http://www.newyorker.com/talk/2008/02/04/080204ta_talk_mcma nus (accessed October 8, 2009).

134 **will be more sensitive to their cause**: Vin Narayanan, "Obama Brings Hope, but the UIGEA Is Here to Stay for Now," January 22, 2009, http://www.casinocity times.com/news/article/obama-brings-hope-but-the-uigea-is-here-to-stay-for-now-176763?contentID=176763 (accessed October 8, 2009).

134 **According to a Harvard study**: S. E. Nelson et al. "Real Limits in the Virtual World: Self-Limiting Behavior of Internet Gamblers," *Journal of Gambling Studies* 24, no. 4 (2008): 463–77.

136 **On a CNET blog discussing**: cnet.com, October 16, 2008, http://news
.cnet.com/8601-17939_109-10059735-0.html?communityId=2008&targetCommu
nityId=2008&blogId=2 (accessed October 8, 2009).

6: INFANTILE REGRESSION AND THE TYRANNY OF THE EMOTICON

138 **"looks like it was plucked"**: Winda Benedetti, "Indulge Your Inner Child with
'Crayon Physics,'" January 13, 2009, http://www.msnbc.msn.com/id/28628780
(accessed October 6, 2009).

138 **2008 survey of 1,200 households**: Entertainment Software Association,
Essential Facts about the Computer and Video Game Industry, 2008, http://www.theesa
.com/facts/pdfs/ESA_EF_2008.pdf (accessed October 6, 2009).

138 **survey by the Pew Internet & American Life Project**: http://www
.pewinternet.org/pdfs/PIP_Teens_Games_and_Civics_Report_FINAL.pdf
(accessed October 6, 2009).

139 **2006 Associated Press/America Online poll**: Fox News, "Survey: Four in
10 American Adults Play Video Games," May 6, 2006, http://www.foxnews.com/
story/0,2933,194659,00.html (accessed October 6, 2009).

139 **all recent top sellers**: James Brightman, 2008, http://www.gamedaily.com/
articles/news/wow-sims-dominate-top-10-pc games-of-07/19191/?biz=1 (last
accessed October 6, 2009).

139 **Sims 2 Web site celebrated 100 million copies**: The Sims 2, *Let's Celebrate!*
100 Million Stories, What's Yours? http://thesims2.ea.com/100million/index.php
(accessed October 6, 2009).

139 **"Create Sims, design their homes"**: Ibid.

140 **characters progress through six stages**: Wikipedia, "The Sims 2," http://
en.wikipedia.org/wiki/The_Sims_2 (accessed October 6, 2009).

141 **clever "cheats" that players discover**: Neoseeker, "The Sims 2 Cheats and
Tips," 2007–2009, http://www.neoseeker.com/Games/cheats/PC/sims_2.html
(accessed October 6, 2009).

141 **As a quick tour of one message board**: Ibid.

143 **"massively multiplayer online role-playing game"**: Wikipedia, "World of
Warcraft," http://en.wikipedia.org/wiki/World_of_Warcraft (accessed October 6,
2009).

143 **11.5 million worldwide subscribers**: Blizzard.com, "World of Warcraft
Subscriber Base Reaches 11.5 Million Worldwide," 2008, http://us.blizzard.com/
en-us/company/press/pressreleases.html?081121 (accessed October 6, 2009).

144 **"You can go from your desktop to being in-game"**: Greg Kasavin, "World
of Warcraft Review," 2004, http://www.gamespot.com/pc/rpg/worldofwarcraft/
review.html (accessed October 6, 2009).

144 **"For one, World of Warcraft has a nice"**: Ibid.

145 **2009 Pew Research Center analysis**: Sharon Jayson, "A Few Wrinkles Are Etching Facebook, Other Social Sites," *USA Today*, January 15, 2009, http://www.usatoday.com/printedition/life/20090115/socialnetworking15_st.art.htm (accessed October 6, 2009).

145 **"A Few Wrinkles Are Etching Facebook"**: Ibid.

146 **"totes," "probs," and "dorbs"**: UrbanDictionary.com, "Strange Facebook Language," January 15, 2009, http://www.urbandictionary.com/define.php?term= Strange%20Facebook%20Language (accessed October 6, 2009).

146 **In World of Warcraft, to "rez"**: Incgamers.com, "Jargon," 2006, http://wow .incgamers.com/forums/showthread.php?t=382799 (accessed April 20, 2010).

147 **"Simlish," a system of communication**: Wikipedia, "Simlish," http://en .wikipedia.org/wiki/Simlish (accessed October 6, 2009).

147 **"Top 50 Internet Acronyms Parents Need to Know"**: NetLingo.com, "Top 50 Internet Acronyms Parents Need to Know," http://www.netlingo.com/ top50teens.cfm (accessed October 6, 2009).

147 **"Now you're ready to learn cyber-lingo"**: JupiterParents.com, "Parent's Guide to Internet Chat Lingo," http://www.jupiterparents.com/children/safety/ safety12.shtml (accessed October 6, 2009).

148 **According to Brazilian linguist Sérgio Costa**: Sérgio Costa, "The Construction/Appropriation of Writing in the Classroom of the 'Fundamental' School in Internet Chat," *Revista de Documentaçao de Estudos em Lingüística Teórica e Aplicada (D.E.L.T.A.)* 22, no. 1 (2006): 159–75.

148 **likened the information age to the advent of printing**: N. Ross, "Written Language May Currently Be Undergoing a Transformation Comparable to the Original Impact of Print," *English Today* 87, no. 22 (2006): 39–45.

148 **"resources for the expression of informality"**: Kristen Philipkoski, "The Web Not the Death of Language," *Wired*, February 22, 2005, http://www.wired .com/culture/lifestyle/news/2005/02/66671 (accessed October 6, 2009).

148 **are partly a "game"**: David Crystal, *Language and the Internet*, 2nd ed. (New York: Cambridge University Press, 2006), 264.

149 **"Netspeak is a development of millennial significance"**: Ibid.

149 **"a giant leap backward"**: Louis Menand, "Thumbspeak: Is Texting Here to Stay?" *The New Yorker*, October 20, 2008, http://www.newyorker.com/arts/critics/ books/2008/10/20/081020crbo_books_menand (accessed October 6, 2009).

150 **"The 'pregnant' pause has been digitally aborted"**: William Safire, "Emoticons," *New York Times*, May 25, 2008, http://www.nytimes.com/2008/05/25/ magazine/25wwln-safire-t.html?fta=y (accessed October 6, 2009).

151 **The first documented use of the emoticons**: Olga Kharif, "The Man Who Brought :-) to Your Screen," *BusinessWeek*, April 23, 2001, http://www.businessweek .com/bwdaily/dnflash/apr2001/nf20010423_785.htm (accessed October 6, 2009).

152 **Geocities' Canonical Smiley List**: Geocities.com, "The Canonical Smiley List," 2008, http://www.geocities.com/dronak/smileys.html (accessed October 6, 2009).

152 **Forty-three individual muscles**: Judy Foreman, "A Conversation with Paul Ekman," *New York Times*, August 5, 2003, http://www.nytimes.com/2003/08/05/health/conversation-with-paul-ekman-43-facial-muscles-that-reveal-even-most-fleeting.html (accessed October 6, 2009).

152 **The Facial Action Coding System, or FACS**: Paul Ekman, Wallace V. Friesen, and Joseph C. Hager, *Facial Action Coding System* (Salt Lake City, UT: A Human Face, 2002).

152 **achieved by contraction of the zygomatic major**: Wikipedia, "Facial Action Coding System," http://en.wikipedia.org/wiki/Facial_Action_Coding_System (accessed October 6, 2009).

152 **FACS has become a popular method**: Judy Foreman, "A Conversation with Paul Ekman."

153 **experiments led by Justin Kruger**: J. Kruger, N. Epley, J. Parker, Z. W. Ng, "Egocentrism over E-mail: Can We Communicate as Well as We Think?" *Journal of Personality and Social Psychology* 89, no. 6 (2005): 925–36.

154 **Sanchez had multiple texting relationships**: Robert J. Lopez and Rich Connell, "Metrolink Engineer Let Unauthorized 'Rail Enthusiasts' Control Train," *Los Angeles Times*, March 3, 2009, http://www.latimes.com/news/la-me-metrolink-hearing4-2009mar04,0,1714392.story (accessed October 6, 2009).

154 **"this time I'm taking a picture of you"**: Ibid.

155 **"I'm gonna do all the radio talkin'"**: Ibid.

155 **A full 47 percent of all texting adults**: *Adults and Cell Phone Distractions, Pew Internet & American Life Project*, June 18, 2010, http://www.pewinternet.org/Reports/2010/Cell-Phone-Distractions.aspx (accessed June 29, 2010).

155 **sent or received 1,742 text messages**: Jennifer Steinhauer and Laura M. Hoslon, "As Text Messages Fly, Danger Lurks," *New York Times*, September 20, 2008, http://www.nytimes.com/2008/09/20/us/20messaging.html (accessed June 28, 2010).

155 **face a twenty-three times greater risk**: Matt Ritchell, "Senators Seek a Ban on Texting and Driving," *New York Times*, July 30, 2009, http://www.nytimes.com/2009/07/30/technology/30distracted.html (accessed October 6, 2009).

155 **ranging from NASCAR to emergency room physicians' associations**: Nationwide, "Nationwide Insurance, NASCAR Driver Jeff Burton Encourage Local Drivers to Stop Texting While Driving," September 3, 2008, http://www.nationwide.com/newsroom/press-release-nascar-jburton.jsp.

155 **consumer research company Nielsen Mobile**: Steinhauer and Holson, "As Text Messages Fly, Danger Lurks."

155 **2010 Consumer Electronics Show**: Ashley Vance and Matt Richtell, "Driven to Distraction," *New York Times*, January 7, 2010, http://www.nytimes.com/2010/01/07/technology/07distracted.html (accessed January 12, 2010).

156 ***Wired News* senior editor**: Kevin Poulsen, "MySpace Predator Caught by Code," *Wired*, October 16, 2006, http://www.wired.com/science/discoveries/news/2006/10/71948?currentPage=1 (accessed October 6, 2009).

157 **MySpace subsequently conducted its own purge**: Robert Lemos, "MySpace Bars 29,000 Sex Offenders," 2007, http://www.securityfocus.com/brief/554 (accessed October 6, 2009).

158 **"true father of psychoanalysis"**: Ernst Jones, *The Life and Work of Sigmund Freud*, vol. 3 (New York: Basic Books, 1957), 24.

158 **"It is first of all a long stem"**: Pierre Janet, *Mental State of Hystericals*, trans. Caroline Rollin Corson (New York: G. P. Putnam's Sons, 1901), 46.

158 **"When I want to write, I find that"**: Ibid., 147.

159 **"It is I, we say, who, before executing it"**: Ibid.

159 **"[T]he automatic writing . . . will help"**: Ibid., 256.

161 **more than half of e-mail users**: Center for the Digital Future, *Annual Internet Survey by the Center for the Digital Future Finds Shifting Trends Among Adults About the Benefits and Consequences of Children Going Online*.

7: LOVE AND SEX RECALIBRATED

163 **the Web site's more than fifteen million subscribers**: *Online Dating*, "History of Match.com," http://www.onlinedatingmagazine.com/history/match-com-history.html (accessed October 7, 2009).

163 **"fastest growing relationship site on the Web"**: Plenty Of Fish, "Welcome to Dating Plenty Of Fish," http://www.datingplentyoffish.com/ (accessed October 7, 2009).

163 **"patented Compatibility Matching System®"**: eHarmony, "eHarmony Is More Than Just Dating," http://eharmony.com/why (accessed October 7, 2009).

163 **enlisting Dr. Helen Fisher**: Chemistry, "Chemistry's Chief Scientific Advisor," http://chemistry.com/drhelenfisher/ (accessed October 7, 2009).

164 **carried by several news outlets**: *Mail on Sunday*, "Revealed: The 'Other' Woman in Second Life Divorce," November 14, 2008, http://www.mailonsunday.co.uk/news/article-1085412/Revealed-The-woman-Second-Life-divorce--whos-engaged-web-cheat-shes-met.html (accessed October 7, 2009); *Mirror*, "Second Life Divorce: Woman Leaves Husband over Virtual Lover," November 13, 2008, http://www.mirror.co.uk/news/technology/2008/11/13/second-life-divorce-woman-leaves-husband-over-virtual-lover-115875-20892166/ (accessed October 7, 2009); Simon de Bruxelles, "Second Life Affair Leads to Real-Life Divorce for

David Pollard, aka Dave Barmy," London *Times*, November 14, 2008, http://women
.timesonline.co.uk/tol/life_and_style/women/relationships/article5151126.ece
(accessed October 7, 2009).

167 **12 billion spam e-mails, of which around 2.5 billion are pornographic**:
Top Ten Reviews, "Spam Statistics 2006," http://spam-filter-review.toptenreviews
.com/spam-statistics.html (accessed October 7, 2009).

168 **online advertising—a 22-billion-dollar industry**: KelseyGroup.com,
"Interactive Advertising Revenues to Reach US$147 Billion Globally by 2012,
According to The Kelsey Group's Annual Forecast," February 25, 2008, http://
www.kelseygroup.com/press/pr080225.asp (accessed October 7, 2009).

168 **"FatFoe™, kiss calorie counting and sweaty exercising good-bye"**: We
Market for You, http://www.wemarket4u.net/fatfoe/index.html (accessed October 7, 2009).

168 **"six pack abs for everyone"**: Total-Abs, http://www.total-abs.com/?hop=
active07 (accessed October 7, 2009).

168 **"BountiFul® breast pills: no surgery, no recovery, results guaranteed"**:
Wonderbreast.com, http://www.wonderbreast.com (accessed October 7, 2009).

168 **"be proud to change your underwear in public"**: The Force, http://boards
.theforce.net/your jedi council community/b10008/28950026/p1 (accessed
October 7, 2009).

169 **11.7 million cosmetic procedures**: CosmeticPlasticSurgeryStatistics.com,
"Trends and Demographic Data," http://www.cosmeticplasticsurgerystatistics
.com/statistics.html (accessed October 7, 2009).

169 **anorexia nervosa seems to be increasing**: R. Brunner and F. Resch, "Eating
Disorders—An Increasing Problem in Children and Adolescents?" *Ther Umsch* 63,
no. 8 (2006): 545–49.

169 **"a disturbing growth industry"**: Bonnie Morris Rothman, "A Disturbing Growth Industry: Web Sites That Espouse Anorexia," *New York Times*, June
23, 2002, http://www.nytimes.com/2002/06/23/health/a-disturbing-growth-
industry-web-sites-that-espouse-anorexia.html?pagewanted=all (accessed October
7, 2009).

169 **"In the Internet age with its endless playground"**: Helen Popkin, "The
Internet Makes Me Feel Fat," *Newsweek*, September 2, 2008, http://www.newsweek
.com/id/156896 (accessed October 7, 2009).

170 **Beauty standards are, of course, dynamic**: Lois W. Banner, *American Beauty*
(New York: A. Knopf, 1984).

170 **"an X-ray, not a picture"**: Mandy Hoemakers, "Sixties Central," 2003,
http://www.geocities.com/FashionAvenue/Catwalk/1038/twiggy.html (accessed
October 7, 2009).

171 **A 2010 survey commissioned by Match.com**: *Match.com and Chadwick Mar-*

tin Bailey 2009–2010 Studies: Recent Trends: Online Dating, Match.com, June 2010, http://cp.match.com/cppp/media/CMB_Study.pdf (accessed June 28, 2010).

172 **study of the online sexual behavior of gay youths**: R. Garofalo, A. Herrick, B. S. Mustanski, and G. R. Donenberg, "Tip of the Iceberg: Young Men Who Have Sex with Men, the Internet, and HIV Risk," *American Journal of Public Health* 97, no. 6 (2007): 1113–17.

173 **fascinating investigation of a syphilis outbreak**: J. D. Klausner, W. Wolf, L. Fischer-Ponce, I. Zolt, and M. H. Katz, "Tracing a Syphilis Outbreak through Cyberspace," *Journal of the American Medical Association* 284, no. 4 (2000): 447–49.

174 **a much larger study, focusing on adult women**: P. M. Padgett, "Personal Safety and Sexual Safety for Women Using Online Personal Ads," *Sexuality Research and Social Policy* 4, no. 2 (2007): 27–37.

178 **A 2008 survey of 1,280 participants**: The National Campaign to Prevent Teen and Unplanned Pregnancy, *Sex and Tech*, 2008, http://www.thenationalcampaign.org/sextech/PDF/SexTech_Summary.pdf (accessed October 7, 2009).

178 **Here is how sixteen-year-old Megan**: MSNBC, "Survey: Teens Sharing Nude Images Online," December 10, 2008, http://www.msnbc.msn.com/id/28141513 (accessed October 7, 2009).

178 **According to the same survey**: Ibid.

179 **six teenagers were facing charges**: Mike Brunker, " 'Sexting' Surprise: Teens Face Child Porn Charges," MSNBC, http://www.msnbc.msn.com/id/28679588 (accessed October 7, 2009).

180 **lust motivates technology**: Quoted in Susan Dwyer, "Enter Here—At Your Own Risk: The Moral Dangers of Cyberporn," in *The Impact of the Internet on Our Moral Lives*, ed. R. Cavalier (New York: State University of New York Press, 2005), 69.

180 **businesses led the way**: Ibid.

180 **Streaming audio, peer-to-peer file sharing**: Tad Miller, "Social Networking Surpasses Porn on the Internet," September 16, 2008, http://blog.search-mojo.com/2008/09/16/social-networking-surpasses-porn-on-the-internet-porn-just-moves-on-to-the-next-technology (accessed October 7, 2009).

180 **"sex" is no longer the most Googled word**: Google, *Google Trends Lab*, http://www.google.com/trends (accessed October 7, 2009).

180 **"The Pill" helped separate recreational aspects**: David Allyn, *Make Love, Not War: The Sexual Revolution: An Unfettered History* (New York: Little, Brown, 2000).

180 **In a 2008 Harris Interactive survey**: CNN, "Survey: Many Would Take Internet over Sex," December 15, 2008, http://www.cnn.com/2008/TECH/12/15/internet.sex.survey (accessed October 7, 2009).

181 **a quarter of an hour a day**: Covenant Eyes, *Internet Pornography Statistics*, http://www.covenanteyes.com/help_and_support/article/internet_pornography_statistics/?c=80 (accessed October 7, 2009).

181 **One in five men**: Family Safe Media, *Pornography Statistics*, 2006, http://www.familysafemedia.com/pornography_statistics.html (accessed October 7, 2009).

181 **More than a third of all downloads**: Ibid.

181 **A quarter of all search engine requests**: Ibid.

181 **users report unwanted exposure**: Ibid.

182 **"meet real sex partners tonight"**: Adult Friend Finder, http://adultfriendfinder.com (accessed October 7, 2009).

184 **as examples of a screenplay or "sexual script"**: Padgett, "Personal Safety and Sexual Safety for Women."

186 **Zick Rubin pioneered the measurement of love**: Z. Rubin, "Measurement of Romantic Love," *Journal of Personality and Social Psychology* 16 (1970): 265–73.

186 **research conducted by psychologist Maria J. Lavooy**: V. M. Scott, K. E. Mottarella, and M. J. Lavooy, "Does Virtual Intimacy Exist? A Brief Exploration into Reported Levels of Intimacy in Online Relationships," *Cyberpsychology and Behavior* 9, no. 6 (2006): 759–61.

187 **"The paradigm has shifted"**: Charles M. Blow, "The Demise of Dating," *New York Times*, December 13, 2008, http://www.nytimes.com/2008/12/13/opinion/13blow.html (accessed October 7, 2009).

188 **"life imitates art far more than art imitates life"**: Oscar Wilde, *The Works of Oscar Wilde* (New York: Lamb Publishing Company, 1909), 38.

8: THE ILLUSION OF KNOWLEDGE

190 **2008 study commissioned by the British Library**: British Library, *Information Behaviour of the Researcher of the Future*, 2008, http://www.bl.uk/news/pdf/googlegen.pdf (accessed October 7, 2009).

191 **"His reasons are as two grains of wheat"**: William Shakespeare, *The Works of William Shakespeare*, vol. 1 (London: Bickers, 1874), 170.

191 **an early authority**: Matt Richtel, "Making Web Sites More 'Usable' Is Former Sun Engineer's Goal," *New York Times*, July 13, 1998, http://www.nytimes.com/library/tech/98/07/cyber/articles/13usability.html (accessed October 7, 2009).

191 **79 percent of online readers scan**: Jakob Nielsen, "Why Web Users Scan Instead of Read," 2005, http://www.useit.com/alertbox/whyscanning.html (accessed October 7, 2009).

191 **"about twenty-five percent slower"**: Ibid.

191 **wanting to be in the driver's seat**: Ibid.

192 **intense competition**: Ibid.

192 **"selfish, lazy, and ruthless"**: Jakob Nielsen, "Information Foraging: Why

Google Makes People Leave Your Site Faster," 2003, http://www.useit.com/alert box/20030630.html (accessed October 7, 2009).

192 **"[They] don't know whether this page"**: Nielsen, "Why Web Users Scan Instead of Read."

193 **eye-tracking study involving 232 subjects**: Jakob Nielsen, "*F*-Shape Pattern for Reading Web Content," 2006, http://www.useit.com/alertbox/reading_pattern .html (accessed October 7, 2009).

193 **"That's how users read your precious content"**: Ibid.

193 **Michael Agger succinctly sums up**: Michael Agger, "Lazy Eyes: How We Read Online," *Slate*, June 13, 2008, http://www.slate.com/id/2193552 (accessed October 7, 2009).

193 **"Bulleted list"**: Ibid.

194 **"Keep things short for the masses"**: Ibid.

194 **"a good editor should be able to cut 40%"**: Ibid.

194 **140-keystroke description of Twitter by Michael Liedtke**: Michael Liedtke, "Can All That Twitters Turn to Gold Amid Gloom?" MSNBC, February 15, 2009, http://www.msnbc.msn.com/id/29183971 (accessed October 7, 2009).

196 **"Over the past few years"**: Nicholas Carr, "Is Google Making Us Stupid?" *Atlantic*, July/August 2008, http://www.theatlantic.com/doc/200807/google (accessed October 7, 2009).

196 **"For many, 2008 was the year that passed"**: Martha Brockenbrough, "Regrettable Trends in Pop Culture: 2008 Edition," 2008, http://entertainment .msn.com/beacon/originalsgalleryvote.aspx?silentchk=1&ptid=b5c78e01-cafa-43cb-84f9-85cd34f13a65&photoidx=8 (accessed October 7, 2009).

197 **"I think I know what's going on"**: Carr, "Is Google Making Us Stupid?"

198 **"Just as the advent of the Colt .45 revolver"**: Howard Rheingold, "Electronic Democracy," http://www.oss.net/dynamaster/file_archive/040323/07063 6573a8a57747e17f626e5b207a6/WER-INFO-16.pdf (accessed October 7, 2009).

199 **"Athens without slaves"**: Ibid.

203 **"Whereas books, newspapers, radio, and television"**: John Gehl and Suzanne Douglas, "From Movable Type to Data Deluge," 2006, http://www.rand .org/multi/parallels/gehl.html (accessed October 7, 2009).

204 **that the 1,000-plus members of the editorial staff of the *New York Times***: Belinda Luscombe, "Arianna Huffington: The Web's New Oracle," *Time*, March 19, 2009, http://www.time.com/time/business/article/0,8599,1886214,00 .html (accessed October 7, 2009).

204 **"We want access to everything"**: James Surowiecki, "News You Can Lose," *The New Yorker*, December 22, 2008, http://www.newyorker.com/talk/financial/ 2008/12/22/081222ta_talk_surowiecki (accessed October 7, 2009).

204 **the *Times* introduced TimesSelect**: Robert MacMillan, "New York Times

to End Paid Internet Service," September 17, 2007, http://www.reuters.com/article/internetNews/idUSWEN10112007091 8?feedType=RSS&feedName=internetNews&rpc=22&sp=true (accessed October 7, 2009).

204 **"the fundamental economics of content"**: Scott Karp, "*New York Times* to Fold TimesSelect, Presaging the Death of Paid Content," http://publishing2 .com/2007/08/07/new-york-times-to-fold-timesselect-presaging-the-death-of-paid-content (accessed October 7, 2009).

205 **include a recommendation to go "hyperlocal"**: Craig Newmark, "Battle Plans for Newspapers," *New York Times*, February 10, 2009, http://roomfordebate .blogs.nytimes.com/2009/02/10/battle-plans-for-newspapers (accessed October 7, 2009).

205 **"Local information is potentially the most valuable product"**: Andrew Keen, "Battle Plans for Newspapers," *New York Times*, February 10, 2009, http:// roomfordebate.blogs.nytimes.com/2009/02/10/battle-plans-for-newspapers (accessed October 7, 2009).

206 **committed $100 million**: Google, *Grants and Investments*, http://www.google .org/projects.html (accessed October 7, 2009).

206 *Newsweek* **announced**: Richard Pérez-Peña, "Newsweek Plans Makeover to Fit a Smaller Audience," *New York Times*, February 9, 2009, http://www.nytimes .com/2009/02/09/business/media/09ncwsweek.html (accessed October 7, 2009).

207 **"democratic swamp of crowd-generated content"**: Keen, "Battle Plans for Newspapers."

207 **"If what you want is real information"**: Gehl and Douglas, "From Movable Type to Data Deluge."

208 **"There is less and less surprise"**: Ibid.

208 **five newspapers in New York and New Jersey**: Eric Sass, "AP Threat: 5 NY/NJ Newspapers Share Content," February 18, 2009, http://www.mediapost .com/publications/?fa=Articles.showArticle&art_aid=100559 (accessed October 7, 2009).

208 **eight Ohio, five Maine, and three South Florida**: EditorandPublisher.com, "More Newspapers Sharing Content—Cutting Competition," *Editor and Publisher*, January 1, 2009, http://www.editorandpublisher.com/eandp/news/article_display .jsp?vnu_content_id=1003926349 (accessed October 7, 2009).

208 **Two formerly bitter rivals**: Ibid.

209 **"Traditionally, what has primarily been an issue"**: Wendy McAuliffe, "Internet Makes Children Lazy, Says Academic," October 12, 2001, http://news .zdnet.co.uk/internet/0,1000000097,2097187,00.htm (accessed October 7, 2009).

209 **increase in the number of Ritalin prescriptions**: PBS.org, *Statistics on Stimulant Use*, 2001, http://www.pbs.org/wgbh/pages/frontline/shows/medicating/drugs/stats.html (accessed October 7, 2009).

209 **most commonly diagnosed behavioral disorder of childhood**: "National Institutes of Health Consensus Development Conference Statement: Diagnosis and Treatment of Attention-Deficit/Hyperactivity Disorder (ADHD)," *Journal of the American Academy of Child & Adolescent Psychiatry* 39, no. 2 (2000): 182–93.

210 **ADHD is defined, in the *Diagnostic and Statistical Manual–IV***: *DSM-IV*, text revision, 92.

210 **involved 752 elementary students**: H. J. Yoo et al., "Attention Deficit Hyperactivity Symptoms and Internet Addiction," *Psychiatry and Clinical Neurosciences* 58 (2004): 487–94.

210 **study in an older age group**: C. H. Ko et al., "Psychiatric Comorbidity of Internet Addiction in College Students: An Interview Study," *CNS Spectrums* 13, no. 2 (2008): 147–53.

211 **"emysphilia"**: June Torbati, "Profs Question Students' Wikipedia Dependency," *Yale Daily News*, http://www.yaledailynews.com/articles/view/19798 (accessed October 7, 2009).

212 **"Morgellons," a total Web invention of a condition**: Wikipedia, "Morgellons," http://en.wikipedia.org/wiki/Morgellons (accessed October 7, 2009).

212 **" . . . creating a citizenry that can't think or read"**: Gehl and Douglas, "From Movable Type to Data Deluge."

9: INTERNET ADDICTION

214 **over forty-five days per year**: *Daily Mail*, "Internet Tops TV as Most Popular Pastime," March 8, 2006, http://www.dailymail.co.uk/news/article-379226/Internet-tops-TV-popular-pastime.html (accessed October 8, 2009).

217 **Internet addiction rates have varied widely**: T. Liu and M. N. Potenza, "Problematic Internet Use: Clinical Implications," *CNS Spectrums* 12, no. 6 (2007): 453–66.

217 **our group conducted a large nationwide survey**: E. Aboujaoude, L. M. Koran, N. Gamel, M. D. Large, R. T. Serpe, "Potential Markers for Problematic Internet Use: A Telephone Survey of 2,513 Adults," *CNS Spectrums* 11, no. 10 (2006): 750–75.

219 **"The Internet is the equivalent of an electronic needle"**: M. C. Miller, "Is 'Internet Addiction' a Distinct Mental Disorder?" *Harvard Mental Health Letter* 24, no. 4 (2007): 8.

221 **"pathological use of electronic media"**: R. Pies, "Should *DSM-V* Designate 'Internet Addiction' a Mental Disorder?" *Psychiatry* 6, no. 2 (2009): 31–37.

221 **Homosexuality, for instance, was until 1973**: J. Drescher, "A History of Homosexuality and Organized Psychoanalysis," *Journal of the American Academy of Psychoanalysis and Dynamic Psychiatry* 36, no. 3 (2008): 443–60.

222 **"clinically significant behavioral or psychological syndrome"**: *DSM-IV*, text revision, xxxi.

222 **they draw parallels with well-accepted *DSM* disorders**: R. Pies, "Should *DSM-V* Designate 'Internet Addiction' a Mental Disorder?"

222 **According to the online measurement service Hitwise**: Verne Kopytoff, "Facebook Moving into Twitter Territory," March 15, 2009, http://www .sfgate.com/cgi-bin/article.cgi?f=/c/a/2009/03/15/BU7816EBGD.DTL&hw= kopytoff&sn=001&sc=1000 (accessed October 8, 2009).

223 **thirty-year-old man who died**: Fox News, "Chinese Man Drops Dead after 3-Day Gaming Binge," September 18, 2007, http://www.foxnews.com/ story/0,2933,297059,00.html (accessed October 8, 2009).

224 **"addictive use of the Internet"**: K. S. Young, "Psychology of Computer Use: XL. Addictive use of the Internet: A Case That Breaks the Stereotype," *Psychological Reports* 79 (1996): 899–902.

224 **developed the Internet Addiction Test**: K. S. Young, *Caught in the Net: How to Recognize the Signs of Internet Addiction—and a Winning Strategy for Recovery* (New York: Wiley, 1998).

224 **tested the Chinese Internet Addiction Inventory**: Z. Huang, M. Wang, M. Qian, J. Zhong, and R. Tao, "Chinese Internet Addiction Inventory: Developing a Measure of Problematic Internet Use for Chinese College Students," *Cyberpsychology and Behavior* 10, no. 6 (2007): 805–11.

225 **The validity of Young's scale**: L. Widyanto and M. McMurran, "The Psychometric Properties of the Internet Addiction Test," *Cyberpsychology and Behavior* 7, no. 4 (2004): 443–50.

225 **In perhaps the most storied case, James Pacenza**: Jim Fitzgerald, "Man Sues IBM over Adult Chat Room Firing," February 18, 2007, http://www.sfgate .com/cgi-bin/article.cgi?f=/n/a/2007/02/17/state/n201859S49.DTL (accessed October 8, 2009).

227 **The first well-designed medication trial**: Dell'Osso et al., "Escitalopram in the Treatment of Impulsive-Compulsive Internet Usage Disorder: An Open-Label Trial Followed by a Double-Blind Discontinuation Phase," *Journal of Clinical Psychiatry* 69, no. 3 (2008): 452–56.

229 **As the *New York Times*'s Martin Fackler**: Martin Fackler, "In Korea, a Boot Camp Cure for Web Obsession," *New York Times*, November 18, 2007, http://www .nytimes.com/2007/11/18/technology/18rehab.html (accessed October 8, 2009).

230 **charging desperate parents $1,200 a month**: Christine Lagorio, "In China, Curing Addiction to the Virtual," CBS News, May 2, 2007, http://www.cbsnews .com/stories/2007/05/02/eveningnews/main2754933.shtml (accessed October 8, 2009).

231 **runs a camp on a military base**: Ibid.

231 **one of over three hundred in the country**: Jonathan Adams, "In an Increasingly Wired China, Rehab for Internet Addicts," *Christian Science Monitor,* January 6, 2009, http://www.csmonitor.com/2009/0106/p01s03-woap.html (accessed October 8, 2009).

231 **The largest was conducted by Dr. Kimberly Young**: K. S. Young, "Cognitive Behavior Therapy with Internet Addicts: Treatment Outcomes and Implications," *Cyberpsychology and Behavior* 10, no. 5 (2007): 671–79.

232 **"any computing system that aids"**: I. M. Marks, K. Cavanagh, and L. Gega, "Computer-Aided Psychotherapy: Revolution or Bubble?" *British Journal of Psychiatry* 191 (2007): 471–73.

233 **evokes Max Planck's maxim**: J. H. Greist, "Counseling in Cyberspace: Your E-Therapist Is on Call," in Aboujaoude and Koran, *Impulse Control Disorders,* 190.

233 **Beating the Blues**: http://www.beatingtheblues.co.uk/connect (accessed October 8, 2009).

233 **FearFighter**: http://www.fearfighter.com (accessed October 8, 2009).

233 **Flying without Fear**: Eliza Hussman, "Aid for Nervous Flyers," November 8, 2009, http://articles.sfgate.com/2009-11-08/travel/17178789_1_iphone-flying-exercises (accessed January 14, 2010).

10: THE END OF PRIVACY

236 **the infant in the earliest phases of development**: S. A. Mitchell and M. J. Black, *Freud and Beyond* (New York: Basic Books, 1995), 43–47.

236 **the child's having a portable image of Mom**: J. Berzoff, L. Flanagan Melano, and P. Hertz, *Inside out and Outside in: Psychodynamic Clinical Theory and Psychopathology in Contemporary Multicultural Contexts* (Lanham, MD: Rowman & Littlefield, 2007), 150.

237 **"True engagement with the other is the result"**: J. Cassidy and P. R. Shaver, *Handbook of Attachment: Theory, Research, and Clinical Applications* (New York: Guilford Press, 2002), 600.

237 **"Individuation is, in general, the process by which"**: G. Wehr, *Jung & Steiner: The Birth of a New Psychology* (New York: Steiner Books, 2002), 103.

238 **"Privacy is partly a form of self-possession"**: L. McCreary, "What Was Privacy?" *Harvard Business Review* 86, no. 10 (2008): 123–30.

238 **Just between December 2008 and March 2009**: Randall Stross, "When Everyone's a Friend, Is Anything Private?" *New York Times,* http://www.nytimes.com/2009/03/08/business/08digi.html (accessed October 8, 2009).

239 **"Among members, a Law of Amiable Inclusiveness"**: Ibid.

239 **"How to Friend Mom, Dad, and the Boss"**: Sarah Perez, "How to Friend Mom, Dad, and the Boss on Facebook . . . Safely," *New York Times,* January 30, 2009, http://www.nytimes.com/external/readwriteweb/2009/01/30/30readwriteweb-how_to_friend_mom_dad_and_the.html (accessed October 8, 2009).

240 **"An application installed by a friend can vacuum"**: Stross, "When Everyone's a Friend, Is Anything Private?"

240 **default setting that Facebook assigns to fifteen of nineteen**: Ibid.

240 **Only about 20 percent of members**: Ibid.

240 **The title itself is a by-product of the Internet age**: Wikipedia, "Chief Privacy Officer," http://en.wikipedia.org/wiki/Chief_privacy_officer (accessed October 8, 2009).

241 **"You have zero privacy anyway. Get over it"**: Polly Sprenger, "Sun on Privacy: 'Get over It,'" *Wired*, January 26, 1999, http://www.wired.com/politics/law/news/1999/01/17538 (accessed October 8, 2009).

241 **became more apparent in February 2009**: Brian Stelter, "Facebook's Users Ask Who Owns Information," *New York Times*, February 16, 2009, http://www.nytimes.com/2009/02/17/technology/internet/17facebook.html (accessed October 8, 2009).

241 **a tracking tool called Beacon**: Louise Story and Brad Stone, "Facebook Retreats on Online Tracking," *New York Times*, http://www.nytimes.com/2007/11/30/technology/30face.html (accessed October 8, 2009).

242 **2006 survey of 100 executive recruiters**: Execunet.com, *Growing Number of Job Searches Disrupted by Digital Dirt*, 2006, http://www.execunet.com/m_releases_content.cfm?id=3349 (accessed October 8, 2009).

242 **sex somewhere online was listed as**: Kate Lorenz, "Warning: Social Networking Can Be Hazardous to Your Job Search," September 24, 2007, http://www.careerbuilder.com/Article/CB-533-Job-Search-Warning-Social-Networking-Can-Be-Hazardous-to-Your-Job-Search (accessed October 8, 2009).

242 **2008 survey of 453 admission departments**: John Hoey, "Ivory Tower Outpacing Corporate America in Use of Social Networking," September 10, 2007, http://www.umassd.edu/communications/articles/showarticles.cfm?a_key=1536 (accessed October 8, 2009).

242 **2006 data from the Pew Internet and American Life Project**: Reputation Defender.com, *Why Does Your Online Reputation Matter?* https://www.reputationdefender.com/myreputation (accessed October 8, 2009).

243 **Almost all respondents to the 2008 Digital Future Project**: Center for the Digital Future, *Annual Internet Survey by the Center for the Digital Future Finds Shifting Trends Among Adults About the Benefits and Consequences of Children Going Online*.

243 **"free Web-based platform that enables patients"**: HealthVault.com, *How HealthVault Connects with Hospitals*, 2009, http://www.healthvault.com/Industry/Ecosystem/hospitals/index.html (accessed October 8, 2009).

243 **RealAge claims to promote**: Liz Clifford, "Online Age Quiz Is a Window for Drug Makers," *New York Times*, March 25, 2009, http://www.nytimes.com/2009/03/26/technology/internet/26privacy.html (accessed October 8, 2009).

244 **is being sold to drug companies**: Ibid.

245 **"Once you start thinking of Google's potential reach"**: Michael Agger, "Google's Evil Eye," *Slate*, October 10, 2007, http://www.slate.com/id/2175651 (accessed October 8, 2009).

246 **whose searches evolved over several weeks**: Ibid.

246 **"dog that urinates on everything"**: Paul Boutin, "You Are What You Search," August 11, 2006, *Slate*, http://www.slate.com/toolbar.aspx?action=print&id=2147590 (accessed October 8, 2009).

246 **"My goodness, it's my whole personal life"**: Michael Barbaro and Tom Zeller Jr., "A Face Is Exposed for AOL Searcher No. 4417749," *New York Times*, August 9, 2006, http://www.nytimes.com/2006/08/09/technology/09aol.html (accessed October 8, 2009).

246 **"60 single men"**: Ibid.

246 **It also included queries about**: Ibid.

248 **story from NPR's *On the Media***: Life Archive, December 18, 2009, http://www.onthemedia.org/transcripts/2009/12/18/06 (accessed April 24, 2010).

249 **"Information on the self-appointed king"**: Richard Tomkins, "Questions Surround WikiLeaks Founder Assange," *Human Events*, July 30, 2010, http://www.humanevents.com/article.php?id=38309 (accessed August 25, 2010).

249 **The video was posted**: Raffi Khatchadourian, "No Secrets," *The New Yorker*, June 7, 2010, http://www.newyorker.com/reporting/2010/06/07/100607fa_fact_khatchadourian (accessed August 25, 2010).

250 **"Secrecy at Apple is not just the prevailing"**: Brad Stone and Ashlee Vance, "Apple's Obsession With Secrecy Grows Stronger," *New York Times*, June 23, 2009, http://www.nytimes.com/2009/06/23/technology/23apple.html (accessed August 25, 2010).

250 **In civil society and in intimate matters**: Peter Levine, "The Internet and Civil Society," in Vedder, *Ethics and the Internet*.

251 **"sought to put power in the hands of the people"**: Deborah Gage, "Web 2.0 Defamation Lawsuits Multiply," February 9, 2009, http://www.sfgate.com/cgi-bin/article.cgi?f=/c/a/2009/02/08/MNOJ15F979.DTL&type=business&tsp=1 (accessed October 8, 2009).

252 **Yvonne Wong is a pediatric dentist**: Deborah Gage, "Dentist Sues over Negative Yelp Review," http://www.sfgate.com/cgi-bin/article.cgi?f=/c/a/2009/01/12/BU4015 8CPE.DTL&type=business&tsp=1 (accessed October 8, 2009).

252 **Steven Biegel, a San Francisco chiropractor**: Ibid.

252 **"charging people whatever [he] feel[s] like"**: Elinor Mills, "Yelp User Faces Lawsuit over Negative Review," January 6, 2009, http://news.cnet.com/8301-13578_3-10133466-38.html (accessed October 8, 2009).

252 **"It's called flaming"**: Gage, "Web 2.0 Defamation Lawsuits Multiply."

253 **in 2008, it took away altogether sellers' ability**: Elinor Mills, "eBay Sellers to Be Banned from Criticizing Buyers," February 5, 2008, http://news.cnet.com/8301-10784_3-9865616-7.html (accessed October 8, 2009).

253 **"No provider or user of an interactive computer service"**: U.S. Code Collection, http://www.law.cornell.edu/uscode/47/230.html (accessed October 8, 2009).

253 **This effectively immunizes Internet service providers (ISPs) and online forums**: K. S. Myers, "Wikimmunity: Fitting the Communications Decency Act to Wikipedia," *Harvard Journal of Law and Technology* 20 (2006): 163.

253 **up 68 percent in 2007 from 2006 levels**: Gage, "Web 2.0 Defamation Lawsuits Multiply."

253 **"It's quite simple"**: ReputationDefender, *My Reputation*, http://www.reputationdefender.com/myreputation (accessed October 8, 2009).

254 **"world's first comprehensive online reputation management and privacy company"**: ReputationDefender, *Company: About Us*, http://www.reputationdefender.com/company (accessed October 8, 2009).

254 **you should opt for their MyEdge service**: Andy Greenberg, "Google-Proof PR?" *Forbes*, May 25, 2007, http://www.forbes.com/2007/05/24/google-search-reputation-cx-tech_ag_0525google.html (accessed October 8, 2009).

254 **"Civilization is the progress toward a society of privacy"**: Ayn Rand, *The Fountainhead* (Indianapolis: Bobbs-Merrill, 1968), 715.

11: MARKING TIME, MAKING MEMORIES

256 **according to a 2007 study of over 500,000 users conducted by Microsoft researchers**: Dinei Florencio and Cormac Herley, *A Large-Scale Study of Web Passwords*, May 8–12, 2007, http://portal.acm.org/citation.cfm?id=1242661 (accessed October 8, 2009).

259 **In a study published in 2007**: B. A. Kuhl, N. M. Dudukovic, I. Kahn, and A. D. Wagner, "Decreased Demands on Cognitive Control Reveal the Neural Processing Benefits of Forgetting," *Nature Neuroscience* 10, no. 7 (2007): 908–14.

260 **"As irrelevant memories are forgotten"**: Lisa Trei, "Forgetting Helps You Remember the Important Stuff, Researchers Say," June 6, 2007, http://news.stanford.edu/news/2007/june6/memory-060607.html (accessed October 8, 2009).

261 **"Any act of remembering reweights memories"**: Ibid.

261 **"The brain is plastic—adaptive"**: Ibid.

261 **"Remembering the past is fraught with competition"**: Kuhl et al., "Decreased Demands on Cognitive Control Reveal the Neural Processing Benefits of Forgetting."

261 **"How Sticky Is Membership on Facebook?"**: Maria Aspan, "How Sticky

Is Membership on Facebook? Just Try Breaking Free," *New York Times*, February 11, 2008, http://www.nytimes.com/2008/02/11/technology/11facebook.html (accessed October 8, 2009).

261 **"2,504 Steps to Closing Your Facebook Account"**: Ibid.

262 **"While your personal computer only keeps one copy"**: Christopher Null, "No Such Thing As 'Deleted' on the Internet," May 21, 2009, http://tech.yahoo.com/blogs/null/142366 (accessed October 8, 2009).

262 **in 2009, in a Cambridge University study**: Rory Cellan-Jones, "Websites 'Keeping Deleted Photos,'" May 21, 2009, http://news.bbc.co.uk/1/hi/uk/8060407.stm (accessed October 8, 2009).

262 **The mission of the Wayback project**: Archive.org, http://www.archive.org/web/web.php (accessed October 8, 2009).

262 **starting to offer access to archived versions**: Archive.org, http://www.archive.org/about/about.php (accessed October 8, 2009).

263 **Forty percent of Twitter tweets**: Pear Analytics, *Twitter Study Reveals Interesting Results About Usage—40 Percent Is "'Pointless Babble,'"* http://www.pearanalytics.com/blog/2009/twitter-study-reveals-interesting-results-40-percent-pointless-babble/ (accessed October 8, 2009).

264 **"The complexity for minimum component costs"**: Gordon E. Moore, "Cramming More Components onto Integrated Circuits," April 19, 1965, http://download.intel.com/museum/Moores_Law/Articles-Press_Releases/Gordon_Moore_1965_Article.pdf (accessed October 8, 2009).

264 **In 1975, Moore revised his prediction**: Gordon E. Moore, "Progress in Digital Integrated Electronics," *Electron Devices Meeting, 1975 International* 21 (1975): 11–13.

264 **This formulation remains accepted**: J. P. Waldner, *Nanocomputers and Swarm Intelligence* (London: John Wiley & Sons, 2008), 44–45.

264 **"integrated circuits will lead to such wonders"**: Moore, "Cramming More Components onto Integrated Circuits."

265 **hoarding is defined as the acquisition of**: Aboujaoude, *Compulsive Acts*, 31–32.

269 **"[People's] very existence will be dictated"**: Elon University/Pew Internet Project, *The Evolving Concept of Time for Leisure, Work*, 2008, http://www.elon.edu/e-web/predictions/expertsurveys/2008survey/internet_time_work_leisure_2020.xhtml (accessed October 8, 2009).

270 **A 2008 report by a New Zealand network**: Alana May Eriksen, "Quarter of Workers' Time Online Is Personal," September 25, 2008, http://msn.nzherald.co.nz/nz/news/article.cfm?c_id=1&objectid=10534055 (accessed October 8, 2009).

270 **According to a 2005 America Online/Salary.com study**: Salary.com, "Per-

sonal Internet Use Ranked as Top Time Wasting Activity," 2005, http://www.salary .com/aboutus/layoutscripts/abtl_default.asp?tab=abt&cat=cato12&ser=sero41& part=Par485 (accessed October 8, 2009).

270 **A 2005 Harris Interactive/Websense study**: Peter Saalfield, *Internet Misuse Costs Businesses $178 Billion Annually*, July 19, 2005, http://www.infoworld.com/t/ applications/internet-misuse-costs-businesses-178-billion-annually-996 (accessed October 8, 2009).

271 **W. Daniel Hillis, who has proposed an impressive monument**: Steven Levy, "The Mind of an Inventor," *Newsweek*, October 10, 2005, http://www .newsweek.com/id/50994 (accessed October 8, 2009).

271 **In the 1980s, as a graduate student at MIT**: Ibid.

271 **"I want to build a computer"**: Ibid.

271 **Connection Machines, or computing behemoths**: L. W. Tucker, G. G. Robertson, "Architecture and Applications of the Connection Machine," *Computer* 21, no. 8 (1988): 26–38.

272 **"When I was a child, people used to talk about"**: Daniel W. Hillis, 2006, http://www.longnow.org/press/articles/ArtFortMason06.php (accessed October 8, 2009).

272 **Worms, viruses, and "Trojan horses" have followed**: Wikipedia, "Timeline of Computer Viruses and Worms," http://en.wikipedia.org/wiki/Timeline_of_ computer_viruses_and_worms (accessed October 8, 2009).

272 **ILOVEYOU**: D. Ian Hopper, "Destructive 'ILOVEYOU' Computer Virus Strikes Worldwide," May 4, 2000, http://archives.cnn.com/2000/TECH/ computing/05/04/iloveyou/index.html (accessed October 8, 2009).

272 **Sobig**: "Who Wrote Sobig?" 2005, http://authortravis.tripod.com (accessed October 8, 2009).

272 **Mydoom**: CNN, "Security Firm: Mydoom Worm Fastest Yet," 2004, http:// edition.cnn.com/2004/TECH/internet/01/28/mydoom.spreadwed (accessed October 8, 2009).

272 **Storm**: Robert Vamosi, "Looking Inside the Storm Worm Botnet," August 7, 2008, http://news.cnet.com/8301-1009_3-10009953-83.html (accessed October 8, 2009).

272 **Conficker**: Gregg Keizer, "Conficker Cashes in, Installs Spam Bots and Scareware," http://www.computerworld.com/s/article/9131380/Conficker_cashes_in_ installs_spam_bots_and_scareware?taxonomyName=Security (accessed October 8, 2009).

273 **"Civilization is revving itself into a pathologically"**: Long Now Foundation, *About Long Now*, http://www.longnow.org/about (accessed October 8, 2009).

273 **"The only way to survive over the long run is to be made of materials"**:

Long Now Foundation, *The 10,000-Year Clock*, http://www.longnow.org/projects/clock (accessed October 8, 2009).

274 **"I know I am a part of a story that starts"**: Ibid.

12: VIRTUALISM, OR THE ART OF BEING MORE REAL THAN REAL

280 **He makes a threefold argument**: Garrath Williams, 2006, *Thomas Hobbes (1588–1679), Moral and Political Philosophy,* http://www.utm.edu/research/iep/h/hobmoral.htm (accessed December 17, 2009).

281 **"the notions of right and wrong"**: Thomas Hobbes, *Leviathan*, ed. Edwin M. Curley (Indianapolis: Hackett Publishing Company, 1994), xxix.

281 **" . . . there is . . . no culture"**: Thomas Hobbes, *A History of Philosophy*, vol. 5, ed. Frederick Copleston (New York: Continuum, 2003), 33.

281 **"If you're looking for a digital Pearl Harbor"**: John Markoff, "Do We Need a New Internet?" *New York Times*, February 15, 2009, http://www.nytimes.com/2009/02/15/weekinreview/15markoff.html (accessed December 16, 2009).

281 **"there is a growing belief"**: Ibid.

282 **"where users would give up"**: Ibid.

282 **"the current Internet might"**: Ibid.

282 **Obama to create a cyberczar position**: Declan McCullagh, "Obama Expected to Announce Cybersecurity Revamp, New 'Czar,'" CBS News, May 29, 2009, http://www.cbsnews.com/blogs/2009/05/29/politics/politicalhotsheet/entry5048128.shtml (accessed October 2, 2009).

282 **Remarks made in early 2010**: Catherine Rampell, "Bernanke Blames Weak Regulation for Financial Crisis," *New York Times*, January 4, 2010, http://www.nytimes.com/2010/01/04/business/economy/04fed.html (accessed January 14, 2010).

283 **The more muscular approach to financial regulation**: Jackie Calmes, "With Populist Stance, Obama Takes on Banks," *New York Times*, January 21, 2010, http://www.nytimes.com/2010/01/22/business/economy/22policy.html (accessed January 22, 2010).

285 **People agonized over the effects**: E. A. Wartella and N. Jennings, "Children and Computers: New Technology, Old Concerns," *The Future of Children* 10, no. 2 (2000): 31–43.

285 **the personal computer in the 1970s, and primitive video games**: M. Shaw and D. W. Black, "Internet Addiction: Definition, Assessment, Epidemiology and Clinical Management," *CNS Drugs* 22, no. 5 (2008): 353–65.

288 **thirteen "enemies of the Internet"**: Reporters without Borders, "List of the 13 Internet Enemies," 2006, http://www.rsf.org/List-of-the-13-Internet-enemies.html (accessed December 15, 2009).

_INDEX

_ABOUT THE AUTHOR

Elias Aboujaoude did his psychiatric training at Stanford University School of Medicine and is an expert in the effects of cyber life and the new digital media. He earned his MD from Stanford and is director of the university's Obsessive Compulsive Disorder Clinic and the Impulse Control Disorders Clinic. Dr. Aboujaoude led the largest U.S. study to date on problematic Internet use, and his work has been featured in the *New York Times*, the *Wall Street Journal*, and the *Los Angeles Times*, as well as on NBC and CNN. He is the author of *Compulsive Acts: A Psychiatrist's Tales of Ritual and Obsession* and the contributor to the "Compulsive Acts" blog at *Psychology Today*.